Mike Walsh

Sams **Teach Yourself**

SharePoint® 2007

2007

in 24 Hours

SAMS 800 East 96th Street, Indianapolis, Indiana, 46240 USA

Sams Teach Yourself SharePoint 2007 in 24 Hours

ISBN-13: 978-0-672-33000-1
ISBN-10: 0-672-33000-8

Library of Congress Cataloging-in-Publication Data:

Walsh, Mike, 1947-
    Sams teach yourself SharePoint 2007 in 24 hours : using Windows SharePoint services 3.0 / Mike Walsh.
        p. cm.
    ISBN 978-0-672-33000-1
  1. Intranets (Computer networks) 2. Microsoft SharePoint (Electronic resource) 3. Web servers. I. Title. II. Title: Teach yourself SharePoint 2007 in 24 hours.
    TK5105.875.I6W345 2009
    004.67'8—dc22
                                2008028445

Printed in the United States of America

First Printing October 2008

Trademarks

Warning and Disclaimer

Bulk Sales

Sams Publishing offers excellent discounts on this book when ordered in quantity for bulk purchases or special sales. For more information, please contact

U.S. Corporate and Government Sales
1-800-382-3419
corpsales@pearsontechgroup.com

For sales outside of the U.S., please contact

International Sales
international@pearson.com

Publisher
Paul Boger

Editor-in-Chief
Karen Gettman

Executive Editor
Neil Rowe

Acquisitions Editor
Brook Farling

Development Editor
Sheri Cain

Managing Editor
Kristy Hart

Project Editor
Andrew Beaster

Copy Editor
Keith Cline

Indexer
Rebecca Salerno

Proofreader
Leslie Joseph

Technical Editor
John Timney

Publishing Coordinator
Cindy Teeters

Book Designer
Gary Adair

Composition
Jake McFarland

Contents at a Glance

Table of Contents

Online Appendixes (available at www.informit.com/title/9780672330001)

About the Author

Mike Walsh has been a SharePoint MVP since October 2002. He works as a Technology Consultant for Logica in Finland, having spent all but one year of his working life living and working in various European countries outside his native Britain.

Mike became an MVP for the SharePoint Team Services (STS) product through actively sharing his STS knowledge in the newsgroup for that product. He has continued to be active in SharePoint newsgroups and (now) forums, mainly for Windows SharePoint Services for both versions 2.0 and 3.0. He has worked on the Ask the Experts stand at several Microsoft European conferences over the years. He was an early beta tester for both Office 2003, including WSS 2.0, and Office 2007, including WSS 3.0.

This is Mike's first full book. He has earlier written a chapter of a book that was a joint effort by a number of SharePoint MVPs.

Dedication

To my father, who died during the preparation of this book after a long illness.

Acknowledgments

It's normal at this point to thank your wife/husband and kids for having put up with the writer during the period in which he or she has been writing the book. I always thought that this was all a bit unnecessary until, that is, I actually had to write a book myself.

Not only was a room (and several computers) totally out of bounds to my wife for several hours a day—and every day for a period of several months—but she also had to put up with me shouting, "I'm working!," when she knocked on the door, even if all she wanted was to say that lunch was ready. As if that weren't enough, I spent most of the rest of the time going through the next chapter in my head, so I now understand all those other authors! So I, too, will start by thanking my wife for putting up with me these past several months.

I also want to thank the SharePoint MVPs as a whole for putting up a bar of excellence that I'd find easy to get under if I were limbo dancing, but which I find far beyond my modest skills even when attempting the equivalent of the Fosbury flop.

In addition to the general thanks to MVPs, I especially want to thank SharePoint MVPs Reza Alirezaei and Jeremy Sublett; their responses to my questions helped me complete a couple of sections. To Berlin's SharePoint MVP Michael Greth for helping me to get a better picture of how MOSS 2007 adds equivalent foreign language versions of pages. The words I use to describe this are, however, entirely my own, so don't blame him for them.

Thanks to Phil Wicklund, a representative for all the people out there who give up their own time to provide free web parts and tools to the SharePoint Community. And thanks to the people from a couple of commercial companies who helped me out when I needed help. You know who you are.

Finally, thanks to the people at Sams (especially Brook Farling), who took a chance with an author with no writing track record other than a single chapter. Also, a special thanks to Sheri Cain for her efforts above and beyond the call of duty. Most of all, however, thanks to those of you who bought this book. I hope my enthusiasm for the product (and many useful screen shots!) makes up for my lack of writing skills.

We Want to Hear from You!

As the reader of this book, *you* are our most important critic and commentator. We value your opinion and want to know what we're doing right, what we could do better, what areas you'd like to see us publish in, and any other words of wisdom you're willing to pass our way.

You can email or write me directly to let me know what you did or didn't like about this book—as well as what we can do to make our books stronger.

Please note that I cannot help you with technical problems related to the topic of this book, and that due to the high volume of mail I receive, I might not be able to reply to every message.

When you write, please be sure to include this book's title and author as well as your name and phone or email address. I will carefully review your comments and share them with the author and editors who worked on the book.

Email: consumer@samspublishing.com

Mail: Karen Gettman
            Editor-in-Chief
            Sams Publishing
            800 East 96th Street
            Indianapolis, IN 46240 USA

Reader Services

Visit our website and register this book at www.informit.com/title/9780672330001 for convenient access to any updates, downloads, or errata that might be available for this book.

Introduction

This book is based on my experience in using the various versions of Windows Share-Point Services throughout the years and on my experience of reading and answering innumerable messages in the SharePoint newsgroups and thus being aware of common problems and misunderstandings.

This book reflects those years of experience by giving considerable space early on to issues that have consistently confused people over the years and by including occasional notes and hints where my experience from the newsgroups tells me such asides will be useful.

Two main products fit the SharePoint 2007 description: Windows SharePoint Services 3.0 (WSS 3.0) and Microsoft Office SharePoint Server 2007 (MOSS 2007).

This book concentrates almost exclusively on the "smaller" of those two products (WSS 3.0). Apart from it being considerably cheaper (WSS 3.0 itself is free) than MOSS 2007, it is simpler to learn and—despite some Microsoft peoples' attempts to pitch MOSS 2007 as the only useful SharePoint product—is a full and useful product in its own right.

Even if you intend to move to MOSS 2007, everything you learn about WSS 3.0 will be of use to you. After all, MOSS 2007 is based entirely on WSS 3.0. MOSS 2007 is a superset of WSS 3.0.

This book covers all the different aspects of working with WSS 3.0, with one exception—programming. Programming is something that probably over 90 percent of users of SharePoint systems never consider doing and which is in any case well covered by several specialist "development" books.

Target Audience for This Book

This book is for beginners in SharePoint 2007. By the time they finish reading it, however, they are likely to be intermediate level.

You will find this book useful whether you are a budding SharePoint administrator, a user who will have some administrative responsibilities, a user who will provide content, or a user who will mostly use content provided by others.

You will also find this book helpful if you have ASP.NET 2.0 programming skills but no SharePoint experience. If this describes you, this book will help you better understand the background that those SharePoint development books often assume. It will also give you a feeling for what you don't need to program because it's already either included or is available elsewhere.

The full-time administrator will in time need to follow up with a specialist book on administration, but for many of the other reader groups (except the programmer!) this book will be enough for their needs for quite a while and maybe forever.

Organization of This Book

Instead of making this a reference book with every exhaustive lists and every parameter described, I've written this book as a teaching tool based on my experience of using SharePoint products for more than six years. Instead of dealing with everything, I have picked out a few more commonly used elements and described them. This approach, in turn, has given me the space needed to discuss topics that many books of this size don't cover, such as using add-in products, sample templates, and third-party web parts with SharePoint sites.

This book gives you an overview of the building blocks that are available to you when creating your own sites. I use these building blocks throughout this book to build and add to a set of test sites.

I developed those sites while writing this book, and I wrote the book in order. Therefore, if you follow it in order you will recognize in your test system most of the screen shots included in this book.

In the long term, this method of instruction will work better for you than if I just focused on one solution area. About halfway through this book (Hour 11, "Using What We've Learned So Far in a Site"), however, I do consider one such solution area and how the things we have learned up to and including Hour 10, "Learning About Authentication and Access Rights," can be used to create sites suitable for that solution area. After all, the real world is out there, and even quality building blocks need to be used in such a way that they suit the demands of that real world. Learning what sort of things to use for that sample solution area should help you when you need to create sites for your own real-world scenario.

Each hour breaks down as follows:

▶ Hour 1, "Introducing SharePoint 2007." This hour introduces SharePoint.

▶ Hour 2, "Installing Windows SharePoint Services 3.0." This hour starts with an already installed Windows 2003 Server (Standard Edition) and shows the steps that you take to first prepare for WSS 3.0 and then install WSS 3.0. (Details of how to install Windows 2003 Server are in Appendix A; details of how to install Windows 2008 Server and prepare it for WSS 3.0 are in Appendix B.)

► Hour 3, "Adding Users and Giving Them Rights." This hour discusses the various types of users; creates users required later and then gives them rights to access the WSS 3.0 site.

► Hour 4, "Using the Administration Site." This hour looks at the Administration site and goes through some actions that usually need to be done there.

► Hour 5, "Planning a Site's Structure." This hour describes the different types of sites and how (and when) to create them.

► Hour 6, "Using Libraries and Lists." This hour is an introduction to libraries and lists and to the relationship between a list and the web part of a list.

► Hour 7, "Creating and Using Libraries." This hour looks at the different types of libraries and at how to add files to Picture Libraries and Document Libraries.

► Hour 8, "Creating and Using Views and Folders." This hour describes how to create and use views and why you shouldn't use folders.

► Hour 9, "Looking at List Types and the Included Web Parts." This hour continues looking at lists and then looks at the web parts that come with the product that aren't directly related to lists (see Hour 6).

► Hour 10, "Learning About Authentication and Access Rights." This hour has more information about authentication and shows how you can change the user being used to access a site or web page.

► Hour 11, "Using What We've Learned So Far in a Site." This hour takes a practical working case where WSS 3.0 could usefully be used and shows how data is collected and then used to build a suitable site structure.

► Hour 12, "Using Wikis and Blogs." This hour looks at the standard Wiki and Blog functions provided by the product and then shows how the Blog functions can be extended by use of a free add-on product.

► Hour 13, "Using WSS 3.0 Search and Installing Search Server 2008 Express." This hour covers the standard WSS 3.0 function and then installs the free Search Server 2008 Express product in order to (in Hour 14) improve the search function.

► Hour 14, "Improving Searches." This hour shows how to use Seacrh Server 2008 Express to improve the search function of the standard WSS 3.0.

▶ Hour 15, "Using Different Versions of the Main Office Products with WSS 3.0." This looks at how the 2003 and 2007 versions of Word, Excel, and PowerPoint work with WSS 3.0. Time is in particular spent on Document Workspaces.

▶ Hour 16, "Using Different Versions of Outlook with WSS 3.0." This hour describes what functionality is available when Outlook 2003 is used with WSS 3.0 and compares this with the much greater functionslity available when using Outlook 2007 with WSS 3.0.

▶ Hour 17, "Sharing OneNote 2007 Notebooks and Access 2007 Tables with WSS 3.0." This hour describes how you can create shared OneNote 2007 notebooks that can be stored on a WSS 3.0 site and accessed and synchronized from different client PCs. It also considers the relationship between Access 2007 tables and WSS lists.

▶ Hour 18, "Using Access 2007 Tables to Produce Reports from WSS 3.0 Lists." This hour uses Access 2007 tables that have been created from WSS lists in order to provide reports on WSS 3.0 lists. Both simple (wizard driven) and complicated (manual, combining two lists) reports are explained.

▶ Hour 19, "Creating Workflows in WSS 3.0." This hour briefly mentions the different methods of creating workflows and then concentrates on the three-stage workflow included in WSS 3.0.

▶ Hour 20, "Using SharePoint Designer 2007 to Create Workflows." This hour follows Hour 19 and shows how to use SharePoint Designer 2007 to produce more complicated workflows than the ones described in Hour 19.

▶ Hour 21, "Using SharePoint Designer 2007 to Create Data View Web Parts." This hour shows how Data View web parts are created and used.

▶ Hour 22, "Making Safety Copies of Your Data and Using Them." This hour takes an end-user (or part site administrator) view of various methods of saving copies of part of a WSS 3.0 installation.

▶ Hour 23, "Enhancing Your WSS 3.0 Sites—Microsoft Official Possibilities." This hour looks at how to install and use (foreign) language templates; application templates and also what is required when using InfoPath 2007 to add value to a WSS 3.0 site.

▶ Hour 24, "Enhancing Your WSS 3.0 Sites—Using Third-Party Web Parts." This hour looks at two commercial web parts and one free web part all of which enable you to enhance your WSS 3.0 site at little or no cost and without writing any code yourself.

Online, you can find some appendixes (www.informit.com/title/
9780672330001):

▶ Appendix A, "Full Installation Details for Windows Server 2003." This appendix gives the full details for how to install Windows Server 2003 so that you can (in Hour 2) prepare for and install WSS 3.0. It is provided for people who have not in the past installed Windows Server 2003.

▶ Appendix B, "Installing WSS 3.0 on Windows Server 2008." Installing Windows Server 2008 and preparing it for the installation of WSS 3.0 is sufficiently different to installing and preparing Windows Server 2003 to make this appendix (which also includes less detailed WSS 3.0 installation information than Hour 2) essential if you have never installed Windows Server 2008.

▶ Appendix C, "Creating a Virtual Machine." This appendix shows how to install a virtual machine system. Even if you do not install this particular virtual machine system (Parallels), you should find it useful when installing any of the other virtual machine systems (listed in the text).

Hardware and Software Used to Write This Book

Finally, a brief word about my working environment when writing this book:

▶ I had a desktop running XP Pro and Office 2003, on which I wrote the chapters (using the publisher's Word 2003 template) and which I also used as a client PC when writing the sections on using Office 2003 applications with WSS 3.0.

▶ I had a portable running Vista Ultimate and Office 2007, which I used as a client PC both for normal browser access to the WSS 3.0 site and for writing the sections on using Office 2007 applications with WSS 3.0.

▶ I had a MacBook (OS X Tiger) running the Parallels virtual machine software. I had a Parallels VM on which I had installed WSS 3.0+SP1 on top of Windows Server 2003 R2. I also used the MacBook to create the VM running Windows Server 2008 (and WSS 3.0), which was needed for the on-line Appendix B.

The screen shots were mostly done using the SnagIt product from TechSmith (www.techsmith.com/screen-capture.asp). The SnagIt Editor, which is part of that product, was used to reduce the size of some screen shots. I heartily recommend SnagIt to you. I had it installed on both my client PCs.

Other screen shots were done using the free Macintosh utility Portrait, which comes with the Macintosh operating system, OS X. These were typically screen shots of actions performed on the server.

That's it. Good luck with your exploration into SharePoint 2007!

HOUR 1

Introducing SharePoint 2007

What You'll Learn in This Hour

▶ Main SharePoint 2007 products
▶ A brief history of the product range

Getting Familiar with the SharePoint 2007 Products

If you look at the latest list of SharePoint 2007 products (at the time of writing), you'll see that the first three products in that list are what I call the "main" products:

▶ Windows SharePoint Services 3.0

▶ Microsoft Office SharePoint Server 2007—Standard Edition

▶ Microsoft Office SharePoint Server 2007—Enterprise Edition

▶ Microsoft Office SharePoint Server 2007 for Internet Sites

▶ Microsoft Office SharePoint Server 2007 for Search Standard

▶ Microsoft Office SharePoint Server 2007 for Search Enterprise

These main products are Windows SharePoint Services 3.0 (WSS 3.0). The two different versions—Standard and Enterprise editions—of Microsoft Office SharePoint Server 2007 are a mouthful, so much so that even Microsoft often calls it just SharePoint Server 2007. In this book, I refer to these products as MOSS 2007.

The three products at the end of this list all derive from the MOSS 2007 product: MOSS 2007 for Internet Sites is actually MOSS 2007—Enterprise Edition licensed for

Internet usage (and not much else). The two search products are really only Microsoft packaging to sell the search aspects (only) of the MOSS 2007 products.

Tip

> Don't assume that (MOSS for) Search Standard is equivalent to MOSS 2007 Standard or that (MOSS for) Search Enterprise is equivalent to MOSS 2007 Enterprise. In fact, Search Standard has tight restrictions on how much can be searched and Search Enterprise doesn't, whereas for MOSS itself the difference between Standard and Enterprise is that Enterprise offers more functionality.

Tip

> Look at the respective prices at http://office.microsoft.com/en-us/ sharepointserver/FX102176831033.aspx. This pricing shows you why, despite these restrictions, some companies choose Search Standard anyway.

Given the cover of the book—which clearly says Windows SharePoint Services 3.0— you might ask yourself why I am even mentioning the two MOSS 2007 products.

The answer is simple. This book deals mainly with WSS 3.0, but almost all the knowledge you acquire by working through this book is equally valid for you even if you have a MOSS 2007 installation to use.

Knowledge of WSS 3.0 will also enable you to use Office 2003 and Office 2007 better. You'll see, too, that you get more functionality when using Office 2007 products with WSS 3.0 than with using Office 2003 products with WSS 3.0.

There is added functionality in both these Office product sets that is available only if the users of them have a SharePoint server they can access.

The good news is that the SharePoint server can be one running WSS 3.0, even if sometimes you might get the impression from (especially) Microsoft presentations that the more expensive MOSS 2007 is needed.

This book includes chapters to help you work through and see this additional functionality. Hours 15, 16, and 17 cover both combinations, because not everyone is working with Office 2007.

Tip

> For Office 2003 users, the added benefits that Office 2007 provides with SharePoint sites might justify upgrading. For some users, the differences compared to using Office 2003 with SharePoint can be *that* important.

While teaching you how to use WSS 3.0, this book also gives you at least an idea about what more MOSS 2007 could offer you in certain areas. All the working sections and diagrams are WSS 3.0 only, but there is the occasional mention of relevant MOSS 2007 additions/differences.

Brief History of the SharePoint Products

The present versions of SharePoint listed in Table 1.1 are version 3 products. So what were the version 1 and 2 products?

TABLE 1.1   Development over Time of the CMS and SPS Products

2001–2002	2003	2007
CMS 2002	CMS 2003	Main path: MOSS 2007 Enterprise
		Sub path: MOSS 2007 Standard
SPS 2001	SPS 2003	Main path: MOSS 2007 Standard
		Sub path: MOSS 2007 Enterprise

Version 1 SharePoint Products

SharePoint version 1 started with a product called SharePoint Portal Server 2001 (SPS 2001).

SPS 2001

SPS 2001 was an internal effort using the same kind of data storage as Exchange, and Microsoft allocated it to the intranet category when it bought a company that made expensive Internet software. Microsoft then renamed that company's product Content Management Server (CMS 2002).

However, the hardware and software costs for CMS 2002 were so high that companies believed that using that for the "unimportant" intranet was overkill, and so they were interested in something less expensive. This was where Microsoft positioned their SPS 2001 product.

SPS 2001, as well as being cheaper than CMS 2002, still ran best when it used numerous servers. However, it didn't need those staging servers, and it didn't need such powerful servers, especially if each major service (such as indexing) was given its own server in the farm.

SPS 2001 didn't need staging servers—not because it wouldn't have been a good design, but because the design assumed that, in an intranet, you could make anything live and then remove it if it was wrong. (At least that's my assumption of how it was regarded.)

Suffice to say, SPS 2001 was cheaper, so many companies ran both CMS 2002 *and* SPS 2001.

Now, neither CMS 2002 or SPS 2001—for the Internet and intranet, respectively—have that much to do with the present products in SharePoint 2007. However, some of their best ideas have trickled down. Table 1.1 shows how CMS and SPS products developed over time.

It looks clear-cut, doesn't it? In fact, Table 1.1 gives a false impression because the product that both versions (MOSS 2007 and WSS 3.0) came from was an internal Microsoft effort that was never intended to become a Microsoft product! It was just supposed to provide services that would be useful to a team.

SharePoint Team Services (STS)

Members of an Office team decided that in a web-based age, there must be a better way of interteam communications than email.

What they decided to write—based on, but adding to, Front Page Server Extensions—were various services. These services included such things as the ability to store and access documents in an easier way than that offered by the file system; to have online discussions (simple and thus nothing like Notes, which was prevalent outside Microsoft at the time); to have a place to announce key meetings (or, who knows, maybe team parties); a calendar; and so on. When those standard things weren't enough, they included the ability to note ad-hoc information and make it easily accessible by team members.

They were concerned with quick results and something they could use immediately. Therefore, there was no major architectural effort: The documents were just stored in the file system, and links to them were stored in a simple table.

But then, other teams wanted it, too. And then teams outside the Office part of Microsoft wanted it. In no time (and with no sales effort), it was being used throughout Microsoft (reputedly by several thousand teams).

I imagine what happened then was that a visiting customer saw it and wanted it, and there was a sudden stop.

This was before CodePlex and other Microsoft initiatives to get unsupported code into the public domain, so someone probably needed to make a choice, and they chose that Microsoft release the code (suitably tidied up, no doubt) as a product.

The Internet and intranet areas were already catered for with CMS 2002 and SPS 2001, respectively, so deciding to make this product for "teams" was an obvious choice.

The *Teams Services* part of the name was natural, and using *SharePoint* in the name was equally obvious a marketing person keen on creating "families" from completely different products.

So, the name SharePoint Team Services (STS) was coined, and *that* is what the present SharePoint 2007 products descend from.

Both these 2001 SharePoint products were virtually unknown except for in a few markets where keen Microsoft people were pushing them. This all changed with the 2003 versions, where version 2 of both the SPS and the STS products were closely tied to the Office 2003 beta process. Via this tie in, the 2003 versions managed to get the attention of Microsoft people in local offices. When the Office 2003 betas became public betas, these people started talking about both SPS 2003 and WSS 2.0.

Version 2 SharePoint Products

Windows SharePoint Services 2.0 (or just WSS with no 2.0, because it was the only WSS at the time) became the new name for SharePoint Team Services 2.0. The STS name was abandoned midway through the private beta process when WSS 2.0 became free to use, provided you had a Windows Server 2003 license.

This connection to a Windows Server 2003 license led to the use of *Windows* in the name and, incidentally, to some confusion at Microsoft. WSS 2.0 was regarded as a (Microsoft) Server division product, but the developers were still part of the Office division. Some duplication of effort occurred in documentation, and often each division seemingly expected the other one to do things, such as provide a support web page.

SPS 2003 was more clearly divided because it was an Office division product and was written by part of the Office division.

Tip

SPS 2003 was an attempt to retain most of what had been in SPS 2001 while using the WSS 2.0 platform. Therefore, it was two separate layers: a WSS layer and a SPS layer. It was messy, but because SPS 2003 was pricey and WSS 2.0 was, in effect, free, Microsoft people naturally described SPS 2003. However, the key product was WSS 2.0 because that was where the main changes had been made.

With WSS 2.0, nearly everything was stored in the database (thus putting an end to the synchronization problems that had often troubled STS users).

Also, WSS 2.0 used ASP.NET. This meant that the "web part" technology became available both in the form of third-party add-ins you could get for free, buy from small companies, or write them yourself. It also meant that you could use the Share-Point subset of ASP.NET to program other additions to your out-of-the-box SharePoint product.

Figure 1.1 shows the move from the version 1 SharePoint products to the version 2 SharePoint products to MOSS 2007.

FIGURE 1.1
Move from STS
and SPS 2001
to MOSS 2007.

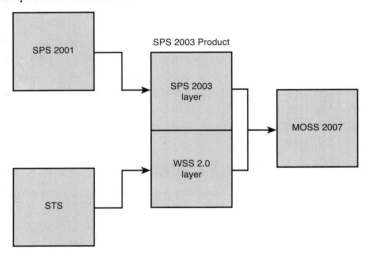

There was still only one installation routine for SPS 2003. If you watched that installation routine carefully, however, you saw that it first installed WSS 2.0 before seamlessly installing the additional SPS 2003 bits.

Version 3 SharePoint Products

This combination of SPS 2003 and WSS 2.0's code bases wasn't satisfactory. Therefore, when the 2007 versions were being developed (as part of the Office 2007 beta process), the SPS parts—called Microsoft Office SharePoint Server 2007 (MOSS 2007)—provided WSS 3.0 with additional functionality.

The main change in WSS 3.0, and thus in MOSS 2007, is the move to pure ASP.NET 2.0, which meant that now ASP.NET 2.0 developers could write code that adds functionality to the SharePoint products.

> In both WSS 3.0 and MOSS 2007, Search uses the same engine. In Hour 13, you see the search in WSS 3.0 is restricted to only a single site and its subsites, and the MOSS 2007 search is more thorough. However, Hour 14 shows how to extend the scope of the WSS 3.0 search by adding Search Server 2008 Express.
>
> ***Note***

Some other changes within WSS 3.0 filled the gaps found in earlier versions:

- You can recover data without restoring an entire earlier copy on a spare server.
- You can have a tree view showing the structure of your site without using a third-party product.
- You can have a menu line showing where you were in the structure, and thus allowing you to jump back to an earlier level without needing to hit your browser's Back button.
- Views are in alphabetic order.
- Folders are improved (but still not that great in some purists' opinions).

So now, we have WSS 3.0: the main foundation product and two main versions of MOSS 2007—Standard and Enterprise. Each version has different levels of additional packaged functionality.

Whenever Microsoft demonstrates SharePoint 2007, its representative invariably mentions all the possible functions of the (top-of-the-line) Enterprise version. Rarely does he clarify that he's describing Enterprise-only functions.

Summary

This chapter familiarized you with SharePoint 2007 products. This chapter examined the historical development of the SharePoint products. You now know that WSS 3.0 is the basis from which all the SharePoint 2007 products derived. Therefore, what you learn about WSS 3.0 in this book (and elsewhere) will be of use to you with all the versions of MOSS 2007 and with other Microsoft products.

Q&A

Q. *Why can't I find function X in my copy of WSS 3.0?*

A. Often, documents about SharePoint functions make no mention of the Share-Point product in which the function is included.

Unfortunately, because the two MOSS 2007 products are in effect WSS 3.0 plus bundled software, many functions are available in only one version of MOSS 2007 (the Enterprise Edition). They are not included in WSS 3.0. (In many cases, they are not included in the Standard version of MOSS 2007, either.)

Q. *Why is X, which was in the 2.0 version, no longer in the 3.0 version?*

A. Microsoft had a good reason to drop some of the functionality found in WSS 2.0. Mostly, it is a good technical reason, but sometimes it's also political.

Workshop

Quiz

1. Which version 1 SharePoint product forms the basis of today's SharePoint product range?

2. Name a couple of improvements in WSS 3.0 compared to WSS 2.0.

3. What do you upgrade CMS 2002 to and via which path?

Quiz Answers

1. SharePoint Team Services (STS).

2. A menu line showing where you are in the site structure; being able to easily recover deleted data.

3. You can upgrade CMS 2002 to either the Enterprise version of MOSS 2007 or (with a loss of function) to the Standard version of MOSS 2007.

You must, however, first upgrade from CMS 2002 to CMS 2003 to use Microsoft's migration tools. (Microsoft also provides tools to migrate from CMS 2002 to CMS 2003.)

HOUR 2

Installing Windows SharePoint Services 3.0

What You'll Learn in This Hour

▶ Computer needs for installing WSS 3.0

▶ Installing WSS 3.0 in the simplest possible way

Computer Type You Need to Install WSS 3.0

A PC with 512MB is enough to install WSS 3.0. However, I never use that little if I can help it. After all, using 1GB of memory speeds up the installation process. (It also speeds up access to the site after WSS 3.0 has been installed).

One alternative to using a new machine is to find a free PC and install either Windows Server 2003 or Windows Server 2008 on it. In this case, 1GB is enough memory for the PC. Another alternative is to use a virtual machine (VM) system running under a standard PC or notebook operating system. 1GB should be assigned to the VM, if possible, which means that the PC or notebook needs to have more memory than that. If you have only 1GB for the PC/notebook, assign slightly less to the VM (such as 760MB).

Tip

I use client PCs running XP Pro (running IE6) and Office 2003; and Vista (running IE7) and Office 2007 to access WSS 3.0. Both of these are normal choices for client access to SharePoint sites.

Installing WSS 3.0

Let's install the simplest installation of WSS 3.0. This particular install uses Windows Server 2003 and installs WSS 3.0 in a workgroup.

We will install the latest version of WSS 3.0, which includes Service Pack 1. This basic version installs the free Windows Internal Database (sometimes referred to as WID). The WID is an embedded version of SQL Server 2005 Express. Unlike that product, however, the WID doesn't limit database sizes. (The normal Express has a 4GB limit.)

Tip

> Some confusion exists about this size-limit issue. The basic installation of MOSS 2007 installs an embedded version of SQL Server 2005 Express. However, the version used by MOSS 2007 has the 4GB limit. Know that the WSS 3.0 version does *not* have this 4GB limit.

Note

> If you want to use a standard SQL Server, don't install WSS 3.0 with the basic installation. In addition, having selected the advanced installation, don't use the Single Server option even if your SQL Server is on the same server on which you are installing WSS 3.0.

The following sections discuss installing WSS 3.0, but here's a brief outline of the steps involved:

1. Install Windows Server 2003.

2. Specify the application server role.

3. Install .NET Framework 3.0.

4. Install WSS 3.0 with SP1.

Step 1: Installing Windows Server 2003

Tip

> I installed Windows Server 2003 R2 with SP2 (Standard Edition), and the screen shots here and in Appendix A reflect this. Appendix A, "Full Installation Details for Windows Server 2003" is online at www.informit.com/title/9780672330001.

Note

> If you use a Windows Server 2003 DVD/CD with no included service pack, your final step in the installation process is to upgrade it to SP2 and later. Therefore, it's simpler and faster to install the version that already includes SP2.

Installing Windows Server 2003 is easy. Just insert the CD and follow the defaults. If you are outside the United States, however, you need to specify a different keyboard, locality, and time zone.

Tip

You can find all the nitty-gritty details regarding the installation of Windows Server 2003 R2 with SP2 (including specifying a different keyboard) in Appendix A, which is online at www.informit.com/title/9780672330001.

At the end of the standard installation process, you'll see the screen shown in Figure 2.1.

FIGURE 2.1
The Ctrl-Alt-Delete page at the end of the Windows installation process.

When you hit Ctrl-Alt-Delete, you'll see a screen recommending that you update this server. It's a good idea to do this now if you can.

As part of this process, you probably need to install the Microsoft Update utility. In both cases, you'll be guided by onscreen instructions.

Step 2: Specifying the Application Server Role

The next step is to specify that the server will be used as an application server. This role is required when you will have websites on a server.

Typically, Figure 2.2 will be visible after you upgrade your server and specify your desired automatic-upgrade type.

To add an application role, follow these steps:

   1. Click Add or Remove a Role.

FIGURE 2.2
The Manage
Your Server
page.

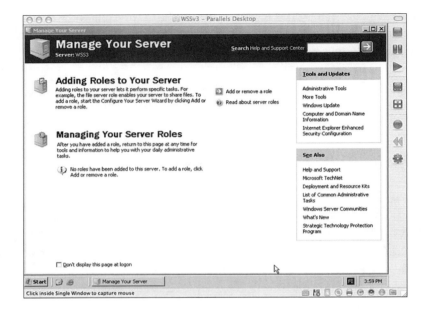

2. On the next screen (Preliminary Steps), click Next. The wizard will then
search for network connections. After this, select the Server Role (see Figure
2.3).

FIGURE 2.3
Specifying the
application serv-
er role.

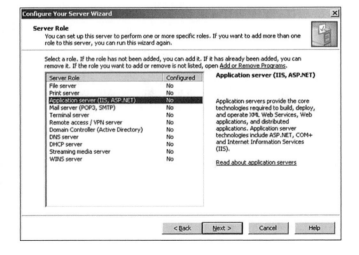

3. After you select Application Server and click Next, you'll see the screen
shown in Figure 2.4. Here, it's important to select Enable ASP.NET (see
Figure 2.4).

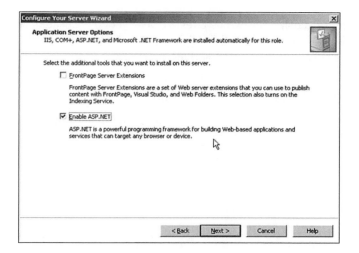

FIGURE 2.4
Select Enable
ASP.NET.

4. Now you see a screen asking you to confirm the options you have selected. Click Next to confirm (see Figure 2.5).

5. Click Finish. The next screen lists the application server role.

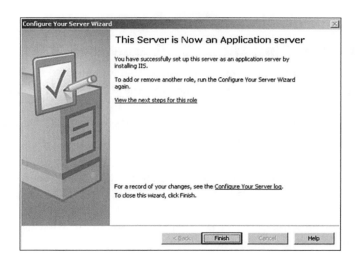

FIGURE 2.5
Confirmation of the application server role.

Note   At this point—and only if this will be a test server—get rid of constant requests for you to answer yes/no (or add to Trusted Sites) for every site you access from a browser on the server. To do this, follow these steps:

1. Select Start > Control Panel > Add or Remove Programs.

2. Select Add/Remove Windows Components.

3. Remove the check mark for the Enhanced Security configuration shown in Figure 2.6. Click Next.

FIGURE 2.6
Turning off Internet Explorer enhanced security.

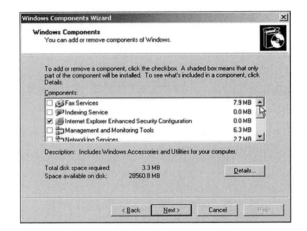

Step 3: Installing the .NET Framework 3.0

Before WSS 3.0 can be installed, another essential step is to install the .NET Framework 3.0. At the time of writing, the download for the Microsoft .NET Framework 3.0 Redistributable Package is at www.microsoft.com/downloads/details.aspx?FamilyID=10cc340b-f857-4a14-83f5-25634c3bf043&DisplayLang=en.

Note   If this preceding URL is no longer current, search for ".NET Framework 3.0" at www.microsoft.com/downloads.

After the download starts, you'll see a screen for dotnetfx3setup.exe where I just select run rather than downloading the file to the server.

Tip   I just run dotnetfx3setup.exe directly, but it's up to you. You can download it to the server (or VM) and run it from there.

Click OK at the next couple of screens, but look closely at Figure 2.7.

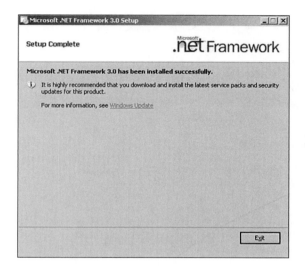

FIGURE 2.7
Confirmation of
the installation
of .NET Frame-
work 3.0.

Follow the recommendation to download and install the latest service packs and
security updates. If you go to Windows Update, two of the updates are the .NET
Framework 2.0 SP1 and .NET Framework 3.0 SP1. You should install both.

Don't worry about both 2.0 and 3.0 being listed. The .NET Framework 3.0 installation installs both. (They are included in the list of programs you see when you go
to Control Panel > Add or Remove Programs.)

Tip

Click the Windows Update link shown in Figure 2.7. This will open a new screen
where you can specify what kind of upgrades you want to install. Do not choose a
type of upgrade yet; first, go back to Figure 2.7 and close it. After that, return to the
Windows Update window.

If you don't first close the screen shown in Figure 2.7, you will find that the
other security updates (listed in Figure 2.8) will be installed but not the two SP1
upgrades; you'll have to go through the Windows Upgrade process again to get
them through.

Note

After you select Custom at the Windows Upgrade page, Figure 2.8 appears. Your list of
updates will most likely be longer than what's shown here, because more time will
have elapsed since the Windows version being installed was created.

FIGURE 2.8
The update page
with two .Net
Framework SP1
downloads listed.

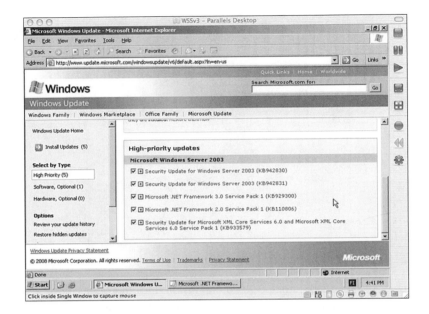

Step 4: Installing WSS 3.0 (With SP1)

Now that the preparatory steps have been made, we can install WSS 3.0 itself. Instead of giving you the URL of this download (which will still point to the "with SP1" version even if a "with SP2" version is out), I'll show you how I always find such downloads.

Go to the WSS FAQ site at www.wssv3faq.com, which is where I keep track of all the key articles (KnowledgeBase articles and downloads for WSS 3.0 and MOSS 2007). There, I click the Articles—2007 Products icon. When that opens, I click the Grouped by Category and Sub-Category link.

By scrolling that page to the WSS category and opening it, you'll see something like Figure 2.9. Several WSS 3.0 downloads will be listed, including Windows SharePoint Services 3.0 with Service Pack 1.

If a WSS 3.0 with Service Pack 2 has come out by the time you read this book, it will be listed there, too, just as the WSS 3.0 download *without* SP1 is listed higher up that page (not visible, but both x64 versions are visible).

Tip

Both the version of WSS 3.0 SP1 and the version without SP1 are listed because several of the backup methods we'll look at in Hour 22 require an identical version of WSS 3.0 for the backup and the restore machine. If Microsoft didn't provide two versions of the WSS 3.0 download, there could be major problems for restorers.

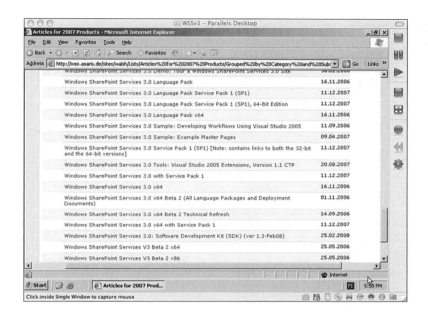

FIGURE 2.9
A list of WSS 3.0 downloads.

When we find the correct web page, we can download and run it. (If you look carefully at Figure 2.10, you'll see the address of the version with SP1.)

FIGURE 2.10
The WSS 3.0 with SP1 download page.

After a few screens, you see Figure 2.11. Here, select Basic.

FIGURE 2.11
Choosing the
kind of installa-
tion.

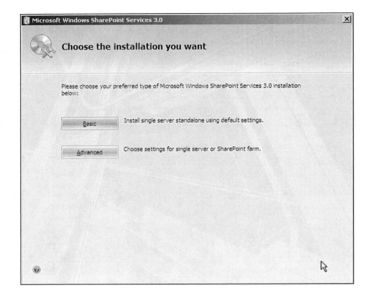

Eventually, the process of installing files to the server is complete and you'll see the
screen shown in Figure 2.12. In this single-server installation, you immediately select

FIGURE 2.12
Deciding to run
the wizard.

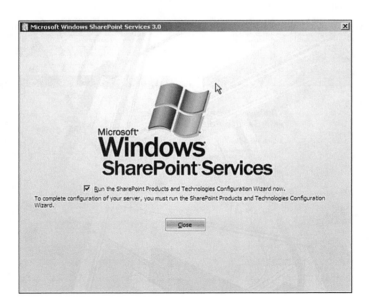

Close, which activates the option to Run the SharePoint Products and Technologies Configuration Wizard (so leave that check mark there).

This is where the real work happens. Be prepared for a process with many (automatic) steps, some of which will take some time (don't panic). By the way, this is the step in the installation process where having assigned 1GB of memory rather than 512MB will pay off.

Click Next and OK on a couple of obvious screens, and then the process starts. Figure 2.13 is an example of what you will see on the screen for about the next 20 minutes as the wizard works though its tasks.

FIGURE 2.13
A typical configuring page.

If everything goes as expected, you'll end up with a Configuration Successful page. When you click Finish, you'll see the screen shown in Figure 2.14, which is the default page of a default WSS 3.0 site.

Summary

This hour concentrated on the steps required to prepare for the installation of WSS 3.0 on a new server running Windows Server 2003 and on the installation of WSS 3.0 itself.

FIGURE 2.14
The default WSS
3.0 site's default
page.

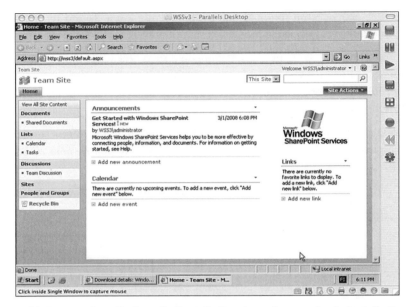

Because this is a test installation, the installation type chosen—basic installation—installs everything on a single server. To keep things simple, the server was installed as the (sole) member of a workgroup.

Q&A

Q. *I'm running out of space in the C: drive on the server. Can I move WSS 3.0?*

A. You can't move the normal files (mostly templates) located in the C: drive. This doesn't matter much, however, because they don't use up much space, so they are not causing the problem (and nor will moving them solve it).

The WSS 3.0 databases account for most of the space used on the C: drive. The default database system (WID) that the basic installation installs always goes to C:, and its databases also go to C:.

There is a way to move those databases, but it is too long to go into here. I do include that method in the WSSv3 FAQ section of my WSS FAQ sites at www. wssv3faq.com (item III.30.04).

Q. *Is the MOSS 2007 basic installation as easy to do as the WSS 3.0 basic installation?*

A. It can be, but be 100 percent sure that you have at least 1GB assigned to the VM (or server); otherwise, the wizard will fail.

My experience has been that the installation can fail at various different places depending on how much less memory than 1GB you have (it gets further with more) and that none of the error messages say anything about lack of memory.

Note that the database system installed in a MOSS 2007 basic installation has a 4GB database size limit, unlike the WID (Windows Internal Database) installed by the WSS 3.0 basic installation.

Workshop

Quiz

1. What benefits do you derive by having more memory allocated within your installation?

2. Which part of the entire installation process takes the longest time?

Quiz Answers

1. More memory means that the installation phase is quicker. (Working with the site after installation is also quicker, but often less noticeably so.)

2. The Configuration Wizard phase.

Adding Users and Giving Them Rights

What You'll Learn in This Hour

- ▶ Different accounts used to access a WSS 3.0 site
- ▶ Creating local users (on the server)
- ▶ Creating SharePoint groups and the benefits of having them
- ▶ Using an AD group
- ▶ Creating a new SharePoint group that has more permissions compared to standard SharePoint group

At the moment, the only way we can access the site we created in Hour 2, "Installing Windows SharePoint Services 3.0," is to use the name (typically Administrator) and password that we specified for the server when we installed the operating system.

The (server) administrator account will be used throughout this book unless specified otherwise. But you need to be aware of the rights that other (non-adminstrator) users can have on WSS 3.0 websites. In this chapter, therefore, you create more users and give them rights to access the sites.

Getting to Know the Different Account Types

Normally, a WSS 3.0 server in a company is part of an Active Directory (AD) setup, and each prospective internal user of the WSS 3.0 site would already have a name (in the form of domain\username) and password.

In Hour 2, we created the simplest standalone server installation—one that perhaps will never be linked to a network—so we're going to create users on the server itself. We then give those users rights to access the site.

Although this is okay for a test site, adding users on the server is usually used only when giving a few outside users rights to access a site that is otherwise accessed only by internal (AD) users.

Note

> The main other possibility to give outside users access rights is a complicated business called *forms authorization*. That's beyond the scope of this book.
>
> If anyone is keen on using forms-based authentication, see Chapter 2 of *RealWorld SharePoint 2007* (ISBN: 978-0-470-16835-6). SharePoint MVP Stacey Draper provides all the information you need to set it up.

Creating Local Users

In this section, we create users. Because this is a test site, the user passwords will be the same as the user name, and the names used will match the rights these users have.

We will add these users:

- ▶ MyAdmin, password MyAdmin
- ▶ MyContrib, password MyContrib
- ▶ MyReader, password MyReader
- ▶ MyReaderPlus1, password MyReaderPlus1
- ▶ MyReaderPlus2, password MyReaderPlus2
- ▶ MyDocLib, password MyDocLib

Tip

> The capital letters shown in the username and password are essential. In the password, they matter. Therefore, we need them in the names so that we can remember the passwords.

In all cases, we specify that the user can't change the password and that the password is permanent. Again, it's a test site, so we can ignore normal security requirements.

Creating a Single User

Follow these steps to create a single user:

1. Go to Start > Administrative Tools > Computer Management. Figure 3.1 shows the Computer Management page.

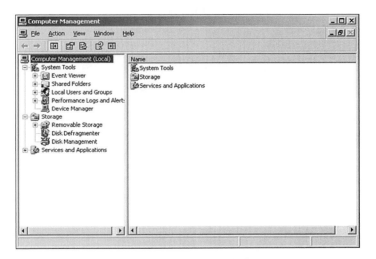

FIGURE 3.1
Computer Management page.

2. In Figure 3.2, select Local Users and Groups and then Users.

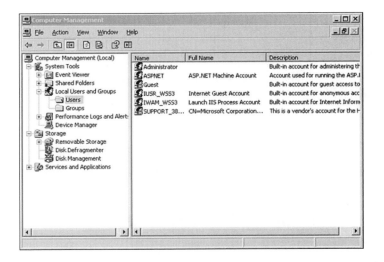

FIGURE 3.2
Selecting users in the Computer Management page.

3. Select Action and then New User. Figure 3.3 shows the completed next page, with the text required to add user MyAdmin.

FIGURE 3.3
A filled-in New
User page.

4. Click Create to return to the empty version of Figure 3.3. From here, you can directly enter the next user from the list.

5. After entering the final user, click Create followed by Close. This gives you Figure 3.4.

This is the same screen as shown in Figure 3.2, but the list of users is longer because it includes the ones just added. Close this window.

Now, let's give some of these users rights to access the site we have created.

Giving Users Rights to Access the Site

Now that we have created the users, we need to tell the WSS 3.0 system that these particular users can access the WSS 3.0 site(s) and what rights these users have when they access the WSS 3.0 site(s).

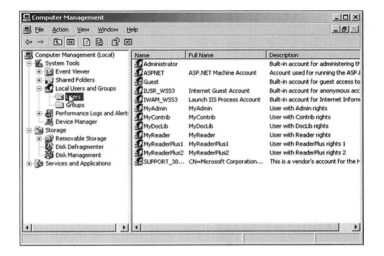

FIGURE 3.4
A longer list of
users.

Follow these steps to achieve this:

1. While still in the virtual machine (VM) or on the server, open Internet
   Explorer and enter http://wss3. After a brief delay, you will see Figure 3.5.

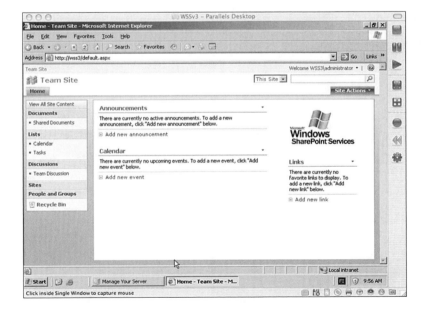

FIGURE 3.5
The default page
of a standard
WSS 3.0 site.

2. Select Site Settings from the Site Actions drop-down. The page shown in
   Figure 3.6 appears.

FIGURE 3.6
The Site Settings
page.

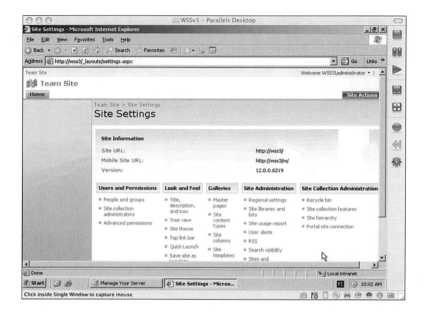

3. Select People and Groups from the top of the leftmost column. The People and Groups page appears (see Figure 3.7).

FIGURE 3.7
The People and
Groups page.

4. Select New and Add Users. You'll get an empty Add Users: Team Site page.

Let's start from the top of that list of users and first specify MyAdmin.

5. Enter **MyAdmin** in the Users/Group box and change the drop-down under Add Users to a SharePoint Group to Team Site Owners (Full Control) (see Figure 3.8).

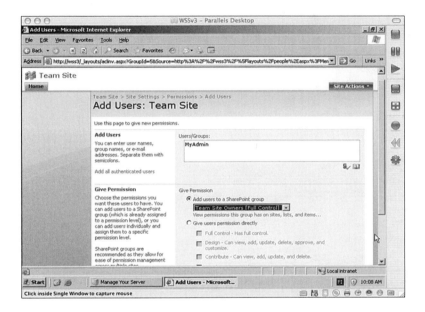

FIGURE 3.8
Adding a user with administrator rights.

6. Click OK. Figure 3.9 appears.

Despite our efforts to call this user MyAdmin to match the password, WSS 3.0 ignores our capital letters and calls it myadmin!

Tip

---

7. Repeat this for MyContrib (allocate to Team Site Members), MyReader (allocate to Team Site Visitors), and MyDocLib (allocate to Team Site Members).

Getting Familiar with SharePoint Groups and Permission Levels

When a user obtains rights to a site, the default behavior is to add that user to a SharePoint group. There are three such default SharePoint groups: Team Site Members, Team Site Owners, and Team Site Visitors.

FIGURE 3.9
A list of users
with
administrator
rights.

The language used here is a bit confusing:

Originally in this chapter (at server level), we *added* users.

But, we have just been *assigning* existing users to a group that has the rights to access a WSS 3.0 site. What we do next is *give users access rights* directly (rather than indirectly via a group) to a WSS 3.0 site.

If you click More in the leftmost column of Figure 3.9, you'll see that at the moment those three groups—Team Site Members, Team Site Owners, and Team Site Visitors— are all there are (see Figure 3.10).

What you also see in Figure 3.10 is that these groups give different levels of permission, respectively:

▶ **Contribute**. Allows you to add, update, and delete (and read)

▶ **Full Control**. Allows you to do almost anything

▶ **Read**. Read-only

FIGURE 3.10
A list of the standard SharePoint groups.

The fourth permission level, Design, is the most powerful one after Full Control. I suspect Microsoft didn't provide this as a default SharePoint group (and thus available from the drop-down) because it wanted to make it difficult to mistakenly give someone this type of power.

Full Control is an option, but the supposition might have been that people are careful when allocating others administration rights but less careful with the lesser rights.

> The inclusion of these three default SharePoint groups represents one improvement in the version 3 SharePoint products compared to the version 2 SharePoint products. They make it easier for administrators to use sensible methods when adding users.

Tip

With SharePoint groups, you can specify that the same SharePoint group has access rights to somewhere else. Then, anyone added to that SharePoint group automatically has access rights to both places.

If you were using direct access rights, you would need to add that new user in both places. Doing so might seem easy enough until you realize that you would have to know *all* the places you need to add the user to (typically more than just two places).

Example of the Benefits of SharePoint Groups

We have our present site, and in time we will have several users in the Team Site Visitors group (= Read rights), several users in the Team Site Members group (= Contribute rights), and a few in the TeamSite Full Control group (= Full Control rights).

Now suppose we create a subsite to that site (doing this is covered later) and we don't want people with only read rights to be able to access that subsite at all. We can just give access rights to that subsite to the Contribute and Full Control SharePoint groups, and the job is done.

Now let's assume the same request, but now all the users are not in a SharePoint group but have all been given Read or Contribute or Full Control rights as individuals.

In this case, we first need to make lists of the people who have Contribute rights and add them to the subsite. Then we must do the same for those users with Full Control rights.

The job is done, for now (with more effort than in the process discussed previously). However, every time we add a new user to the site and give that user Contribute rights, we must also remember to give that user Contribute rights to the subsite (and as more subsites are added, this process quickly becomes a nightmare).

Example of Using AD Groups

Just as you can add a number of individual users to a SharePoint group or give them individual rights, you can also add an entire AD group to a SharePoint group or give that AD group an "individual" right.

One typical example of this is if you have a site for the Personnel department.

You might not want to give anyone but members of the Personnel department's AD group (= ADPersonnel perhaps) access rights. And therefore, you typically create a Personnel site, remove anyone listed with rights to access the site (even perhaps the administrator), and then give rights to ADPersonnel to Contribute to the site.

Tip	In this scenario, you typically give that AD group an "individual" access right.

Creating a New SharePoint Group

Let's look at why the users we created in section "Creating Local Users" included two users called MyReaderPlus1 and MyReaderPlus2.

Our intention is to have a number of users who have more permissions than a reader, but fewer permissions than a contributor. To do this, we first create a new SharePoint group called ReadPlus:

1. At Figure 3.7, select New > New Group. Figure 3.11 appears.

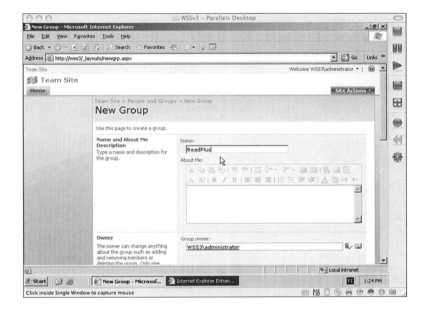

FIGURE 3.11
Creating a new SharePoint group.

2. Fill in the name of the SharePoint group. Make sure that you go to the end of the page and select Read—Can View Only for the options that are there before you click Create.

Amending the Permissions of a SharePoint Group

Our new SharePoint group ReadPlus still has only the standard rights of the normal Team Site Visitors SharePoint group. So, we need to amend the permissions of ReadPlus:

1. Select Site Permissions in the leftmost column. A screen appears showing ReadPlus listed along with Team Site Members, Team Site Owners, and Team Site Visitors.

2. Select ReadPlus. On the menu item, select Settings and then Permission Levels from the drop-down. The Permission Levels page appears (see Figure 3.12).

FIGURE 3.12
The Permission Levels page.

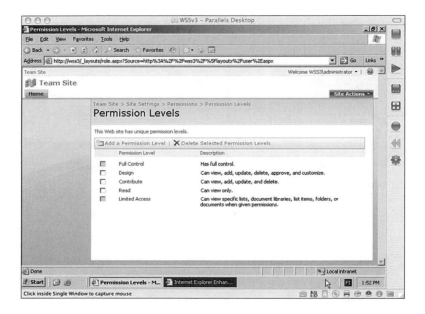

3. Select Add a Permission Level from the menu line. Figure 3.13 shows the Add a Permission Level page.

   I've started writing Read Plus Delete Versions as the name—I made it as far as Read Plus only—and have written a description explaining what this set of permissions is.

4. Scroll down and specify all the standard Read permissions.

Tip

Some of the lower permissions will already be selected when you come to them because they are connected to permissions that are higher in the list.

5. Select Delete Versions.

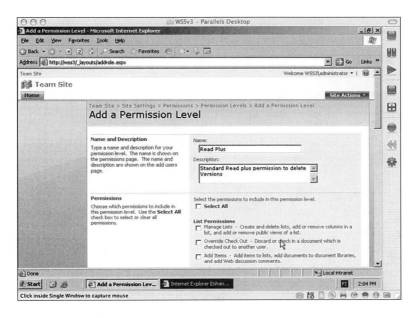

FIGURE 3.13
Adding a permission level.

6. Click Create. Now the Permission Levels list includes Read Plus Delete Versions (see Figure 3.14).

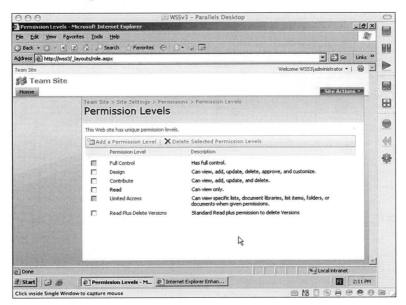

FIGURE 3.14
The Permission Levels page, now with Read Plus Delete Versions.

7. In the so-called breadcrumb trail (which shows where we came from), select Permissions. This takes you to the Permissions: Team Site page (see Figure 3.15).

FIGURE 3.15
The list of Share-Point groups (and users).

8. Click ReadPlus. This takes you to Figure 3.16.

What's selected here at the moment for the Read Plus SharePoint group is the Read permission.

FIGURE 3.16
The revised list of available permissions.

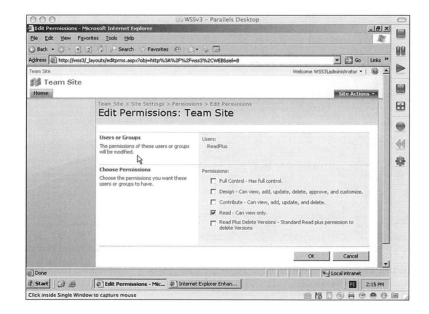

9. Select Read Plus Delete Versions and unselect Read, which is redundant because all its permissions are also included in Read Plus Delete Versions.

10. Click OK. We now clearly have an additional SharePoint group called ReadPlus that has the Read Plus Delete Versions set of permissions.

Following this, we can use the same procedure as in Figure 3.8 to give access rights to the site to both MyReaderPlus1 and MyReaderPlus2 and to allocate them to the site group ReadPlus, which is now included in the drop-down as ReadPlus [Read Plus Delete Versions].

Summary

This hour examined which rights users have when they access sites and how these can be specified. We created users local to the server, assigned these to existing site groups, and created a new site group with a different set of permissions.

Q&A

Q. *Can you specify two (or more) permissions for the same SharePoint group?*

A. You wouldn't normally because you would have SharePoint groups that overlap permissions with other SharePoint groups. That is, one set of permissions includes all the individual permissions of another set of permissions.

However, there is nothing in the system to stop you from having a set of permissions that covers only most of the permissions in another set of permissions, yet also includes one additional permission. In that case, some of the users might need to belong to the sum of those permissions, and the SharePoint group those users are in would need both sets of permissions.

Q. *Wouldn't it have been possible to create a new set of permissions (called DeleteOnly) where only the delete permission was selected? Then it would have been possible to specify the normal Read set of permissions and the DeleteOnly set and have the same effect as the method you used.*

A. Yes, in SharePoint you can often obtain the same result in many different ways. In this case, I personally prefer the approach I took, but it's only a matter of opinion.

Workshop

Quiz

1. What are the three main users to whom you can give access rights to a site?

2. What is the principal advantage in giving a SharePoint group access rights to a site compared to giving such rights directly to a user?

Quiz Answers

1. Local users on the server, SharePoint groups, and AD groups.

2. The main advantage is that it's common for the same set of users to be given access rights to the same sites. By using SharePoint groups, this becomes less of an administrative nightmare.

HOUR 4

Using the Administration Site

What You'll Learn in This Hour

▶ Ensuring access to the WSS 3.0 site

▶ Working with the Administration site

In this chapter, we do a couple of practical and necessary things with the Administration site.

Ensuring Access to the WSS 3.0 Site

Let's make sure that we can access the WSS 3.0 site from the host machine (if a virtual machine, VM) or from another server in the network:

1. Check the TCP/IP settings for networking by opening the command prompt and entering **ipconfig /all** (see Figure 4.1).

FIGURE 4.1
The result of ipconfig/all.

Here you'll be able to see whether you have a network address (as in the example) or a local address for the VM's host machine.

2. If you are connected to the network but don't yet have a network address available, go in the server at Control Panel > Network Connections > Local Area Connection and choose Disable. Go there again and choose Enable. Now check with `ipconfig/all`.

Tip

> If disabling and enabling doesn't affect things, look at your VM's definition of the network adapter in use.

3. Once that's clear, note the TCP/IP address.

Now that we can access the site from the host of the VM or from another machine (theoretically, at least), let's first make sure that nothing in the server is blocking access.

To do that, you need to confirm that the Windows Firewall is disabled. (It is usually set to on when you install either R2 or SP2, or even Windows Server 2008.) If it isn't, that will stop us from accessing our WSS 3.0 site from anywhere other than from within the server itself.

1. Go to Start > Administrative Tools > Services and scroll to Windows Firewall (see Figure 4.2).

FIGURE 4.2
Checking the state of Windows Firewall.

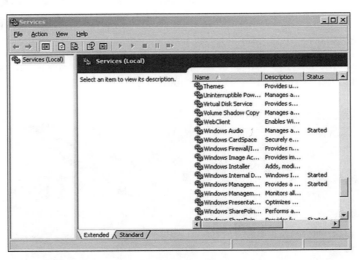

2. Double-click Windows Firewall. If the Startup Type indicates anything other than Disabled, set it to Disabled (see Figure 4.3). Click OK.

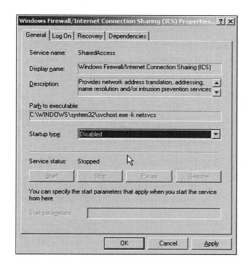

FIGURE 4.3
Disabling the
Windows Firewall
service.

> Simply disabling it is the brute-force method. It works and, for a test site, it's all we
> need. If you set up a production site, investigate the Windows Firewall in detail.

Note

Now that we can access the site, let's look at the Administration site. There are two
things we need to do there right away: configure Search and configure Alternate Access Methods. The following section shows how to access the Administration site and
how to do those two key configurations when there.

Working with the Administration Site

When you install WSS 3.0, you install two sites: the site you have already seen (called
http://wss3 after the name of the server) and a separate Administration site
(http://wss3:<*portnumber*>).

In this case (because we did a basic installation), the port number for the Administration site is chosen at random and is fixed. (In my case, it is 17770.)

   1. To go to the Administration site, go to Start > All Programs >
       Administrative Tools. The Administration site is listed as SharePoint 3.0
       Central Administration. The site opens in a browser (http://wss3:17770/
       default.aspx).

Note

> Unlike the situation with earlier SharePoint versions, you no longer need to be local to the server to access Central Administration, which I regard as a good thing. Others are more security conscious, however, and block such access.

2. At a page titled Central Administration (see Figure 4.4), you'll see a list of the tasks that the system thinks you should do.

FIGURE 4.4
An initial list of administrator tasks.

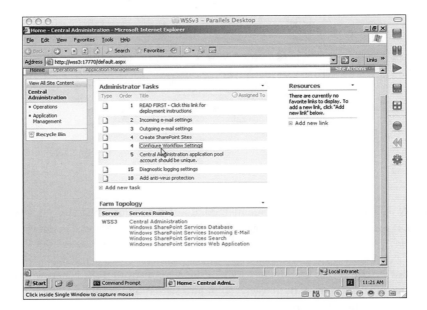

We will configure two features from that list: Search and Alternate Access Methods. (We won't go through all of those tasks because doing so requires an entire book. Here we're mainly concerned with the content of a site, not how to configure it.)

Configuring Search in the Applications Management Section of Central Administration

Looking at Figure 4.4, notice that our server WSS3 appears, along with a list of the services that it is running. One service is Windows SharePoint Services Search. The logical conclusion is that after we add some content and wait, we'll be able to use Search.

Yes, it *is* logical, but that's not how it works. For Search to actually work and not just be a "running" service, we need to specify on which server our data is stored. To do this, follow these steps:

1. Go to Application Management (see Figure 4.5).

FIGURE 4.5
The Applications
Management
page.

2. In the SharePoint Web Application Management section, click Content
Databases. The Manage Content Databases page appears (see Figure 4.6).

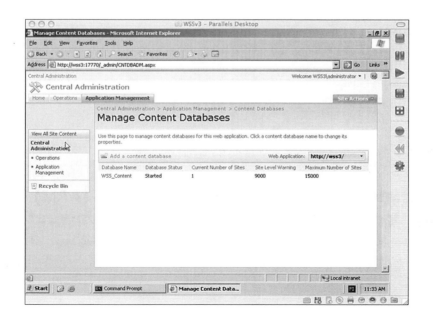

FIGURE 4.6
The Manage
Content Data-
bases page.

3. Select WSS_Content. The next page is called Manage Content Database Settings. Scroll halfway down this page and add WSS3 to the Search Server field. You will see Figure 4.7.

FIGURE 4.7
Specifying the name of the server containing the content databases.

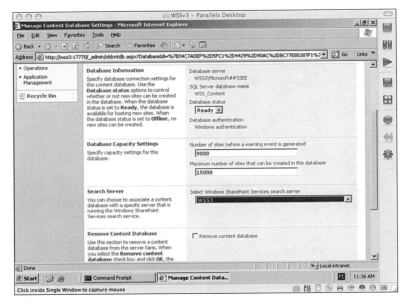

4. Finish configuring the Search feature by clicking OK.

Note

We have only one server, and the databases containing the data are stored in that one server. What's more, the installation routine knows this because that is where the installation routine set them up. (Basic installation didn't give us an alternative.) However, Search still needs to be told explicitly, "The data I want to search is stored on server *X*."

The need to specify which server to search isn't obvious by any means. If you don't configure this, however, your search will not work.

Configuring Alternate Access Methods (AAM) in the Operations Section of Central Administration

We've made one change starting from the Application Management page. Now it's time to make another important change this time starting from the Operations page. To do this, click Operations in the leftmost column to display Figure 4.8.

FIGURE 4.8
The Operations page.

Use the Alternate Access Mappings part of Global Configuration at the upper right.

First, however, let's do a few experiments using a browser on a different machine in the network and from the browser of the host system of the VM. (If you don't have your site in a network, just use the browser in the host system of the VM.)

A Few Site Access Tests

The first test is to write **http://wss3** in the browser and see what results.

Using my Mac's (= host system) browser (Safari), I got a long message ending with "can't find the server wss3." Using Firefox on the Mac, I received the authentication box and then a Google search for wss3. Using my home system's browsers (XPPro/IE6 and Vista/IE7), I got similar messages. Using my work machine's browser (XP Pro/IE6), however, I got a request for authentication, and then the site's default page opened.

If that works (*if*), we're fine, because you'll be able to click any of the internal links and (because wss3 is known) they'll work, too.

But that probably didn't work, so let's try using the TCP/IP address we jotted down earlier.

The second test is to use **http://192.168.1.197** (or the equivalent for the work machine tests) to access the site.

The Mac first asked me for authorization (administrator/password), but then told me it can't open http://wss3/default.aspx because it can't find wss3. The home PCs both asked for authorization and went to the site just fine (showing http://192.168.1.197/default.aspx). But, the internal links would not work. The work machine (using the TCP/IP address that it has been given when in the work network) asked for authorization (and was given the correct name/password). It "thought" for a long time before asking for authorization again. Finally, it loaded the default page (which showed http://wss3/default.aspx; so, it's been converted again). The same happened there via Firefox. In both cases, because of the conversion to wss3, the internal links worked.

As these tests demonstrated, there is no consistency. What's more, all these tests were on intranets.

Note

> An Internet access is never going to find wss3. Any attempt to go to a TCP/IP address will always lead to internal links (which will always point to http://wss3/nnn not working).

Configuring Alternate Access Mappings

You can use alternate access mappings to fix the problem of access to the site itself and especially the problem of access to links within the site.

Note

> Joel Oleson wrote a good Microsoft paper on alternate access mappings (http://technet2.microsoft.com/windowsserver/WSS/en/library/c8ccffce-5162-46af-a3ef-1d7914e8efee1033.mspx?mfr=true).

Here are the steps required to configure Alternate Access Mappings:

1. Return to the Operations page (refer to Figure 4.8). Click Alternate Access Mappings. Figure 4.9 shows the Alternate Access Mappings page. Both sites that are known should be listed here (http://wss3 and http://wss3:17770).

   The user interface that you need to follow to add alternate addresses isn't all that good; let's walk through it.

2. First click Edit Public URLs. You'll see the screen in Figure 4.10 or the equivalent screen with SharePoint – 80 in yellow after Alternate Access Mapping Collection (or a screen that has nothing in that same location).

3. To get to the screen with SharePoint – 80 (if you don't see it already), click Central Administration (top right) or the blank item that might be there. Then click Change Alternative Access Mapping Collection.

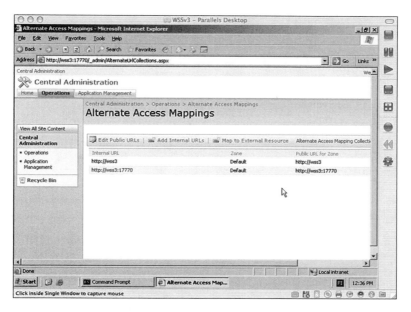

FIGURE 4.9
Defining alternate access mappings.

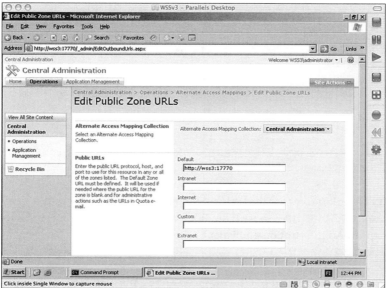

FIGURE 4.10
The Edit Public URLs screen.

You'll now see the Select an Alternate Access Mapping Collection page (see Figure 4.11).

4. Double-click SharePoint - 80 to display the Edit Public Zone URLs screen (see Figure 4.12). Notice that in addition to the Default field (http:/wss3), there are fields for Intranet, Internet, Custom, and Extranet.

FIGURE 4.11
The Select an Alternate Access Mapping Collection page.

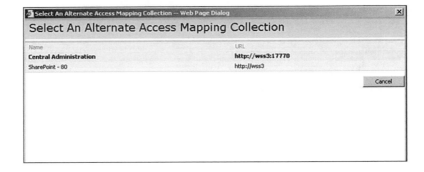

FIGURE 4.12
Defining alternate access mappings.

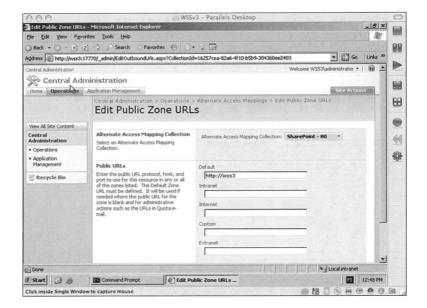

5. It's logical in this case that we will fill out the Intranet field with http://192.168.1.197, so we'll do that. (We then repeat the process for the Central Administration equivalent, where we'll use http://192.168.1.197:17770.)

Now when you try to access the site using http://192.168.1.197 you **will** access the site. More important, when you get to the site, the internal links will still work even though they continue to point to http://wss3/etc.

Figure 4.13 shows my settings for a *different* WSS 3.0–based site where I keep a copy of my WSS FAQ site (http://192.168.1.199 on that same home network) in a VM on the Mac. Notice that all the available fields contain values.

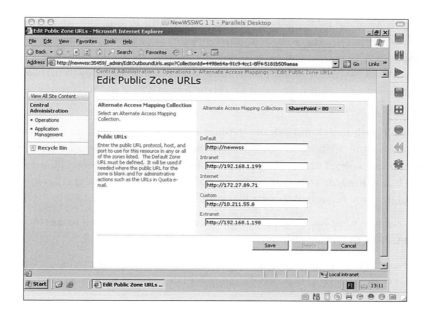

FIGURE 4.13
A complete set
of public zone
URLs.

In order from the top, here are the addresses I have listed:

▶ **Intranet**. The TCP/IP I have for the VM on the home wireless network if I start the Mac before the Vista-based PC

▶ **Internet**. The TCP/IP I have for the VM if I'm running the Mac on the office network

▶ **Custom**. The TCP/IP I have for the VM if I am running the Mac with no network connected

▶ **Extranet**. The TCP/IP I have for the VM on the home wireless network if I start the Mac after the Vista-based PC

All of these addresses are constant except for the office network. If I haven't had my Mac connected for a few days, I get a new TCP/IP address. So, I first check the TCP/IP with `ipconfig/all`, and then amend the last three numbers of this TCP/IP address in this field. (I do the same for the equivalent Central Administration address field.)

Note

The key thing about these addresses is that you have the default URL and up to four alternative addresses. The names (Intranet, Internet, and so on) are irrelevant. Nothing happens differently if you enter an intranet address in the Internet field and vice versa. Just include all the alternative addresses that people are likely to use. For documentation reasons it is however best to use the Intranet field for the Intranet address and so on.

I am using the intranet and extranet settings for two different versions of the same thing (access into my home network). That's just me being lazy. Because I had a spare extranet entry, I just used it for a possible URL (if my Vista-based PC had been started before the Mac's VM and had thus grabbed the URL ending in .199) in order to avoid the need to amend the intranet value (to .198) if that happened.

As you can see, after you've got past the odd menu choices required to specify these different URLs, the whole process is straightforward.

If you have ISA Server, however, read the Joel Oleson article I mentioned earlier, because configuring alternate access mapping for ISA Server is not clear cut.

Summary

This hour concentrated on the Central Administration site. It showed how to change the site's default settings for Search. The hour concluded with defining alternate access mappings. These mappings enable you to ensure that people accessing the site via different URLs can still have full functionality when using the site.

Q&A

Q. *Can you amend the port number that is used for the Central Administration site after the installation is complete?*

A. You can amend it later with a `stsadm` statement in the command line:

```
stsadm -o setadminport -port <port> (where <port> is for instance "12345")
```

You can find more information about this—including where to do this—at http://technet2.microsoft.com/WindowsServer/WSS/en/library/8e7b1668-cd69-488c-b10b-04b9c91ce9711033.mspx.

Q. *Do you recommend changing the port number of the Central Administration site?*

A. No. On the positive side, if you change the port number, you can always use the same port number for all your servers. And therefore, you don't need to remember the number being used for one particular site.

On the negative site, it's risky to assume that all the SharePoint code will correctly use the revised port number. I would always be worried that something had been set on installation (with port 98765) that would no longer work after a change (to port 12345).

Workshop

Quiz

1. Do you need to be on the server to access Central Administration?

2. Why doesn't Search work out of the box?

3. Which alternate access method field do you need to fill in to cater for users who will be entering your site via your extranet?

Quiz Answers

1. No, you can access Central Administration via the browser provided this possibility has not been shut down for security reasons.

2. Search works only if the Search server is told which server contains the databases that it is searching.

3. The answer isn't the obvious "the Extranet field." In fact, any of the fields (Intranet, Internet, Extranet, or Custom) will do. However, it is good practice to use the Extranet field.

HOUR 5

Planning a Site's Structure

What You'll Learn in This Hour

- ▶ What sites are
- ▶ Creating a site
- ▶ Templates used to create a site
- ▶ Which site to use for which situation

Basic Information About Sites

Before we can start thinking about a site's structure and contents, we first need to know more about sites in general. Our standard installation of WSS 3.0 created two sites: a "normal" one (http://wss3) and a "special" one (http://wss3:17770).

The words *normal* and *special* are by no means official.	**Note**

The normal site isn't used for any particular purpose and can have subsites. The special site administrates the entire WSS 3.0 system using routines provided by Microsoft as part of the software package. This site doesn't include a function for creating a subsite.

Note

> The Central Administration site is the only special site that comes with WSS 3.0.
>
> MOSS 2007, on the other hand, has a few special sites:
>
> ▶ MySite, is a site that all users can define for themselves (if not blocked by the administrator). It's used for the dual role of having a personal page containing information that the user wants to make available to others and a more personal page that the user uses as his usual entry to the system and that contains the information that the user wants to see personally.
>
> ▶ Shared Services Provider (SSP) is a site for the central administration of additional services.

Here are a few often confusing terms that you will come across:

▶ **Web application**. Any Windows Internet Information Services (IIS) website that is in the SharePoint system (here, for instance, the default site).

▶ **Top-level site**. A site that is at the top of a site + subsite structure (even if there are no subsites).

▶ **Site collection**. A set of sites and subsites. There are exceptions to this definition. For example, the Central Administration site is regarded as a site collection even though it has no subsites.

Creating a Site

In this section, you create a subsite to our default site to see what different kinds of sites can be created. These steps show you how to create a Meeting Workspace site:

1. Let's start with that default page, as shown in Figure 5.1. Select Site Actions and then Create from the drop-down.

2. In Figure 5.2, we select Sites and Workspaces (at the far right). This action brings you to Figure 5.3. I've entered BookSite1 as the site name and used it in the URL.

3. Scroll down the page until you reach the Template Selection section (see Figure 5.4).

   When we create a site, we have a choice of what type it will be. For a standard WSS 3.0 installation, there are two groupings of site types: Collaboration and Meetings. For each, there are subtypes. Figure 5.4 lists the options for Collaboration, and clicking Meetings gives us a choice of five different meeting workspaces.

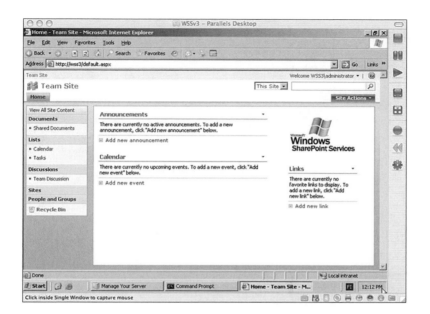

FIGURE 5.1
WSS 3.0 default
web page.

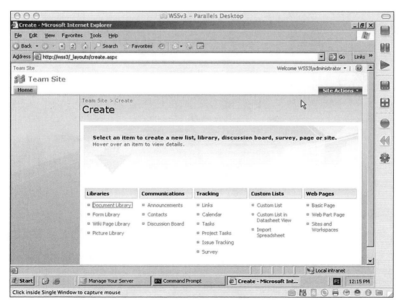

FIGURE 5.2
Standard Create
page.

The difference between *sites* and *workspaces* is explained in the section, "Q&A."   ***Note***

FIGURE 5.3
Creating a new
SharePoint site.

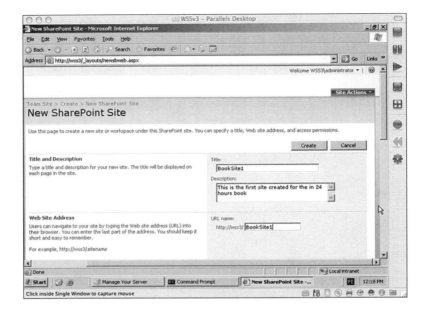

FIGURE 5.4
Selecting a tem-
plate when creat-
ing a site.

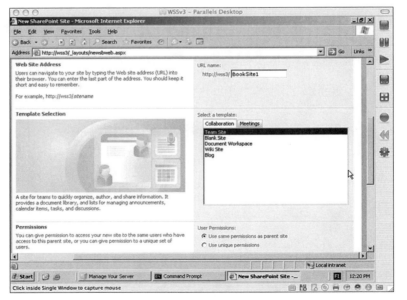

Note MOSS 2007 offers several more site types with subsites. The Publishing site type,
which is one of those extra types, is notorious because even though it provides

some useful additional functionality it doesn't contain functionality that most people regard as standard.

Each template gives us a different look to the page and a different set of functions. The original default template is a "team site," which is the most commonly used type.

Tip

Avoid blank sites. It might be appealing to start off with an empty screen, but unfortunately "different set of functions" means that you will be missing functionality. Therefore, you might not be able to later add something you really want.

Use the team sites unless you have special needs, such as creating a wiki (see Hour 12, "Using Wikis and Blogs").

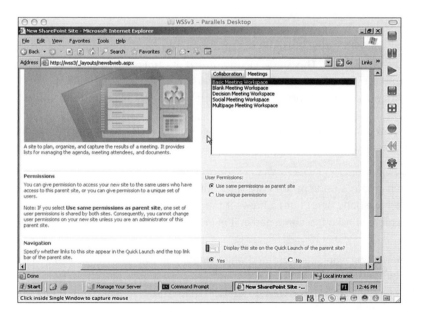

FIGURE 5.5
Selecting the Basic Meeting Workspace template.

   4. Make BookSite1 a meeting workspace just so that you can get a feel for the difference in look. Select Meetings, and then Basic Meeting Workspace, as shown in Figure 5.5. For now, accept the defaults. Click Create.

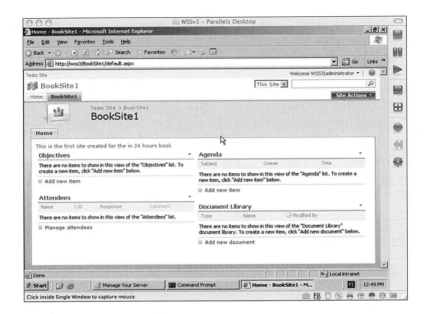

As you can see from Figure 5.6, this is a completely different look to that of the default site. This site is clearly aimed at a meeting or series of meetings (as you can understand from the inclusion of Agenda, Objectives, Attendees, and a document Library for documents relevant to the meeting).

We cover what lies behind the things you see on the site's page in the next hour. For now, concentrate on sites.

Tip

You can create a workspace in two ways: either from within an Office application or (as we have done here) from a browser that is accessing a site. Although they look the same and have the same name, it is important that you note the difference:

▶ A meeting workspace created while creating an Outlook meeting is a site for that particular meeting.

▶ A meeting workspace created when in the browser is a site that offers a suitable look and functionality for a meeting.

▶ A meeting workspace created while creating an Outlook meeting is a site outside any site structure.

▶ A meeting workspace created when in the browser (like BookSite1) *is* in a site structure and is thus a member of a site collection.

Using Templates

A *template* is a ready-made set of code that is used to create a site. The code contains both a look (site design, colors, fonts) and a feel (what functions are available to use in connection with the site).

In addition to Microsoft providing templates, it's possible for us to create new templates and have them appear either under the existing Collaboration and Meetings group names or under our own group name. Typically, templates aren't created by scratch. Instead, they are generally created by amending a site that was created with a standard template and then using the Save as Template function to create a new template with a different name.

Let's walk through an example. Here, we'll change the color of a standard team site. Let's use BookSite1.

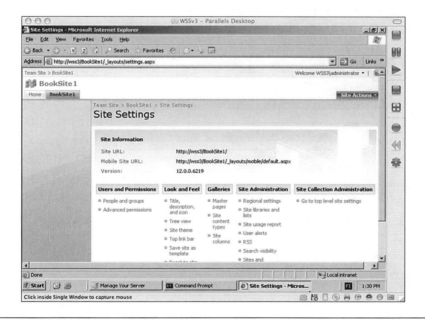

FIGURE 5.7
Specifying site settings.

Note

Your browser should be pointing at BookSite1. If it isn't, click Home and then click BookSite1 in the leftmost column.

1. In Figure 5.6, select Site Actions and (from the drop-down) Site Settings. Figure 5.7 appears.

FIGURE 5.8
Selecting a
theme when
amending a
site.

FIGURE 5.8
Selecting a
theme when
amending a
site.

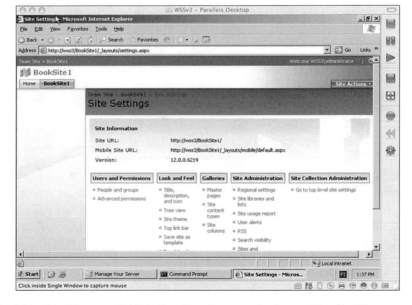

FIGURE 5.9
Selecting a tem-
plate when creat-
ing a site.

> **2.** Select Site Theme, which is listed in the second column. The Site Theme
>   page appears, as shown in Figure 5.8.
>
> **3.** Scroll through the various themes in the rightmost column. Select Cardinal,
>   which is the reddest.

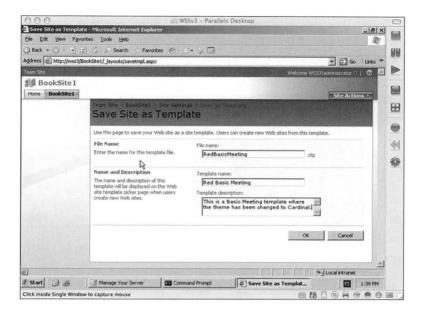

FIGURE 5.10
Saving a site as
a template.

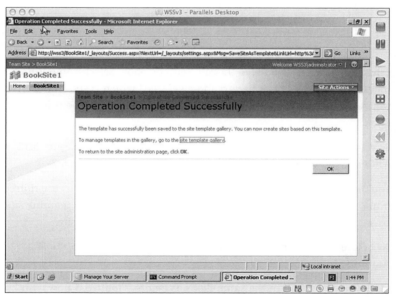

FIGURE 5.11
The template is
safely in the site
template gallery.

4. Click Apply. Figure 5.9 shows the result.

5. Find Save Site as Template in the second column. Complete the form as I have done in Figure 5.10.

6. Click OK. The new site template, Red Basic Meeting, has been saved to the site template gallery (see Figure 5.11). If you want, you can click the link to that gallery in Figure 5.11 to see what it looks like.

FIGURE 5.12
The Site Settings page after a sub-site has been created.

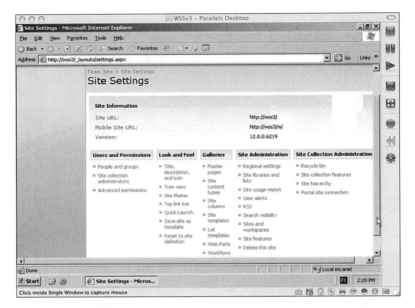

7. Clicking OK takes us back to the Site Settings page. Select Home from the menu row to get us back to our "top-level site," which is still in blue. Here, we create a second subsite to this top-level site, which will be called BookSite2.

8. Select Site Actions and Settings. Compare what we get (see Figure 5.12) with what we had when we went to this page last (refer to Figure 5.7).

   You're not mistaken. There are different (and more) entries in the right column. The system is reacting to the fact that we now have a genuine site collection (site + subsite) rather than just a single top-level site.

9. As before, we will go to Sites and Workspaces via the link in the Sites Administration column.

10. Click Create and fill in the same fields as before (Figure 5.5 now with BookSite2 rather than BookSite1 and with a description of Uses the Basic Meeting template but with the Cardinal theme).

11. Scroll to the bottom of the page, where we see Figure 5.13.

12. Select Custom to see the new Red Basic Meeting template. Select that. Click Create.

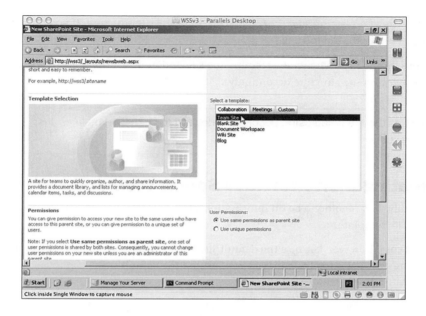

FIGURE 5.13
The site tem-
plates that are
available if we
have chosen
Save Site as
Template.

You just created a second subsite (BookSite2) to the default site, and this second subsite looks the same as our amended first site (BookSite1).

So now we know that if we want to have a standard look to sites that is different from the look provided by Microsoft, we can do it.

Designing Your Site: Where to Put the Sites and Which Templates to Use

When creating a site, you have choices. You can choose where to put the site and what kind of site it is.

Creating a Wiki (or Blog or Meeting) Site

There are standard templates for Wikis, Blogs, or Meetings, so if you want to create one of these types of sites you will normally use the standard template provided for them.

In each case we have the choice between creating our new site as a subsite to the default site or creating a new top-level site.

In the case of wikis or blogs (see Hour 12), there's normally no point in having them under the default site in the site structure, so just create a new site.

In the case of a Meeting site, that could be part of the site structure. If you think it is, create it under the default site.

Always think about why you're creating the site and make it a new site or a site within the existing site structure accordingly.

Tip

> Don't delete the default site. People who do tend to get problems later. Just ignore it if you aren't using it.

Creating a Site for Your Sports Club

Generally, this is going to be an information site. Therefore, you will choose the Team Site template.

In this case, however, because the default site is already a team site, there's no need to create any new sites. Instead, you can just use the default site.

Tip

> Note the warning about the cost of connecting to the Internet in the FAQ section at the end!

Let's close this section on private sites with a couple of thoughts about access rights.

When you create a top-level site, you can decide whether anyone can access it (anonymous) or whether you will restrict it to particular users (and which rights they will have).

You'll remember that we already created a cross-section of users with different access rights and added them to the site.

When you create a subsite, the default choice is that whoever can access the top-level site (or, because subsites aren't necessarily only at level two in a structure, the site above the subsite) can also access the subsite and with the same rights. This is known as *inheriting permissions*.

The other choice is to not inherit permissions, meaning that no one can access the site until you specifically grant that person access rights on that site.

Now suppose we have our Sport's site and we let everyone access that, but we also want to keep some things private, such as finances. One way is to create a subsite that doesn't inherit permissions and then specify individually those few people who need to be able to access and amend that information.

> Another way is to create a SharePoint group with standard Contribute rights and then make the members of the finance committee members of that SharePoint group. Then give the group access rights to the subsite. Then when the committee changes, just replace some of the members of that SharePoint group.
>
> ***Tip***

Creating a Site for Your Company

With company sites, the main choice is likely to be between a single site (no doubt the default site) with a subsite structure and several different top-level sites (probably also with a subsite structure). The main considerations here are administration needs, the size of those sites, and perhaps even the number of top-level sites the design requires.

You potentially have increased administration needs because the various settings are specified for an entire site collection. If you don't want to have the same settings for all your sites, you must have different site collections (= different top-level sites).

The size of those sites is important for backups and restores (for which the size of the content database is important). Each site collection must be contained in a single content database. Therefore, if you have a lot of sites with a lot of data, you might need to use different site collections (which can have their own content databases) to keep the sizes reasonable.

What is *reasonable*? It's difficult to say, but today more than 200GB is considered unreasonable (a couple of years ago, that figure was 50GB).

Finally, it's not advisable to have more than roughly 50 site collections. So, if you are thinking about using a site collection for each subsidiary and you have more than 40 subsidiary companies today, think again. Instead group your subsidiaries together with one group of companies per site collection.

Summary

This hour covered different sites. It showed how to create sites and amend their look. From this new-look site, a template was created from which new sites could be generated.

The hour concluded with a brief look at which kinds of sites are suitable for common private and work areas.

Q&A

Q. *What is the difference between sites and workspaces?*

A. There isn't one. Workspaces are sites, too. The difference is probably historical.

Originally, there were only sites. Then, in SharePoint version 2 products, it became possible to create sites from Office 2003 products (and not just in the browser). Such sites were called document workspaces (connected to Excel, PowerPoint, Word) and meeting workplaces (connected to Outlook).

In present versions of SharePoint, both kinds are called workspaces, even though the meeting workspaces are sufficiently different to justify their own type button.

Q. *I want to connect my private website using WSS 3.0 to the Internet. Can I just do it?*

A. No. Connecting to the Internet involves licensing costs. These costs could drive you to using a commercial web host for your site. If you are running WSS 3.0, an Internet Connection license for the server costs a few thousand dollars. This is on top of the normal licensing requirement for the operating system used on the server (and database licensing costs if SQL Server 2K; 2005 or 2008 is used).

Workshop

Quiz

1. What are the two main groupings of site templates?

2. How does the Site Settings page change after a subsite has been created?

3. Can we create our own company look and duplicate it?

Quiz Answers

1. Collaboration and Meetings.

2. There are more options in the Site Collection Administration column after subsites have been created.

3. Yes. One way is to make changes to an existing site, save the result as a template, and then use that newly created template when creating all future sites.

HOUR 6

Using Libraries and Lists

What You'll Learn in This Hour

▶ Main areas of the default site page

▶ Differentiating between a list and the web part of a list

▶ When the content of two web parts of the same list is identical—and when it is not

Understanding the Basic Site Elements

In order to introduce the concept of lists and libraries the first section of this hour will look at the content of the standard website with special note of the links to lists and libraries that it contains.

Our test site's default page shows the two subsites that we created (see leftmost column in Figure 6.1). This column is called the Quick Launch section.

The Quick Launch section contains a number of links that enable you to do such things as

▶ Share documents (Documents section)

▶ Work with calendars and tasks (Lists section)

The main section of the page looks like it consists of two columns. These columns are called zones.

Note

You could have a horizontal zone above these two columns (and/or below it, too). It depends on the page definition. A zone can also be empty, in which case, the other zones grow to fill the gap.

FIGURE 6.1
The WSS 3.0 de-
fault web page.

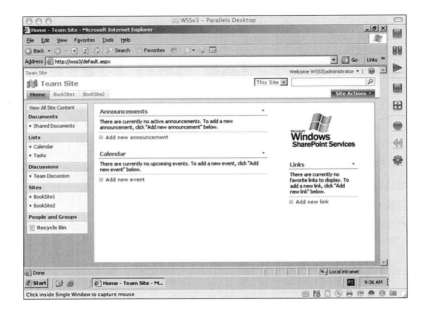

This part of the page also contains links, but its main use is to display information.
(No information is currently indicated in Figure 6.1.)

The list that follows looks at some of the places where links to lists or libraries can be
seen. It looks especially at which lists and libraries are accessible from the different
locations.

1. Calendar appears both in that leftmost column and in the main section of
   Figure 6.1. Select View All Site Content in the Quick Launch section.

2. Look at Figure 6.2. (I scrolled the page to make the comparison easier.)
   You'll see that, in addition to the items that were in Quick Launch, there
   are also Announcements and Links, which were previously listed only in
   the main section.

3. Click Site Actions (upper right), and click Create.

In Figure 6.3, we see most of the things we saw in Figure 6.2. However, we also have
various other things listed, such as the following:

▶ Form Library, Wiki Page Library, Picture Library (Libraries)

▶ Contacts (Communications)

▶ Project Tasks, Issue Tracking, Survey (Tracking)

▶ Custom List (2 versions), Import Spreadsheet (Custom Lists)

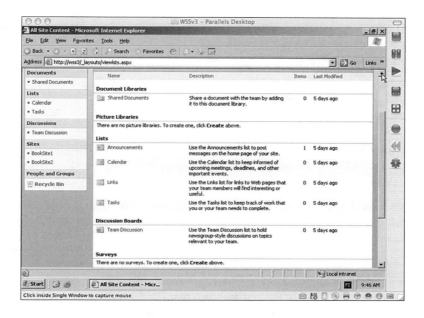

FIGURE 6.2
The View All Site
Content page.

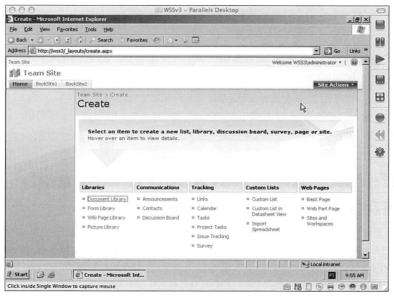

FIGURE 6.3
The administra-
tor's Create
page.

Now that we have seen that, depending on where you are, there is a different amount of lists and libraries available, here's a brief explanation of the differences of what we have seen in Figures 6.1 through 6.3.

They will be discussed in reverse order for clarity reasons.

▶ **Figure 6.3**. Contains a list of all the SharePoint library and list types that this template provides for our possible use.

Note

Import Spreadsheet isn't a type of list, but by using it, you create a list from a spreadsheet.

▶ **Figure 6.2**. Contains a list of all the SharePoint libraries and lists that Microsoft has created in its site template from the selection of library and list types available for use in Figure 6.3.

Microsoft has chosen not to create lists and libraries from **all** the list and library types available to it.

Note

The sentence "Microsoft has chosen..." explains why some of the names in Figure 6.2 differ from the names in Figure 6.3. When using the list type Announcements to create a list in a standard team site, Microsoft called that list Announcements. When using the library type Document Library to create a library, however, Microsoft called that library Shared Documents.

▶ **Figure 6.1**. Contains the lists and libraries that Microsoft decided to list in the Quick Launch section and/or in the main section of the default site's web page.

Before we use some of these options, we must change the look of the default website. Let me first clear up a couple of things.

Differentiating Between a List and Library

A list is how SharePoint stores like data in the same place. An example of a list is a Calendar where as we have seen the items of the list are dates and descriptions of what will happen on those dates. A library is a kind of a list. The difference between a library and any other kind of list is that the main function of a library is to store files, whereas the main function of a list that is not a document library is to store data.

A library has versioning because it stores files; a nonlibrary list doesn't.

Note

I use the word *list* as the name for lists that aren't libraries. I use the word *library* for lists that are libraries. I use the phrase *all kinds of lists* when I mean both.

Differentiating Between a List and a List's Web Part

Tip

People new to SharePoint have problems differentiating between a list and a web part, so don't skip this section. It will save you time later!

The short explanation of the difference between a list and a list's web part is that what you see in the main section of the default site is a web part representation of a list; it's not the list itself. (However, that explanation is useful only after you read the next section and do the exercises.)

We've established that Shared Documents is a library that Microsoft created from the library type Document Library. There's a link to it in the leftmost column; when that is selected, the document library named Shared Documents opens.

We've also established that Calendar is a list that Microsoft created from the list type Calendar. Clicking the Calendar link takes us to the list named Calendar.

There is also something called Calendar in the center/right area. This is a web part that Microsoft called Calendar. If we click the Calendar, we go to the list Calendar (again).

Note

Are you keeping count? So far, we have three different "calendars":

▶ List type Calendar
▶ List named Calendar
▶ Web part named Calendar

Wouldn't it have been useful if Microsoft had given them different names?

Creating a Calendar List and a Calendar Web Part

All these calendars are making us crazy, right? Follow these steps to end up with three different names for Calendar:

1. First (and you should be still at Figure 6.3 if not go there by clicking "Site Actions" and "Create"), select Calendar and create a new calendar called My Test Calendar. Leave the default setting (Yes) of Display This List on the Quick Launch (see Figure 6.4).

FIGURE 6.4
Creating a new calendar called Test Calendar.

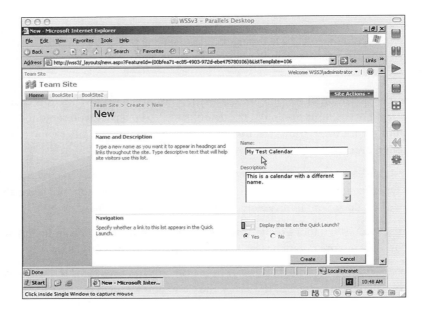

After clicking Create, you'll see that the Lists section of Quick Launch now contains three items: Calendar, Tasks, and My Test Calendar. It would be better if new links were not added at the end, but they are.

Tip

SharePoint Designer 2007 can be used to put the links in Quick Launch sections in any desired order. (Later in the book we'll use SharePoint Designer 2007 to create workflows and a special kind of web part called a Data View web part.)

2. If not already there, go back to the default page (by clicking Home on the horizontal menu line). Select Site Actions > Edit Page. Figure 6.5 shows the page that you can now edit.

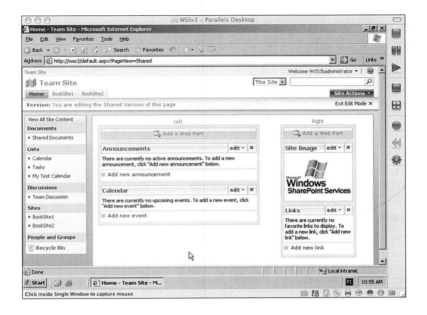

FIGURE 6.5
The Edit a Page
web page.

3. Select Add a Web Part in the center column. A list appears, showing all the lists and libraries we can create a web part from, followed by a list of all the web parts we can add to the site (see Figure 6.6).

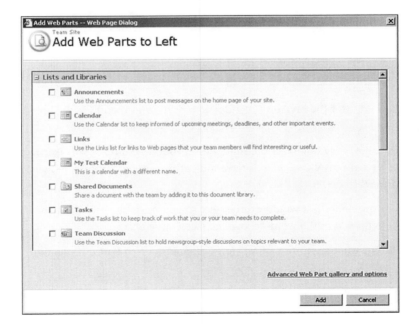

FIGURE 6.6
Adding the web
part representa-
tions of lists and
libraries to a
page.

Note Hour 9, "Looking at List Types and the Included Web Parts," discusses adding other kinds of web parts to a site. In this hour, we just create web parts from lists and libraries.

4. Select My Test Calendar and press Enter.

    As shown in Figure 6.7, the web part that is now listed at the top of the center column is called My Test Calendar (which is not what we want).

FIGURE 6.7
The Edit Page web page with My Test Calendar.

Click Edit (for the My Test Calendar web part), and then Modify Shared Web Part.

A window now opens on the right with a couple of drop-downs (see Figure 6.8). (<Current View> is an interesting option; we cover that when we look at views in detail.)

5. For now, go to that window and select Appearance by clicking the plus sign (+) to the left of the word *Appearance* (see Figure 6.9).

6. Change the present title of My Test Calendar to Web Part of Calendar. Click OK.

    While we are here, let's get rid of the original calendar. To do so, click the X at the top right of the Calendar web part to close it (see Figure 6.10).

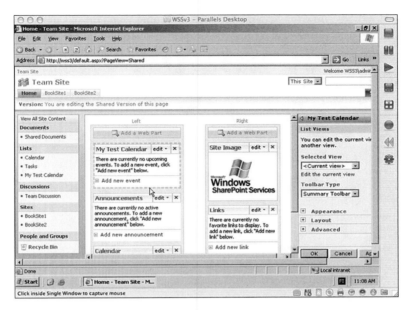

FIGURE 6.8
Modifying the My Test Calendar web part.

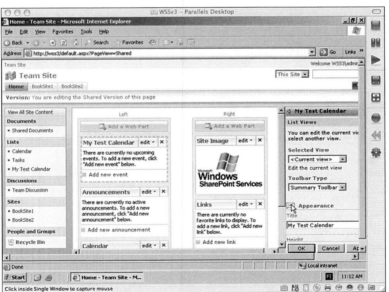

FIGURE 6.9
Modifying the title of the My Test Calendar web part.

Note

Closing the calendar does not remove it from the code of the page; it marks it as nonvisible. If you want to delete it from the code of the page, click Edit > Delete.

7. Select the Announcements web part by clicking the line to the right of the word Announcements. Without letting go of the mouse button, drag the selected area upward. When you reach the name Web Part of Calendar, you'll see an orange line above the name. Now you can let go.

FIGURE 6.10
The default page
with Web Part of
Calendar.

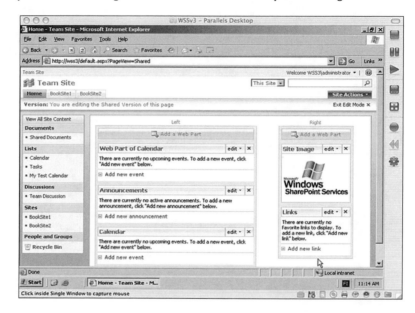

The order should be Announcements and then Web Part of Calendar, as in Figure 6.11. (If it isn't, try the drag and drop again.)

FIGURE 6.11
The default page
after a web part
"drag and drop."

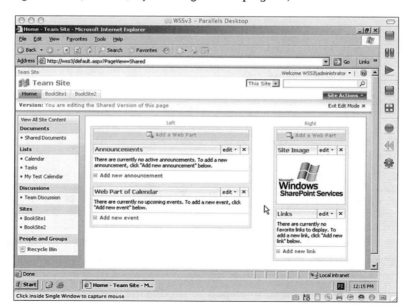

8. Select Exit Edit Mode (or the X next to it). We're now back at the default page, just out of Edit mode.

9. You'll see that we still have Calendar listed in the Quick Launch section. We could leave it there, but because we'll use the new calendar instead, we might as well remove that listing. Before we do so, however, let's make use of the fact that for the moment we have two different calendars to show the complete separation between the Calendar List "Calendar" and the Calendar List "My Test Calendar." The following sublist creates a calendar entry in "Calendar" and shows that that entry isn't in My Test Calendar:

> **1.** Click Calendar > New. I use 3/7/2008 and make it an all-day event (see Figure 6.12). You should use your "tomorrow's date."

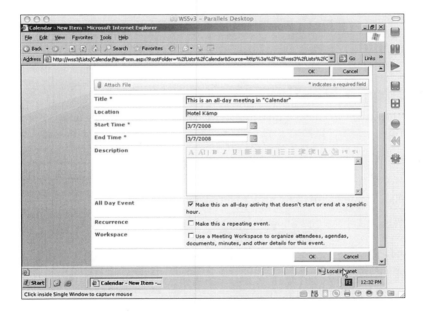

FIGURE 6.12
Creating a calendar entry.

> **2.** Click OK. Notice that we have something marked for March 7, 2008 (see Figure 6.13).

> **3.** Open My Test Calendar and look at the same date. You will see *nothing*!

As promised, even though both calendars were created from the Calendar list type, they are completely separate, and entries into one are not reflected in the other.

Note

FIGURE 6.13
The calendar entry in the Calendar document library.

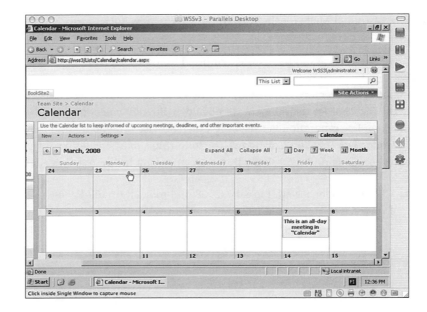

Creating a Meeting

Follow these steps to create a meeting and see that it is now visible on the home page:

1. While still in My Test Calendar, specify a meeting called Once Only Meeting. Check the All Day Event check box (because that is fastest).

2. Click Home again to go back to our default page.

3. Under Web Part of Calendar, there is a listing of Once Only Meeting.

The next steps add a second web part that is also based on the "My Test Calendar" list.

1. Edit the page again via Site Actions > Edit Page.

2. Use Add a Web Part > My Test Calendar > Add.

There are now two calendars with different names (see Figure 6.14). Both calendars show the same meeting, but we only added it to a single calendar.

When you add to a web page a web part based on a particular list, that web part includes the contents of that list. Therefore, if you have two web parts that both are based on the same list, both will have the same contents.

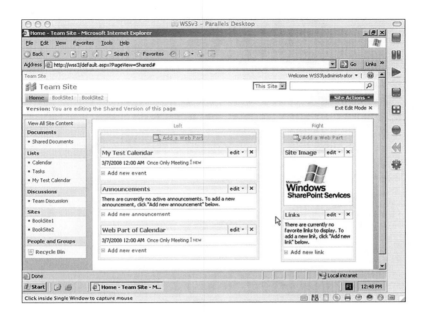

FIGURE 6.14
Two web parts of the same Calendar list.

To make sure that the ramifications of this are clear, let's add an event to the lower of our two calendars:

1. Click Add New Event in the Web Part of Calendar section.

2. This time, we'll add a meeting for 2009. (Create an hour-long meeting on 3/4/2009 called Next Year's Meeting. Make it repeating, monthly, and with two occurrences.)

3. Now both My Test Calendar and Web Part of Calendar will show all three meetings (see Figure 6.15).

Let's summarize what we have so far:

▶ There is a list type called Calendar.

▶ From that list type, we can create any number of differently named calendars.

▶ These differently named calendars have different content.

▶ A Calendar X list is the place where data is stored.

▶ The web part of the Calendar X list is a representation of the Calendar X list.

▶ Two (or more) web parts with different names but derived from the same Calendar X list contain the same content (unless they use a different view—see Hour 8, "Creating and Using Views and Folders").

FIGURE 6.15
Two web parts,
both with three
meetings.

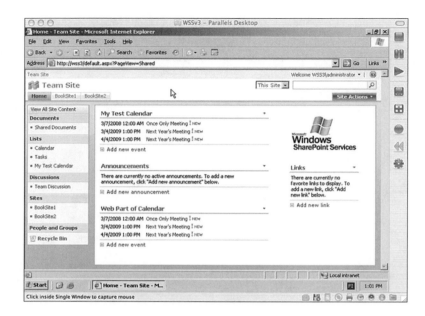

Summary

This hour explained that there are list and library types from each of which you can create one or more independent lists and libraries.

In this hour, you also learned that what you see on the default page is not the list or library itself, but a web page representation of the list or library. In addition, if you have two or more such web page representations of a single list or library, calling them different names will not change their total content.

Q&A

Q. *Why does opening a site in the browser take so long?*

A. Every time you first open a site in a newly opened copy of a browser, the browser needs to download ActiveX components.

You can avoid this delay by using a browser such as Firefox or Safari which don't have ActiveX support and thus don't download any ActiveX components. However when using them you don't have functionality that requires ActiveX.

For most users, this lack of ActiveX support doesn't matter. After all, there are usually other less-direct ways to solve a problem for which the ActiveX support provides a direct answer. However, an administrator should make sure to have access to a machine running Internet Explorer 5.x and later.

Q. *Is Shared Documents the only document library that is shareable?*

A. No. All document libraries are as shareable as the document library that Microsoft created as part of its standard Team Site template and chose to call "Shared Documents." It's just a name—they could have picked a better one in my opinion.

Workshop

Quiz

1. Why are two calendars listed on the default page?

2. What are the major differences between the two calendars on the default page?

Quiz Answers

1. Because Microsoft decided when creating its Team Site template that this is how the page would look.

2. One is a link to the list called Calendar. The other is a web part representation of the list called Calendar. (The official name of this web part representation of a list is the "List View web part.")

HOUR 7

Creating and Using Libraries

What You'll Learn in This Hour

▶ Understanding the different libraries
▶ Creating a picture library and a document library
▶ Differing ways to add images and files

Different Types of Libraries

The list of libraries shown in Figure 6.3 (in Hour 6, "Using Libraries and Lists") contained four library types:

▶ **Document library**. Standard library type used for the majority of file types. We'll use this library type in upcoming examples.

▶ **Form library**. Designed to be a storage location for forms created in InfoPath 2007. When you create a form in InfoPath 2007 and "publish" it, it publishes to a form library.

▶ **Wiki page library**. Stores wiki pages.

▶ **Picture library**. Stores images (formerly called an image library).

All these library types store files. Each type allows versioning to be specified, but they differ in the kinds of files that they are designed to store.

InfoPath 2007 is beyond this book's scope, so it's not discussed in this chapter.	***Note***

Note

Hour 12, "Using Wikis and Blogs," covers wikis.

Note

A picture library differs from a standard document library mainly in the way the files are presented. For example, a thumbnail view and a slide view are available, but neither makes sense for documents.

Creating and Using a Picture Library

In this section, we create a simple picture library and add images to it.

Creating the Picture Library

To create the picture library, go to Home and select Site Actions and Create (see Figure 7.1). We now have an empty picture library (see Figure 7.2).

FIGURE 7.1
Creating a picture library.

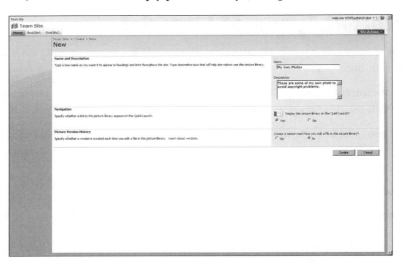

You'll want to add some files to the picture library. The usual way to add files (and this goes for a document library) is to use the browser.

Using the Single-Upload Method

To add files to your picture library by using the single-upload method, you must first select the Upload option.

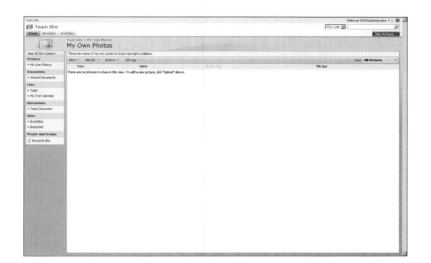

FIGURE 7.2
An empty picture library.

Note

Although here we use Upload to upload an image to a picture library, the technique is identical for uploading a single file to a document library; thus, these steps are not repeated when we discuss the document library. So, even if you don't think you'll use a picture library, read through these instructions.

Here's how you can upload one document at a time:

1. Use Browse.

2. Find a suitable image file.

3. Select the image file.

4. Upload the image file.

Repeat the action for more pictures. At this point—in TV cook style—I've uploaded three images. Now I'll upload a fourth, still using the single-upload method (see Figure 7.4).

When you add a single picture, you get the chance to add metadata. In this case, the fields that can be completed are those included in the picture library as it is delivered. As you add another picture, fill in some of the fields.

Using the Multiple-Upload Method

You can simultaneously add several files to your picture library by using the Upload Multiple Files link (refer to Figure 7.3).

FIGURE 7.3
Adding a
picture.

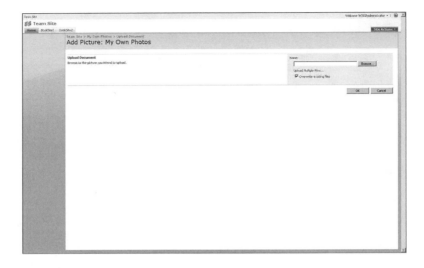

FIGURE 7.4
A single picture
with fields to
fill in.

> ***Tip***
>
> Can't see the Upload Multiple Files link? It means you are not using Internet
> Explorer as your browser or your client is not running a suitable Office version.
> (The Office versions that make Upload Multiple Files visible are Office 2003 Pro
> and Office 2007.)

Note

There is an alternative way to achieve the same result of being able to upload multiple files. Instead of clicking the word *Upload* in Figure 7.2, select the small arrow to the right of the word *Upload*. This gives you a drop-down with the option of Upload Picture or Upload Multiple Pictures.

Note

Windows SharePoint Services often provides different ways to achieve the same result.

Here's how to upload multiple files by using the Upload Multiple Files link:

1. Starting at Figure 7.3, choose Upload Multiple Files.

Note

Figure 7.5 is included so that you are not worried if you see it. (You might not see it. Don't worry about that, either!) If you didn't see Figure 7.5, you will instead have loaded Microsoft Office Picture Manager directly (see Figure 7.6).

FIGURE 7.5
A request for authentication when starting Office Picture Manager.

Note

The fact that a multiple upload will load the Microsoft Office Picture Manager is yet another reason for the requirement that you have certain Office versions on your client before you can use multiple upload!

Tip

The Office Picture Manager screen is likely to show you images from a directory that you don't want to select your photos/images from.

FIGURE 7.6
Choosing a directory in Office Picture Manager.

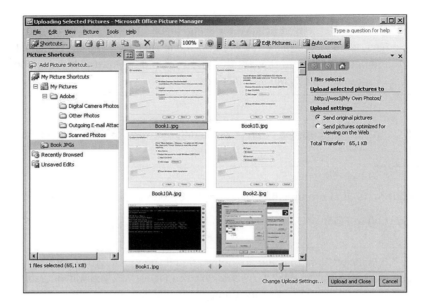

2. If it does, select Add Picture Shortcut (see Figure 7.6) to add to the My Picture Shortcuts list the directory containing the images you want.

Tip

In Figure 7.7, I've added (and selected) the TouristInHelsinki20070510 directory (see the leftmost column).

3. Scroll down the central section to the photos you want to use. Select them using click (the first one) and Ctrl-click (the second one).

4. Select Upload and Close. The pictures will upload to the picture library, and the Office Picture Manager application will close.

5. Before returning to the picture library, a screen offers you the chance to go back to the picture library to select more images to upload. In this case, we'll just click Go Back to My Own Photos on that screen. Doing so takes us back to the picture library (see Figure 7.8).

Although we've added metadata to one of those pictures, all the pictures look the same. Nothing indicates that one picture has metadata associated with it and the others not.

As mentioned earlier, if you select Upload Multiple Pictures, the pictures are uploaded to the picture library with the metadata fields empty.

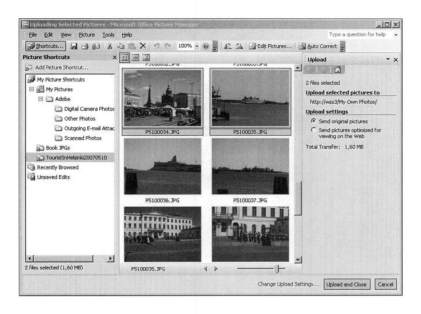

FIGURE 7.7
Selecting pictures in Office Picture Manager.

FIGURE 7.8
The picture library with content.

> This is logical. Otherwise, uploading a number of pictures would mean "Stop! Give me metadata for picture 1," "Stop! Give me metadata for picture 2," and so on. The upload would take forever.

Note

To see whether we have metadata, we must double-click a picture. If we want to amend or add metadata, we must select Edit Item in the menu line (see Figure 7.9).

FIGURE 7.9
Checking and
adding metadata
for a picture.

Note   The Upload Multiple Pictures option offers a quick way to upload numerous
images from a single directory. If you require the images to be itemized, however,
the total time needed might be more than that required for single uploads.

Tip   There are other ways to upload documents to a library (as discussed in the
document library coverage). Even so, only the browser-based single-upload
method allows for metadata entry at the time of uploading to the library.

Creating a Document Library

Just as a Picture Library stores images, a Document Library stores documents. Document Libraries are more widely used than Picture Libraries, so we will mostly use them throughout this book.

So that we have something to work with in our document library, I've created several files (most with little real content) in Acrobat, Excel, PowerPoint, Notepad (so, normal text files), and Word. (I did this on a PC running Office 2003, so these are Office 2003 versions.) These files should give us enough initial data to see how document libraries are used.

These are the files; the number of files; and the file types. The filenames indicate which company is associated with them:

▶ Excel (7) 2 HP, 3 IBM, 1 MS, 1 Sun

▶ PDF (4) 2 IBM, 2 MS

▶ PowerPoint (1) MS

▶ Text (3) 2 HP, 1 MS

▶ Word (5) 2 HP, 3 MS

Be patient. It won't be long and you'll see why I've created files that are supposed to be from different companies.

Note

We'll start by creating a new document library (instead of using the existing one, Shared Documents):

1. If you aren't already at the Home page, click Home and select Site Actions > Create > Document Library (at the upper left of the Create page).

2. Leave the default as Display on the Quick Launch, but amend the second radio button pair so that we have versions allowed.

3. Leave the final drop-down at its default value. Notice that this specifies the type of document that will be created for this document library if you click New Document when opening the document library.

   In this case, I've left this at the default value of a Word 97-2003 document (see Figure 7.10).

There is actually one good reason for having a special template here: if you are an administrator and want your users to use a different template when writing documents for a particular document library than they normally use.

One good reason for that is if you want them to always fill in some additional properties whenever they create a new Word document.

Tip

In that case, you create a Word document, add properties, and then give all those properties dummy values. You then save the Word document as a template (Our-CompanyTemplate perhaps) and make sure that template is available in the drop-down that appears in Figure 7.10.

Then, when a user creates a new document via the New Document item and chooses the OurCompanyTemplate template, there will be a screen with two sections. The top (horizontal) section will contain all those new document properties with their dummy values. The lower section will contain the space for writing the document itself.

FIGURE 7.10
Creating a document library.

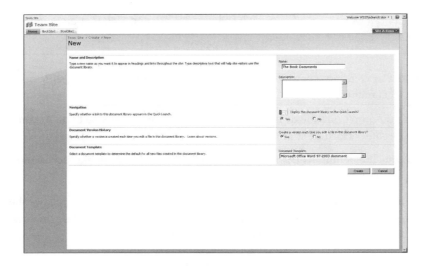

Note   To see the screen in two parts, select Office (upper-left corner) > Prepare > Properties.

Alternative Methods for Uploading Files to a Document Library

You just learned two ways to upload items to a library. In this section, those methods apply to files being uploaded to a document library.

Because the methods are the same, there's no point in repeating them here. Instead, let's look at a couple of alternative methods.

One method involves opening the document library in one window and changing the view used (upper right of screen) to Explorer view (leftmost part of Figure 7.11).

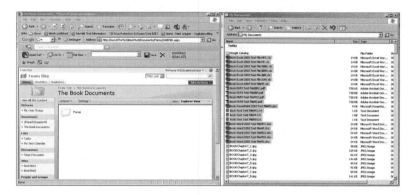

FIGURE 7.11
Copying files to a document library using Explorer view.

Then, open Windows Explorer in another window and select the files you want to upload (rightmost part of Figure 7.11).

Most often, you can just drag and drop the documents from right to left (in Figure 7.11). On a few client systems, however, this doesn't work. In that case, select the files and then press Ctrl-C on the right side and Ctrl-V on the left side (that is, copy and paste); this alternative method always seems to work.

> In both cases (drag and drop / copy and paste), the files are copied, not moved.

Note

Just as with the multiple-upload option in the user interface, you won't have yet had an option to fill in any fields with additional information about the documents being uploaded.

So, all the system knows is that I have uploaded the document, when, what the filename is (what kind of document it is), the file size, and a few more things we can't see in Figure 7.12.

After we've copied the files, it is better to leave Explorer view.

> If you cannot see Explorer view in the drop-down at the rightmost side of the screen, your administrator has removed this view.
>
> Explorer view is slightly dangerous, and some administrators play it safe by completely removing it.

Note

Removal tends to happen only after the *n*th user has done something he shouldn't have while in Explorer view. Don't blame the administrator if you can't see Explorer view. After all, users can still use the Upload Multiple Files option from the user interface (if they have a suitable Office version).

FIGURE 7.12
Showing the up-
loaded docu-
ments in
Explorer view.

The second main way to perform multiple uploads (there are some less-usual methods that I don't discuss) involves using local drives.

Here is an outline of two approaches using that method:

1. Assign a document library to a local drive via a statement in the command line like this (where the URL of the document library is http://servername/xxx/doclib1):

    ```
    Net use X: \\servername\xxx\doclib1
    ```
(If this isn't enough explanation for you, ignore this method.)

2. Copy your files from (for instance) your PC My Documents folder to X:, or follow the following method using My Network Places:

    ▶ Define the document library in My Network Places.

    ▶ Open the My Network Places entry.

► Copy and paste (or drag and drop if it works) the files from Windows Explorer to it.

Now let's go back to Figure 7.12. What you see is that the system knows the kinds of file that have been uploaded to the document library and has suitable icons for them.

At this stage, all seems fine. All the different kinds of files have appropriate icons.

If we then change the view (again at the upper right of the screen) to All Documents, we get Figure 7.13. Carefully look at this figure before reading the text that follows it.

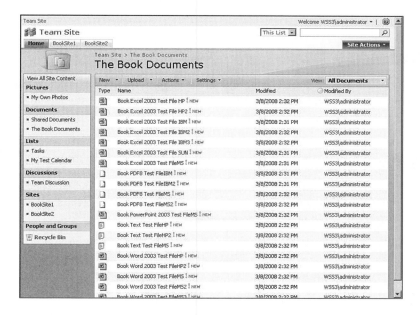

FIGURE 7.13
Checking the All Documents view.

Did you spot the oddity? There is no longer an "appropriate" image for the PDF files.

Note

The Word files are now shown, so you can now verify that that icon is present, too. Having the PDF icon missing in action is something that was a "feature" of the SharePoint v2 products, too, but I always expected the mistake to be corrected in the SharePoint v3 products. But, it's still there, although, oddly, corrected in the much less common Explorer view.

It's actually just something the administrator can fix quickly by

1. Creating (or finding) a PDF image of the right size

2. Going to the server

3. Finding the directory that contains the other images

4. Copying the new PDF image to it

5. Amending a file in another directory that lists file types (and adding a line for PDF files)

Because these instructions aren't enough for you to do it yourself, track down a Microsoft article with more details: Go to www.microsoft.com and use the search term "pdf icon sharepoint," which should give you KB article 837849.

Summary

This hour looked at a picture library and a document library. It showed how files are uploaded to them, which data is available on those files, and how the files are displayed on the default page for the library.

Q&A

Q. *What is the point of adding metadata? I just want to quickly add content, so surely uploading a lot of files simultaneously is the best method even if I can't in the same process add metadata.*

A. Adding metadata both allows you to set up meaningful views (see Hour 8, "Creating and Using Views and Folders") and enables you to improve the quality of your searches (Hour 14, "Improving Searches").

There's a discussion later (in the section about folders in Hour 8) about why it's not a good idea to attempt to replace the file system by uploading large quantities of files in bulk.

Q. *You talked about creating a template for use in a document library. What are the steps for doing this?*

A. Here is what you do:

1. Open the document library.

2. Choose Settings.

3. Choose Document Settings.

4. Choose Advanced Settings (leftmost column).

5. Select Edit Template. This opens the default template in Word, and you can amend it.

6. Save as the template with a new name.

This saves the template in Forms alongside default.dot. (That is, both templates are stored in Forms, so default.doc is still available if you want to change back to it.)

You are then taken back to the Advanced Settings page, where the name of the default template has been replaced with your new template.

Now when you click New in the document library, you will see your new template (perhaps with your company logo, if you so desire) rather than the old standard one.

Workshop

Quiz

1. What are two main ways to upload files to a library when using the user interface?

2. When is the Multiple Upload option not available?

3. What is the major problem with using the Multiple Upload option?

Quiz Answers

1. The single-upload method and the multiple-upload method.

2. If the client system is not running Internet Explorer (5.x and later) or is running Internet Explorer but isn't running Office 2003 Pro or Office 2007.

3. Metadata cannot be added during the upgrade process when using the Upload Multiple Files option.

Creating and Using Views and Folders

What You'll Learn in This Hour

▶ Creating and naming a new field
▶ Creating views using the new field's different values
▶ Creating folders, even though you should not use them

A view is a way to present the contents of a list or library to a user. It is typically used for Document Libraries to divide the presentation of the library's contents into subsections or to list them in a particular order.

A folder is the equivalent of a directory in the file system. Documents can be added to a folder contained within a document library rather than to the document library's main storage level.

Creating a Suitable Column for a View

Later in this hour, we'll create Views. To do that, we need to have a column/field in the document library that we can use when creating those views. So in this section, we create a column called Company and populate it with the name of computer companies. This enables us to later create, for instance, a view where only IBM documents are listed to the user.

Follow these steps to create a column for a view:

1. Go to http://wss3 and select The Book Documents.

2. Select Settings. In the drop-down, select Create Column. Figure 8.1 appears.

FIGURE 8.1
Creating the Column page.

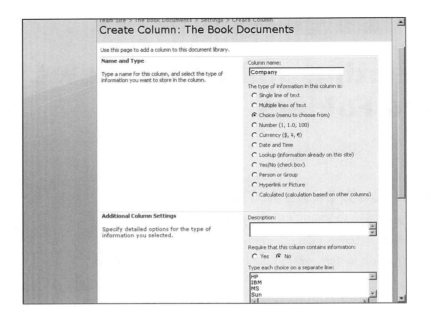

(I have already added some information to this figure.)

Note

Both the words *field* and *column* are used in documentation. *Column* is used because, when you open a document library, the new field Company will appear in the list as a column (if it is selected to be listed, that is).

In the database table where all these things are stored, it's a field, of course. Confusing, isn't it?

3. You have many different options for the The Type of Information in This Column Is section.

It would be swamping you with too much information to go through all the options, so here are the ones I use most often on my sites:

▶ Single Line of Text

▶ Choice (which allows you to specify the possible contents of this field/column)

▶ Date and Time (using the Date Only option for that column)

▶ Yes/No

> Below the area of the screen shown in Figure 8.1, there is a tricky option: Allow Fill-In Options. If this isn't selected the user is restricted to using one of the values that the administrator has previously defined for this column/field.
>
> If you don't (as an administrator) allow additional values, you open the door to a stream of phone calls or emails asking you to add something.
>
> If you do allow this option, you will be bound to get alternative spellings of the same thing (which, naturally, the system will not regard as being the same thing), and you will have to occasionally tidy the mess.

Note

4. We have the option to Add to Default View. Here, we'll leave it in.

Now we're at the screen shown in Figure 8.2.

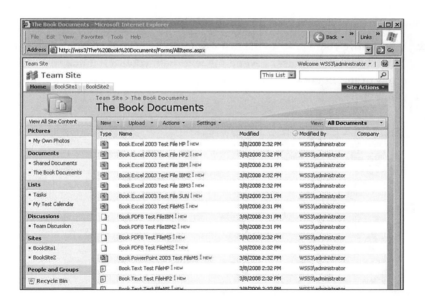

FIGURE 8.2
No values in the column we just added.

Can you spot the issue in Figure 8.2? We want to add a value in the Company column for each row in the list, and we don't seem to be able to.

Here's a list of our present options:

▶ We can click the icon in the Type column and it will open the document.

▶ We can click the field name (which is in the Title column) and it will open the document.

Neither icon will allow us to add a value to the Company column. It's still a perfectly valid view for presenting the data, but it's also a good idea to provide at least one view where the user *can* add values to columns.

Three Editing Solutions for a View

You have three ways of creating such a view.

Editing a View with a Drop-Down

One solution, which is editing a view with a drop-down, requires no changes to the list shown in Figure 8.2. To use this solution, follow these steps:

1. If you move your cursor to the first row under the Name column and then carefully move the cursor beyond the text itself, you'll see a box with an arrow at the end of it (see Figure 8.3). Click it to open the page shown in Figure 8.4.

FIGURE 8.3
One way of editing the contents of a row.

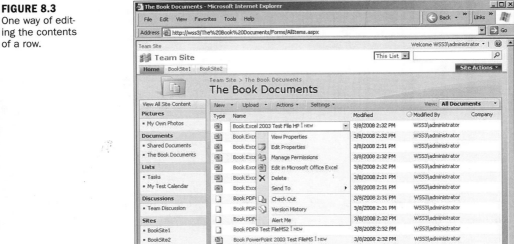

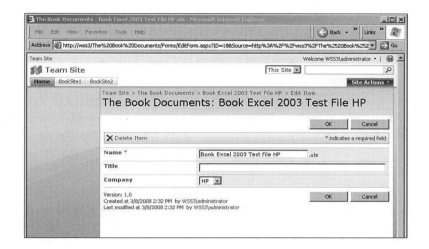

FIGURE 8.4
Changing
the contents of
a row.

2. To add a value to Company, choose Edit Properties. I select HP from the Company drop-down (see Figure 8.4).

Tip

To open the document in Excel for editing, choose Edit in Excel. To save this back to the document library after amendment, choose Save.

The options of clicking the icon or the name only open the document in read-only mode. In this mode, you spend more effort to get the revised version back to the document library.

Note

The Name field is the place where the filename is stored; the Title field is where you give a file a meaningful name that can be used in a list.

Do not use Title in a list rather than Name. There is no possibility of right-clicking a Title field in the way we clicked the Name field.

Editing a View by Adding an Edit Column

Another solution, editing a view by adding an Edit column, works even if we have the Title field listed and not the Name field (and not so incidentally also works with any browser).

This solution is to create a new view that includes an Edit field. Let's create a view called All Documents Edit (probably not what you'd use in real life):

1. Choose the Settings menu item followed by Create View, and then Standard View.

2. Fill out the form as shown in Figure 8.5. In this figure, Edit (Link to Edit Item) is 12th on the list. Change its position to 1. Doing so pushes down all the other columns. Then, ignore the rest of the form except for the OK.

Figure 8.6 shows the result of that effort.

FIGURE 8.5
Adding an Edit icon.

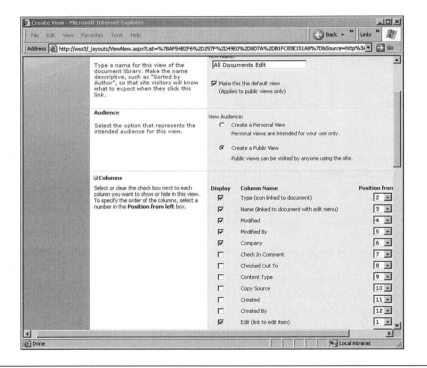

Note

The Edit icon at the start of the rows is clear, but why are the documents arranged differently than Figure 8.2?

The order difference is because the previous All Documents was in Name order. This view isn't in any order because we ignored all the options in Figure 8.5 after the column selection.

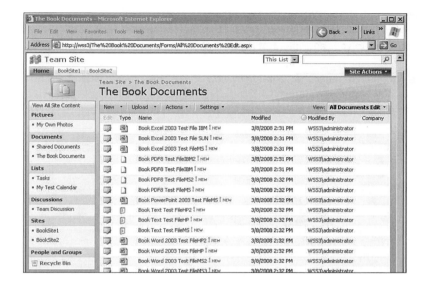

FIGURE 8.6
Adding an Edit
icon, continued.

3. Click the Edit icon at the beginning of a row to get the screen shown in
   Figure 8.4.

Both the use of the Name field's dropdown and the use of an additional column
containing an Edit icon mean that you can edit a **single item** and then specify the
company.

Editing a View by Using Datasheet View

Finally, to get a value in the Company column, you can edit a view by using
Datasheet view. Doing this speeds up editing when there is a list of more than just a
few items. This solution is similar to the just-discussed solution in that we must create
a new view.

This time, we'll create a Datasheet view: Go to Settings > Create View > Datasheet
View. I name this Datasheet view (Maintenance). The parentheses indicate that it's
not really a view that users are expected to use in normal circumstances.

This time, I've said that it should be sorted by name (and that it will not be the
default view; *not* being the default view is default here).

Note

> My tests have shown that either that first column appears or not. Don't worry if it isn't present in your equivalent of Figure 8.7.
>
> It's a curiosity no more that Datasheet view shows this column whereas Standard view (of the same view) doesn't.

FIGURE 8.7
Using a Datasheet View to add a value to the Company column.

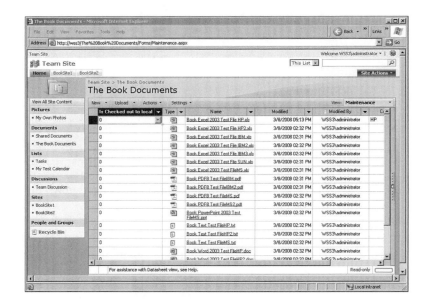

The point of using Datasheet view is that you can

▶ Change several or all rows and then leave the page

▶ Use the drop-down in the column (row) to choose the value

▶ Copy the values in cells just like you can in Excel (but only like to like)

Doing a combination of these, we can complete the Company column with the appropriate values in all rows.

Note

> There is no OK button, so you must ensure that the changes go through. To do this, select a different view after you fill in the values on the page.

Figure 8.8 is what often appears after you try to change the view.

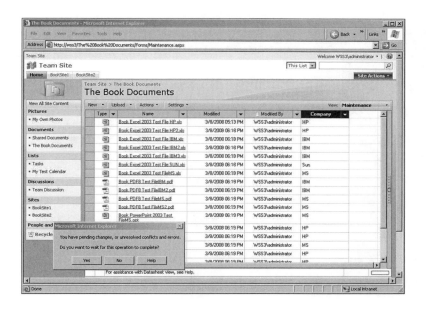

FIGURE 8.8
Making sure the
changes in
Datasheet view
go through.

Figure 8.8 is a common message after every large change made when using the
Datasheet view in a list/library. (Click Yes, of course.)

Creating a View That Includes All Documents

Now that we have a Company value for each document, we can (finally) create a
view that uses those values. To do this, follow these steps:

1. Choose Settings > Create View > Standard View. This time, we focus on the
   second half of the screen.

Before you scroll down, remove the tick for Company. (Reading offline? Figure 8.5
shows this section). If we leave it there, we'll have a view called HP in which only
items where Company=HP are listed, and we'll have a column called Company,
which for all rows will contain HP. That's pointless!

Tip

2. Name this view **HP**. Then, scroll down and complete the Sort and Filter fields
   (see Figure 8.9).

FIGURE 8.9
Setting sorting
and filtering for a
view.

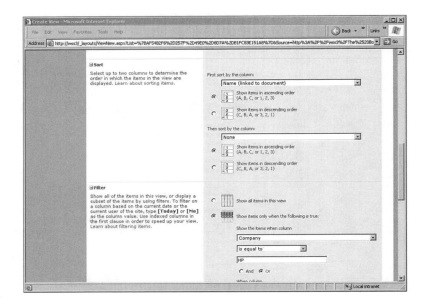

3. Click OK, and repeat the whole thing for IBM, MS, and Sun.

Tip

If you do this for fields/columns where the names are long, enter the name in the View Name field (make sure it is exactly the same name you had in the Choice field), and copy (Ctrl-C) this name and paste it (Ctrl-V) in the Filter field.

I often play even safer by opening the list in a second browser and then going to Document Settings and the Choice field. That way, I can copy the exact value and then paste this value into first the Name row and then into the Filter row.

Creating a Filtered View

Next, let's create a view that could be used if you want to split a single report into HP, IBM, MS, and Sun sections:

1. Choose Settings > Create View > Standard View. This time call it Grouped By Company. Remove the tick for Company and sort the view by name.

2. Do not enter a filter. Complete the rest of the page as shown in Figure 8.10. (Note that I chose Grouping = Expanded.)

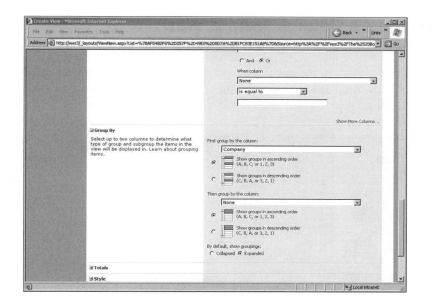

FIGURE 8.10
Looking at the Group By element when specifying a view.

3. Click OK. Figure 8.11 shows the result.

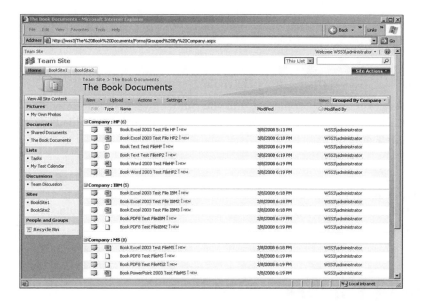

FIGURE 8.11
A completed Grouped By view.

This is a useful overview of that document library's contents, although I'm going to make a judgment call and say that we don't need to see the date a document was modified, so let's remove it from the view.

Deleting a Column from a View

To delete the Modified column, follow these steps:

1. Select Settings in the menu line, and choose Document Library Settings from the drop-down. Then scroll the screen to see a list of the views (see Figure 8.12).

FIGURE 8.12
Amending a view.

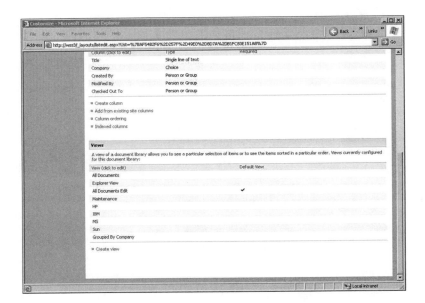

2. Select Grouped By Company, and you can remove the tick for Modified. Click OK to open the Book Documents page without the Modified column (see Figure 8.13).

Note

In Figure 8.13, you can also see (at the topmost right corner) where to select the HP, IBM, etc. views. Select IBM to see a list of only the IBM documents.

Using Folders

Now that you've seen how views can be used to separate the documents stored in a single document library into subdivisions, let's look at folders, which are an alternative method of doing this.

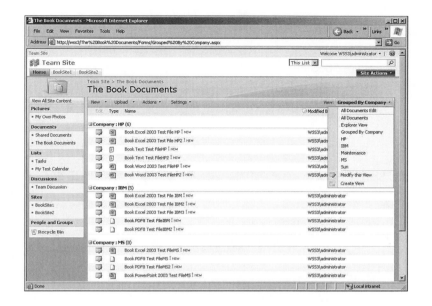

FIGURE 8.13
A revised view.

Tip

> Most people with several years of experience with SharePoint do not recommend using folders. Instead, they prefer alternatives: having several document libraries or using views. (They usually prefer to use both.)

However, we have two problems with folders:

▶ Implementation isn't particularly good.

▶ Folders encourage bad habits when transferring data from "normal" systems (that is, from the file system).

A quick demonstration will show you a few problems with folder implementation:

1. Go to BookSite1 and open the document library.

Note

> It's called Document Library in this site template (not Shared Documents). The Microsoft people obviously ran out of inspiration.

2. Select New > New Folder (see Figure 8.14). Name this folder **HP**.

3. Repeat this process (New > New Folder) to create folders for IBM, MS, and Sun. Figure 8.15 shows the result.

FIGURE 8.14
Creating a
folder.

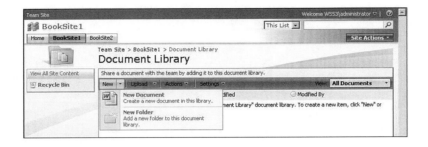

FIGURE 8.15
Folders are
now available
for use.

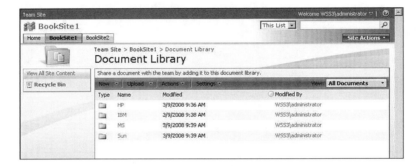

4. Populate the folders with the same test files we used earlier in this hour. To do so, click the folder icon before the word *HP* or on the word *HP* itself to open the folder. Then use the upload actions we've used before. Repeat this process for the IBM, MS, and Sun files.

Tip

Use the "breadcrumb" section above the title Document Library. Click 1 to go back to a screen where you can open the next folder.

5. Now use the breadcrumb to go back to the Document Library level and upload some other files (preferably with more appropriate names for your business than those shown in Figure 8.16).

6. Click Name at the top of the column. This sorts the contents of the document library in name order (first ascending and, after a second click on Name, descending).

7. The folders all come first, followed by all the files. Click Name again, and all the files come first and then all the folders. That's perhaps acceptable.

8. Now create a file in Notepad and add it to the IBM folder.

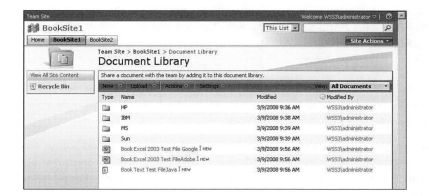

FIGURE 8.16
A document library with both views and folders.

> Open the IBM folder first. I forgot to do that, which is why there's a text file in Figure 8.16!

Tip

9. Go back to the Document Library level and click Modified (twice).

When we click Modified, which sorts the date and time at which something in SharePoint was added or amended, we ought (you would think) to first see the folder IBM, the contents of which have been modified last, followed by the individual files we uploaded, followed by the other folders.

In fact, we get the screen shown in Figure 8.17.

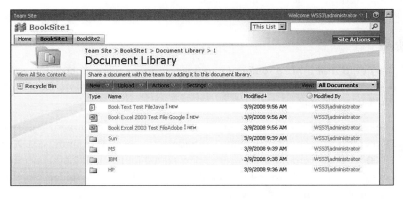

FIGURE 8.17
Problems with sorting when folders are involved.

All that is considered in the sort order is when the folder was created; when the contents of the folder were amended is completely ignored.

Note

From Figure 8.17, you also have no way of seeing that new content has been added to the IBM folder.

That's one of the functionality problems with folders. Another one is what happens if you do a search. The search identifies the folder in which a document that contains the search term is included, not the document itself.

However, the main problem with folders is that they encourage bad habits. They encourage you to copy your entire file system to a single WSS 3.0 document library, which also means that you don't bother getting rid of documents that no longer are relevant.

By comparison, the process of creating a view means that you need to analyze the files that are in the file system first (to create suitable views). This means that, during the analysis process, you become aware of no longer relevant files and sets of files and do not upload them to the WSS 3.0 document library. You also divide your relevant files into different document libraries.

Summary

This hour showed you how to create views and folders. It gave you the benefits of using views to subcategorize the documents in a document library, and you learned some of the disadvantages of using folders.

Q&A

Q. *I've heard that if I use folders I can have up to 4 million documents stored in a single document library. If that's true, why are you recommending that I don't use folders?*

A. The recommended maximum limit for documents in a document library is 2,000 for document libraries without folders. However, that limit is 2,000 x 2,000 for document libraries with folders (2,000 folders and 2,000 documents per folder), and thus your 4 million documents when using folders. So, that statement is technically correct.

Some papers say this limit is 5 million. This is a hard number, whereas the 2,000 number that leads to the 4 million total is a "recommended maximum" only. You can have 2,001 or 2,002 or….

There are many reasons why this wholesale transfer of files from the file system is not desirable, including the following:

▶ Ease of use when accessing the files

▶ The results of searches

▶ The storage space required (up to 80 percent more space can be needed for storage in the SharePoint databases than is required for the same files in the file system)

▶ Backup requirements

Q. Are there, in your opinion, any good uses for folders?

A. In my opinion, just one.

You might want to consider folders if you have a copy of a website that was created by a fairly old tool such as Site Sweeper. These old tools typically created a single index.htm file with links to files that were placed in folders one level below the index.htm file.

The index.htm file can be uploaded to the document library and the files it references can be uploaded to a folder in the document library.

The reason this is a good use of folders is because it really can't be done any other way, given the way these Site Sweeper type applications work.

Workshop

Quiz

1. When creating a view, which type of column do I use when I want to ensure that it always contains specific text strings?

2. With folders, what two functionality problem areas are there?

3. Why is it a bad idea to copy the file system to a WSS 3.0 document library that uses folders?

Quiz Answers

1. I use the Choice type of field because in this field type I can specify a list of possible values (and, incidentally, a default value).

2. Sort and search.

3. It's a bad idea to copy the file system because this encourages the mass copying of files, which means that no effort is made to weed out documents that are no longer relevant or active.

HOUR 9

Looking at List Types and the Included Web Parts

What You'll Learn in This Hour

- ► Purpose of list types
- ► Which web parts are delivered with WSS 3.0 that are not just representations of lists and libraries
- ► Purposes of standard and nonlist web parts

Understanding List Types

The WSS 3.0 product includes several list types. This section discusses some of these list types.

> *Note*
>
> Refer to Figure 6.3 in Hour 6, "Using Libraries and Lists," for a complete list of the possible list types. They're shown in columns called Communications, Tracking, and Custom Lists.

Announcements List

The Announcements list is intended for use as a web part on a website's default page to present readers of the site with up-to-the-minute and important information. The Announcements List is almost always on the default page so that as many people as possible see this information. Be wary of changing the default view. The standard default view is designed especially for use on the site's default page. Amending it might mess up the look, and it's impossible to create a new view with the same look.

Contacts List

The Contacts list contains useful contacts for readers of the website.

So, for instance, if a computer services company uses the site for one of their customers, the Contacts list would consist of contact information for people in that customer company (and also probably for people from the computer services company who work with that particular customer).

You cannot combine the contacts information in the site's Contacts list with your Outlook contacts. Even if it is possible, there will be two separate Contacts items in Outlook, not just one that combines both sources. (For more information, see Hour 16, "Using Different Versions of Outlook with WSS 3.0.")

Discussion Board

Naturally, the Discussion Board is used for discussions. There are both threaded and non-threaded options for the look of this list.

The Discussion Board hasn't improved much since SharePoint Team Services 2001, so don't expect much functionality beyond the simple "write a message, get a reply" level of functionality.

Links List

The Links list's main function is to list useful web addresses with accompanying descriptions. I use it in my websites to list and link to both useful SharePoint articles and Knowledge Base articles.

The problem with the Links list is that the URL field consists of two parts: the URL itself and the description.

So, for instance, when you open a Links list, you will see a description listed in the URL field. When you click the description, the system will actually use the URL to go to the web page.

This isn't a problem for users who tend to be happy to see something meaningful rather than an obscure website address. But, it can be a problem for administrators because Datasheet view (which normally allows for bulk changes) does not list a Description field; thus, it's impossible to populate the Links list in bulk from, say, an Excel spreadsheet containing a URL column and a Description column.

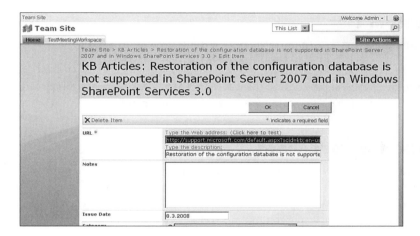

FIGURE 9.1
Editing a single
Links list item.

The way around this is to add an additional column, perhaps called Site Description, and use this in the Datasheet view along with the URL column. In this way, you can bulk populate a Links list.

If you do this, all you will have is a URL field containing a URL! In other words, there's no corresponding description. In such cases, what would be showing in Figure 9.1 would be the URL, not the description.

So after a bulk populate, it's necessary to edit each single item individually, because then the Description field is available. Here, it's possible to copy the contents of the Site Description field into the Type the Description entry box. It might not be the fastest process overall, but it's not that demanding.

Calendar List

Typically, the Calendar list is used as a calendar only for the area covered by the website (for instance, for the customer company in the preceding example).

Like the Contacts list, the Calendar list is not merged with any Outlook calendar. If the Outlook version allows it, however, this calendar will appear in Outlook alongside the Outlook user's own calendar.

Tasks List

The Tasks list relates to workflow. Workflows are covered in Hour 19, "Creating Workflows in WSS 3.0," and Hour 20, "Using SharePoint Designer 2007 to Create Workflows," and so are not mentioned further.

Custom List

A Custom list isn't as custom as you might think. All that it seems to be is a list that doesn't already (in contrast to the others) have a predefined role.

Typically, it stores simple data. I use it to store FAQs, where I have a Single-Line Text field for a question and a Multi-Line Text field for an answer.

Import Spreadsheet

In WSS 3.0, the Import Spreadsheet option provides a way for you to move an existing Excel spreadsheet to a WSS 3.0 site. If you use this option, a list is created from a set of cells contained in a spreadsheet. The result is a list in which each field/column name matches its respective column in Excel.

The list created from the Import Spreadsheet option and the Excel spreadsheet from which it's derived are not connected. Changes made later to the spreadsheet are not reflected in the list. Once the list is compiled, the spreadsheet and the list are two completely independent entities.

Tip

> Always delete the spreadsheet after you create the list from it. This forces your users to only update the list.

Using Standard Web Parts with the Team Site

Now that you understand the various list types, let's look at the standard web parts that are listed when you add a web part (see Figure 9.2). I will set up a separate site for testing these web parts.

Creating a Site to Test Web Parts

If you want a site where you can test web parts, you must first create one. Let's start at the default page:

1. Click Home if you are not there already.

2. To create the site, select Site Actions > Create > Sites and Workspaces.

3. Name the site **Web Parts Test** and name the part URL **WebPartsTest**.

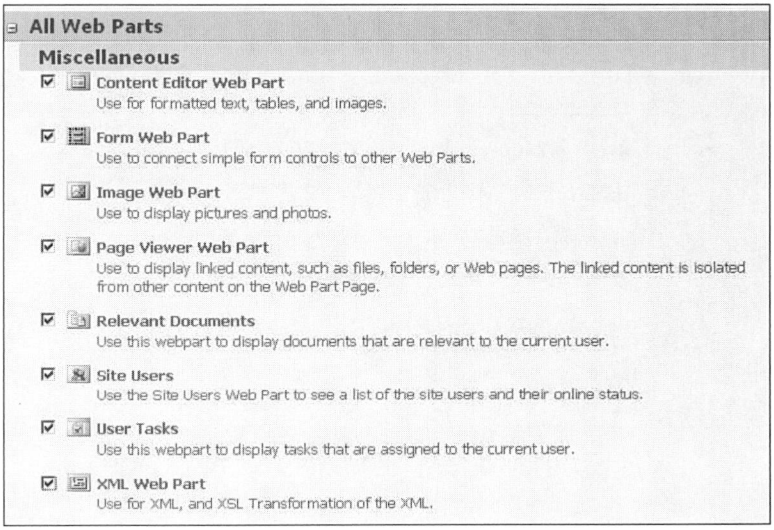

FIGURE 9.2
List of the sup-
plied web parts.

4. Change the color of the site so that it's easy to know where you are. Select Site Actions > Site Settings > Site Theme. Choose Verdant for a nice green look.

Adding Web Parts to the Test Site

To add a web part to your test site, follow these steps:

1. Go to Web Parts Test on the menu line and select Site Actions > Edit Page > Add a Web Part (in the left of the two columns).

2. Scroll down the page and select all the listed web parts. You should now see Figure 9.2.

3. Click OK. You should now see Figure 9.3.

You can see that all these new web parts have their default name, which is the same as the type of web part. This is potentially confusing, so we'll change those names along the way.

Removing Some of the Previous Web Parts

Let's tidy the page by deleting Announcements, Calendar, and Links lists. (For now, we'll leave the web part with the WSS image.) In addition, rename all the newly added web parts Test *XXX* (where *XXX* is the present name). The final bit of tidying requires moving some of the new web parts to the rightmost column.

FIGURE 9.3
The default page with added web parts.

To remove the Announcements web part, click the downward-pointing arrow in the upper part of the Announcements web part. Then click Delete in the window that appears at the right of the screen.

You'll receive a warning that you are *permanently deleting* the web part. Ignore this warning.

Note

What does *permanently deleting* mean here? Not much, because if you click Add a Web Part again, you'll find that you can select Announcements and thus re-create the Announcements web part you just deleted (only empty of items posted to it, of course).

The Announcements list that the Announcements web part was a representation of has not been removed!

Continue by deleting Calendar and Links in the same way. Transfer the bottom four web parts to the rightmost column.

Transferring Web Parts from One Column to Another

You can transfer web parts from one column to another by following these steps:

1. Click the same arrow at the top right of the web part and select Modify Shared Web Part. First, amend the title so that it becomes **Test Relevant Documents**.

> **Tip**
>
> For most of the other web parts, you must click Appearance first to access the Title field.

2. Scroll down until you see Layout. Open it.

3. Change Zone to Right and Zone Index to 2.

> **Tip**
>
> It's helpful to use increments that are greater than one when specifying the position of a web part in the zone. (The zone here is the right side of the main part of the screen.)
>
> So, specify 4, 6, and 8 for the other three web parts you are moving here.

4. Repeat for Site Users, User Tasks, and XML. Change just the names (by adding **Test**) of the web parts that are left in the zone.

5. Move the WSS image to the bottom of the column by editing it and specifying that the zone index equals 10.

Let's now look at the individual web part types.

Understanding Different (Nonlist) Standard Web Parts

This section provides introductions to the web parts included in the Team Site template, but they are not just representations of Lists or Libraries.

Content Editor Web Part

The Content Editor web part often makes part of a zone in a SharePoint look dissimilar to a zone in a SharePoint site. Here's an example of that:

1. At Figure 9.4, click the Open the Tool Pane link within the Content Editor web part.

FIGURE 9.4
Defining a
Content Editor
Web Part.

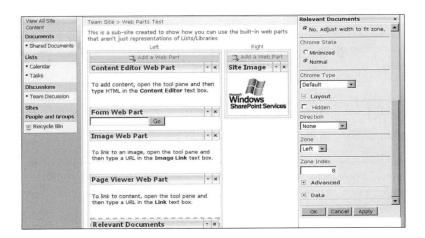

2. You'll see a new column on the right side. Click Source Editor. Enter this HTML code:

```
<H3><center><color="#FF0000">Key Personnel</color></center></H3>
<center><table border=2 cellspacing=2 cellpadding=5>
<tr><bold>
<td>Finance</td><td>IT</td>
<td>Manufacturing</td><td>Personnel</td>
</bold></tr><tr>
<td>Jim McPherson</td><td>Woody Winchester</td>
<td>Robin Goodfellow</td><td>Lucius Cassio</td>
</tr>
</table></center>
```

3. Click OK. You should get something like what's shown in Figure 9.5.

Form Web Part

The Form web part (at least in the way it is most commonly used) is the single entry box with a Go button (refer to Figure 9.5). It doesn't look like much, but as you'll see, even the simplest version of this web part type (which is all we look at here) is useful.

To use the Form web part, we first need some data, and then we run through how web part connections work (something else that is simple, but useful).

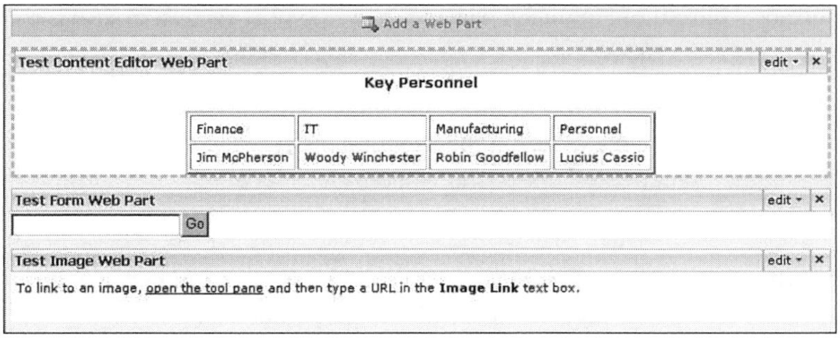

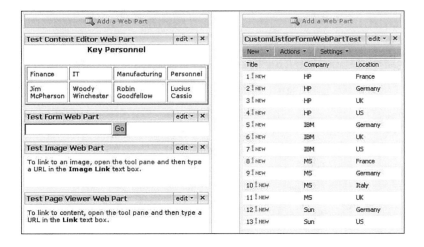

FIGURE 9.5
An example of using the Content Editor web part.

To show how this works, I created a custom list, added two columns to it, and populated the columns with some data. (If you want to do this yourself, look at the rightmost column of Figure 9.6 to see which columns and values were added.) Once that was done, a web part of that new list was available.

FIGURE 9.6
Stage one of showing how to use the Form web part.

In the same page used for earlier exercises, I did the following:

1. I selected Add a Web Part in the rightmost column.

The list of possible web parts appeared and the new web part was listed.

2. I selected it.

3. I clicked OK.

The rightmost column of Figure 9.6 contains the web part version of that new List.

Note

> The Title field is compulsory. Otherwise, I wouldn't put any value there. The 1 to 13 values are just dummy values. The key information is the repeated company names and the nonrepeated (for each company) locations.

Now that that web part is available, we can set up a connection between it and another web part on that page (a so-called *web part connection*):

1. Click the small arrow next to the Edit button in the web part of the list we've just created and added values to.

2. Then, on Connections, select Get Sort/Filter From. Now we have a number of possible web parts to connect to. In Figure 9.7, however, we have just one choice: Test Form Web Part.

FIGURE 9.7
Starting web part connections.

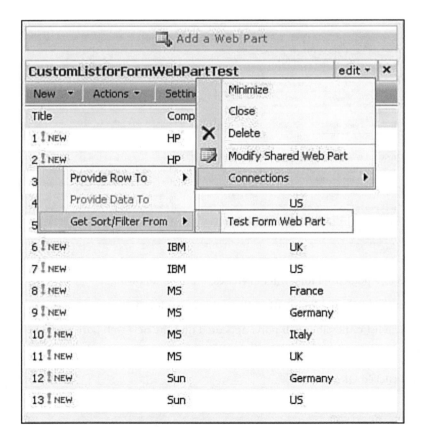

3. Select Test Form Web Part. A pop-up appears (see Figure 9.8).

4. There is only one column in our standard Test Form web part, so that drop-down has a single entry. Accept T1 and click Next.

5. The following screen is a similar pop-up, this time for the CustomListforFormWebPartTest web part. (This name is too long, so I call it as CL1 from now on.) In this web part, we have a choice of all three columns. Select Company, and click Next.

Now we see Figure 9.6 again.

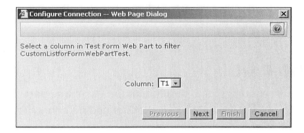

FIGURE 9.8
Configuring the web part connection.

6. Write **IBM** into the Test Form Web Part field and click Go. You now see Figure 9.9 (compare with Figure 9.6).

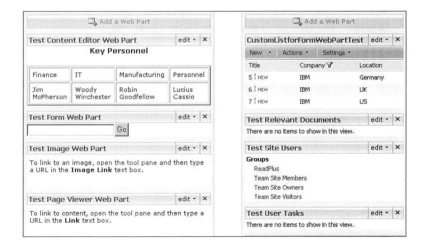

FIGURE 9.9
The result of entering IBM into the Form web part.

Entering IBM in the Form web part that was connected to CL1 has filtered the information that CL1 shows us. CL1 the list still contains rows for HP, IBM MS, and Sun, as does CL1 the web part of that list (because we are still using just the standard view for it). However, CL1 the connected web part *displays* only the information about the company the user of this page chose to specify in the Form web part.

Note

> If you are in Edit (Page) mode when you do the test, IBM will vanish from the box. So, try the test again; but this time, click Exit Edit Mode in the upper-right corner of the page. The first thing you'll see is that <null> (blank) is the initial value of the Form web part box, and so the CustomListforFormWebPartTest connected web part shows empty.
>
> Entering IBM returns you to Figure 9.9, but now the entry box is no longer empty and contains IBM.

Image Web Part

The Image web part enables you to position an image on any part of a page to which a web part can be added. Other methods of adding images to a page require coding changes, so they are less straightforward.

With the Image web part, you need to point at an image that all the people accessing the page have the rights to see. One such location is the /_layouts/images/ directory, which is the storage location for the homepage.gif image (the WSS logo). You can verify this by looking at the Site Image web part (which is a standard Image web part that has been renamed) via Modify Shared Web Part.

Another way to guarantee that everyone can access the image is to create a site (or subsite) that everyone has access rights to (safest way is to allow anonymous access, see Hour 10, "Learning About Authentication and Access Rights") and within that site create an image library. Upload your images to this newly created image library. Then, use an appropriate version of the image from the image library in the URL field of the Image web part.

Tip

> One way to get an "appropriate" version is to open the image library and right-click one of the images that, at this point, appears in a reduced-size form. Select Copy Link Location. Enter this link into the URL field of the Image web part (Ctrl-V) and click Test Link.
>
> You'll probably see more than you want to (not just the image, but the image's metadata). So, on this test image, again right-click. Select Copy Location and enter this new value into the URL field of the Image web part. Now at least you'll just have an image being displayed.

Page Viewer Web Part

The Page Viewer web part does just one thing, but it does it well. It allows you to in-corporate any page that can be accessed from the Internet into your WSS 3.0 site. For instance, a page in an Internal Dell WSS 3.0 site could include a (public) HP Hard-ware Announcements web page so that Dell people can quickly see new HP an-nouncements.

To get the following example (see Figure 9.10), modify the web part and enter **http:// www.wssfaq.com** into the URL field.

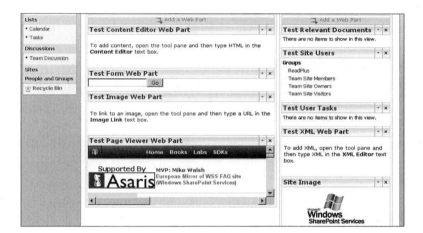

FIGURE 9.10
An example of using the Page Viewer web part.

Relevant Document Web Part

A relevant document is a document that the user who is accessing the page ("me") has done something with. (The choices are Has Created, Has Checked Out, and Has Last Modified). The results of this web part look similar to those generated by the User Tasks web part (see Figure 9.11).

Site Users Web Part

The Site Users web part shows the administrator at a glance which groups of users can access the site.

In Figure 9.9 and Figure 9.10, you can see this web part displaying ReadPlus, Team Site Members, Team Site Owners, and Team Site Visitors. This is the result of using the default selection for this web part type (Show People and Groups with Direct Permis-sions on the Site).

Some other possible options are

FIGURE 9.11
An example of using the User Tasks web part (in the right column).

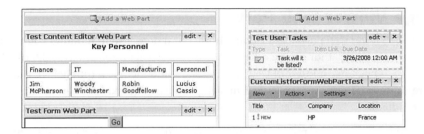

▶ Show People in This Site's Member Group

▶ Show People in the Group: (Where You Specify the Group)

User Tasks Web Part

The User Tasks web part is similar to the Relevant Documents web part in that it shows only items that have been entered elsewhere (in this case, naturally, in a Tasks list rather than in a Documents list).

The other difference is that the Relevant Documents web part offered a number of options in the Data section, but here there is just one (Display Item Link column: Yes/No).

Figure 9.11 shows an example of a simple Tasks web part (that I created especially for this test) and how it would display in this User Tasks web part.

Note   I moved the web part up the column.

XML Web Part

The XML web part is similar in operation to the Content Editor web part. The main difference is that whereas the Content Editor web part offers both a Source Editor for HTML coders and a Rich Text Editor for people who don't want to write code, the XML web part offers only a Source Editor.

Because writing XML code is beyond the scope of this book, I'll leave it to the XML experts among you to wonder about how you could use XML code in a web part.

Summary

In this hour, we looked at the list types that haven't been mentioned earlier and examined what they are good for and potential problems associated with their use.

We then looked at the default web parts that come with WSS 3.0. We saw when each of them is used, and you saw (when appropriate) actual examples of their use.

Q&A

Q. *I can't find the /_layouts/images/ directory. Where is it in the file system?*

A. Find this directory here: C:\Program Files\Common Files\Microsoft Shared\web server extensions\12\TEMPLATE\LAYOUTS.

Workshop

Quiz

1. What do the Contacts list and the Calendar list have in common?

2. I want to add a web part to my page. When I choose Site Actions > Create, however, I don't see any web parts that were discussed in this hour.

Quiz Answers

1. Both lists can be synchronized with some versions of Outlook, and yet the copy of both lists in Outlook is separate from your Outlook Contacts and your Outlook calendar.

2. You don't see any web parts because what you do see when you select Create are lists and library types (and sites!) from which you can create a new list or library or site. To add a web part to a page, go to Site Actions > Edit Page.

HOUR 10

Learning About Authentication and Access Rights

What You'll Learn in This Hour

▶ How anonymous users and authenticated users can be allowed access to our sites

▶ Getting familiar with the built-in authorization levels (SharePoint groups) and how to use different users without closing the browser

▶ User levels and the rights associated with them

This hour expands on Hour 3, "Adding Users and Giving Them Rights," by looking at how you can make anonymous users or all authenticated users able to access a site. It also looks at how to change the logged on user when accessing the site and the differences logging in with a different level of user makes to what can be seen and what can be done.

We created new users and assigned them to SharePoint groups in Hour 3. Go back to that hour if you need to refresh your memory about SharePoint groups and their privileges.

Note

Learning About Anonymous Access and All Authenticated Users

This section looks at a few special cases of groups of users: anonymous users and all authenticated users.

Anonymous Access

It is possible to have anonymous access to a site. Therefore, a new group of users could be given access rights to a site: anonymous users.

A common question about the WSS 2.0 products was "Why can't I set anonymous access? Why is the option grayed out?" The option was unavailable until after anonymous access in Windows Internet Information Services (IIS) had been set up. After that was done, the anonymous option became available in the WSS 2.0 system.

Curiously, this runaround is still necessary, but in a different way. You can now specify anonymous access in WSS 3.0 without first adding it to IIS. Specifying it in WSS 3.0 also generates the addition to IIS. Anonymous users still cannot access the site, however, because IIS is defined so that (anonymous access is allowed but) "users are allowed to access nothing." So, you still have to go into IIS if you want those anonymous users to actually access something.

Note

> Several questions and answers with instructions about how to set up anonymous access in WSS 3.0 can be found in the section, "Q&A."

Allowing anonymous access isn't a sensible choice for many sites. You may decide that you don't want anonymous users to be able to access even a restricted amount of your site's information. If that's the case, you can restrict access to the site to only users who have specifically been given rights to the site, or you can consider giving all the users who are logged in to your domain such rights. In the latter case, you should give authenticated users access rights to your site.

All Authenticated Users

The All Authenticated Users group is a special set of users that is available when a WSS 3.0 server is in a domain.

Tip

> There's a set of users called Everyone. It is good practice to give only the All Authenticated Users group rights to access the site and not the Everyone group.
>
> If the Everyone group were given access rights, anybody using a computer connected to the network could access your WSS 3.0 site. Restricting access to the All Authenticated Users group, however, ensures that the users who can access our site are logged in to the domain.

Setting up access for authenticated users is simple to do.

Go back to Hour 3 and look at Figure 3.8, where we added MyAdmin. On the left-most side (toward the top), you can see an Add All Authenticated Users link. Upon clicking that link, NT Authority\Authenticated Users appears in the User/Groups box, which in Figure 3.8 was used to enter MyAdmin.

Typically, you confirm that the Add Users to a SharePoint Page drop-down is Team Site Visitors [Read]. This confirmation ensures that authenticated users only get Read rights. Click OK to finish.

Note

The availability in WSS 3.0 of the Add All Authenticated Users link encourages us to use this group rather than the Everyone group. Sometimes, Microsoft thinks of everything!

Figure 10.1 shows the result of having added Authenticated Users and having given them Read rights by assigning this set of users to the Team Site Vistors SharePoint group.

FIGURE 10.1
Showing authenticated users in the Team Site Visitors SharePoint group.

Getting to Understand the Rights of Different Kinds of Users

So far, even though we've created different users and assigned them to one of the existing SharePoint groups or to a new specially created SharePoint group, we've always been logged in as administrator. I use this access right throughout this book unless otherwise stated.

The second half of this hour looks at how we can log in as someone else and the effect of doing so on what we can do in a site and what we can see of the site.

Logging In to a Site as Someone Else

In WSS 3.0, logging in as someone else is simple. Just as with Vista, you can use the authority of a normal user most of the day and "run as an administrator" when you are doing something "special."

When accessing WSS 3.0, you can switch users as follows:

1. Go to the Home page. Look at the upper-right corner of the screen. You will see text similar to "Welcome WSS3\administrator," with a small arrow to the right of the text (see Figure 10.2).

FIGURE 10.2
Signing in as a different user.

2. Click the arrow. You get the standard login box, and you can now log in (see Figure 10.3).

FIGURE 10.3
Logging in as MyReader.

Notice that "Welcome WSS3\administrator" is replaced by "Welcome WSS3\ myreader." Otherwise, everything seems to be the same. Or is it?

Effect on the Default Site of Logging In as Somebody Else

Figure 10.4 shows what the screen now looks like.

In fact, two differences now exist:

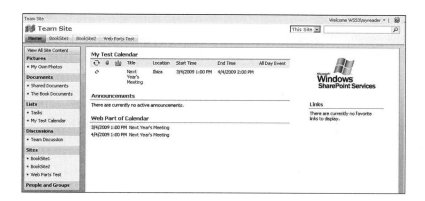

FIGURE 10.4
The home page when logged in as MyReader.

▶ Near the upper-right corner when logged in as administrator, there was a Site Actions drop-down. Now there isn't.

▶ Before, there was a Recycle Bin below People and Groups. Now there isn't. (In Figure 10.2, this is unfortunately not visible.)

The general reason why these two items have vanished is the same. A reader doesn't have the rights to use either of these items:

▶ The user MyReader has Read rights, and a reader can't make site specification changes.

▶ The user MyReader has Read rights, and a reader can't delete anything.

Now log in as MyContrib. Before you do and before you look at Figure 10.5, however, think about whether one or both of the previously mentioned items will then be present or whether they will both still be missing.

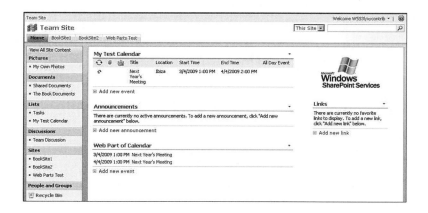

FIGURE 10.5
The home page when logged in as MyContrib.

That's right. The Recycle Bin is back because a contributor does have Delete rights. Site Actions didn't make it, however, because again, even a contributor can't make changes to the site.

What if you've given someone Design rights?

Note

This is oddly only possible out of the box by choosing to give a user his/her own rights, when Design is an option.

Tip

A better way than doing this is to first create the group that Microsoft failed to include (call it Team Site Designers) and give that group Design rights. Upon doing so, you can add users to a SharePoint group with Design rights.

Note

At this point, you must make a decision. Use the techniques that were specified in Hour 3. First, create a user MyDesign. Then, in this site (logged in as an administrator), use New in People and Groups to add MyDesign to the site and give MyDesign Design rights.

Figure 10.6 shows what the home page looks like if you are logged in as MyDesign.

FIGURE 10.6
The home page when logged in as MyDesign.

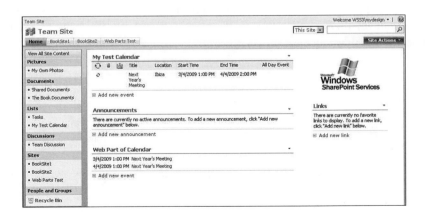

You're right again. This time, both the Recycle Bin and Site Actions are present because the designer can make some amendments to the site.

Note that this doesn't just apply on this page: If you select People and Groups (which, remember, was available for all the kinds of users), for example, you see the same list of names for each site group. You'll also see a different number of horizontal menu items. In the drop-down for each, you'll also see a different number of possible actions (see Table 10.1).

TABLE 10.1   Cross-Reference of Access Rights and Menu Items for People and Groups

Access Rights	Menu Item 1	Menu Item 2	Menu Item 3	Differences
	New	*Actions*	*Settings*	
Administrator	2	3	5	Remove Users
Design	0	2	0	
Contribute	0	2	1	View Group Permissions
Read	0	2	0	

> Things are never as they seem. Obviously, the standard Design rights do not completely overlap the standard Contribute rights.

Note

> Sometimes it is worth spending the time—especially when investigating someone else's site—to look exactly at what permissions have been granted, rather than (as I, too, would have normally done) expect a standard and logical non-overlapping set of rights behind the standard SharePoint group names.

Tip

Effect on Site Settings of Logging In as Somebody Else

Let's closely look at what happens to the Site Settings screen when logged in as administrator or as designer. Select the same menu item (Site Actions) and select the same item from the drop-down list (Site Settings).

Not much left of all those options, is there? Again, the screen is changed to reflect just what that particular user (within or not within a SharePoint group) has rights to do.

FIGURE 10.7
Site Settings
when logged
in as
administrator.

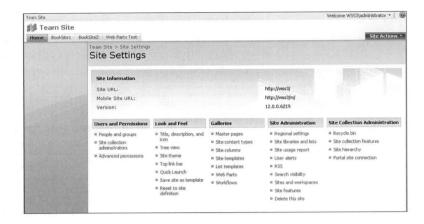

FIGURE 10.7
Site Settings
when logged
in as
administrator.

If the user doesn't have rights to do something, almost without exception the user doesn't see it.

You'll remember that Administrator was the name of the administrator of the server (or VM) on which we had installed WSS 3.0. Also recall that when we created our additional web application and site collection (for the Web Parts Test site) that we said that wss3\Administrator (the same guy) was the site collection administrator.

Wss3\Administrator is also the site collection administrator for the main site. So what happens if we have someone with Administration rights who isn't a site collection administrator? We can use the same "sign in as a different user" method, and we already have an administrator who isn't a site collection administrator (MyAdmin), so let's sign in as her/him and go to Site Actions > Site Settings again.

Figure 10.9 shows more possibilities than Figure 10.8, but an entire column (Site Collection Administration) is missing, as is the Site Collection Administrators link in the first column.

FIGURE 10.8
Site Settings
when logged in
as MyDesign.

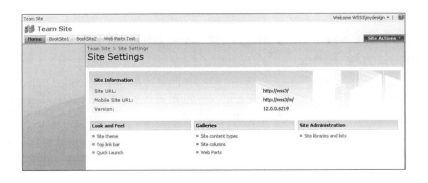

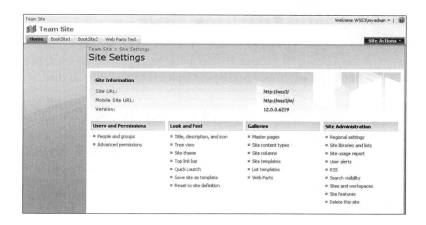

FIGURE 10.9
Site Settings
when logged in
as a mere site
admin.

Both of these omissions are fairly obvious, but it's interesting that a site administrator isn't even allowed to see who the site-collection administrators are.

What about the omission of workflows? We cover that in Hour 19, "Creating Workflows in WSS 3.0." But, you would have thought that creating a workflow wouldn't need a very high-level administrator, right?

> Actually, it's a trick question. Look at the workflow item again. It's in the Galleries section. In other words, it is a list of workflows that only the site-collection admin can see.

Note

Many readers will probably have just one name and password combination to access SharePoint sites. For those readers, were the preceding sections a complete waste of time?

Not necessarily. You might be wondering why your friend Joe, who works just down the corridor, can see more on his screen than you can. You might also be trying to follow another SharePoint book and wondering why you don't see the options it describes. This is actually a tricky one. One of the usual reasons for this is that the book you are reading is describing something in MOSS 2007 that doesn't even exist in WSS 3.0. In that case, even Joe (if he is using WSS 3.0) won't see it.

I believe it's better to be open about these things rather than to hide them. So, no, you didn't waste your time reading the preceding sections. Now if you discover that you are missing access to something you need in your work, you know (if Joe has that access) that you just need to be moved to a different SharePoint group. I'm not saying that will happen if you ask, but if you don't ask, you certainly won't be moved.

General Security Principles Apply

Of all the users we created together in Hour 3, one has so far not been used: MyDocLib. We haven't used it because I want to use MyDocLib as an example when showing you how to restrict access to a list within a site to a particular group.

First, however, there's one thing about SharePoint security that you need to know: SharePoint security does *not* break any standard security rules. Therefore, when restricting access to a document library, you can only allow someone to access the document library in question who also has the rights to access the site (or subsite) in which the document library is located. If you want someone to be allowed to access a document library but not be allowed to access the site containing it, the only solution is to create a special site that that person *can* access and put the document library there.

Note

Treat "access" here as an example. You can't give them Contribute rights to the document library if they have only Read rights to the site. Again, doing so would break standard security rules.

Specifying Special Access Rights for a Document Library

Now that you know the general principles, check again that MyDocLib has been given rights to the main site. Go back to being the administrator and access People and Groups. You should see Figure 10.10. If MyDocLib is not listed there, add it.

FIGURE 10.10
Checking that MyDocLib is listed in the Team Site Members group.

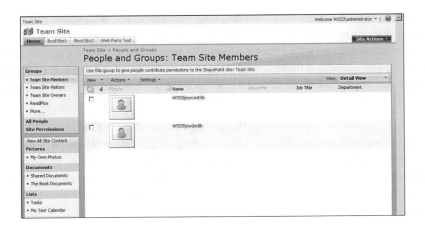

Now that we know that MyDocLib has access rights to the main site, there is nothing stopping us from giving MyDocLib access rights to a document library in the site. To do this, follow these steps:

1. We have two libraries, so let's open Shared Documents from the link in Quick Launch. At the moment, this library is empty. Add at least one document to it so that it's a reasonable test.

2. Access Settings (menu line) and Document Library Settings (drop-down). Figure 10.11 is the top part of what you'll see.

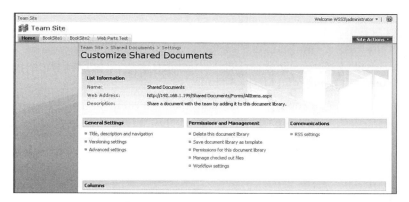

FIGURE 10.11
Customizing shared documents.

3. In the center column (Permissions and Management), there's a Permissions for This Document Library item. Select it. You will see Figure 10.12.

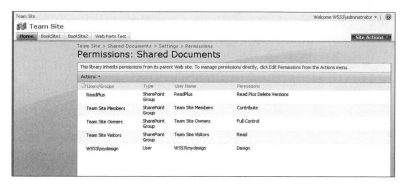

FIGURE 10.12
Standard permissions for a document library.

4. Select Actions and Edit Permissions. You'll receive a warning that you are going to specify specific permissions for this document library. Click OK.

   As Figure 10.13 shows, this is the same list of SharePoint groups and users that Figure 10.12 had. Now, however, there's an additional menu item (New) and probably more items behind the Actions menu item.

FIGURE 10.13
Starting to amend the standard permissions for a document library.

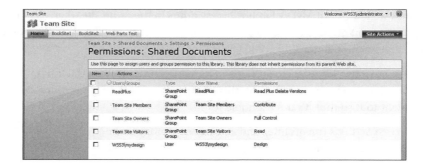

In this case, we intend to end up with a document library that can be accessed by all the administrators (= members of the Team Site Owners SharePoint group) and MyDocAdmin.

This is just an example, but is perhaps the most common use of restricting permissions for a document library. To do this, we can first select all the rows except Team Site Owners and select Remove User Permissions (see Figure 10.14).

FIGURE 10.14
Removing some user permissions.

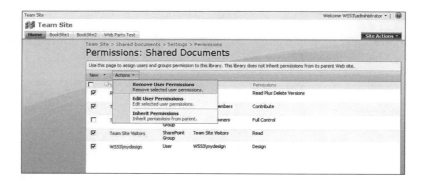

5. Click OK when the warning message appears.

Note   You can always easily add these groups back. Therefore, I don't understand the necessity of this warning. I understand a warning message when you remove things forever. But here...?

6. The list now shows only Team Site Owners. The final step is to add MyDocLib, so select New and Add Users (see Figure 10.15).

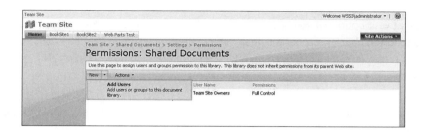

FIGURE 10.15
Adding users.

Figure 10.16 shows the situation before checking the username you've typed in (always a good idea). Figure 10.17 shows an extract of the same screen after the username has been checked.

Note that I have given this user direct permissions.

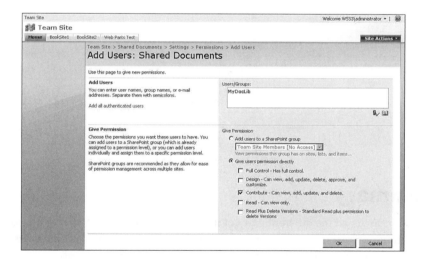

FIGURE 10.16
Adding a user to
Shared Docu-
ments.

FIGURE 10.17
Adding a user
after having
checked the
username.

Tip

> Look at your options if you had tried to add the user to a SharePoint group. You could do this, but except for the Team Site Owners newsgroup that has access rights to the site, all the other SharePoint groups are listed as <Name> (No Access).
>
> Adding MyDocLib to any of them would not give MyDocLib any access rights to the document library, which is certainly not what we had in mind. (The answer to what would happen if we assign MyDocLib to the group Team Site Owners [Full Control] is in the section "Q&A.")

Now we have achieved our aim, and both the administrators and this single user can access the content in this document library (see Figure 10.18). No one else can, though!

FIGURE 10.18
Only the administrators and one user have access rights.

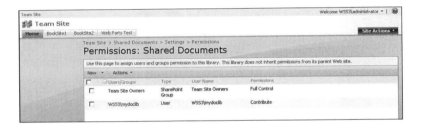

Summary

This hour discussed the different types of users who can access WSS sites. After covering both anonymous access and the All Authenticated Users group (all the users logged in to the domain), the hour examined the effect different permissions have on the look of WSS sites and the different options that are available.

The hour finished with a look at how WSS 3.0 applies general security principles, using an example of what happens when access rights to a document library are restricted to administrators and one particular user only.

Q&A

Q. *At what level do I specify anonymous access?*

A. You specify anonymous access at the web application level.

A web application is a bunch of sites accessible via the same port number. Doing the basic installation has created one web application (http://wss3) at port 80 (that is, the default site). All the sites we have added so far have been subsites to that site and are thus included in that same web application.

Even if we were to add a new "top-level" site to start off a new site collection (which, remember was a top-level site with its subsites [and sub-subsites]), that top-level site would still be in the same wss3 web application.

It's good practice to separate the anonymous access content from the normal content. One way to do this is to create a new web application. As part of that process, specify anonymous access for the web application and add a top-level site to it.

Checking that anonymous access is set is covered later in this section. For now, here are the basic instructions for creating a new web application where you specify that anonymous access is allowed, followed by the instructions for creating a new top-level site:

1. Open Central Administration > Application Management.

2. Create or extend a web application (upper left).

3. Create a new web application.

4. Note the port number, and accept the defaults until halfway down the page.

5. Change Allow Anonymous to Yes.

6. Enter **Administrator** and *<password>* in the "Create New Application Pool" section.

7. At the bottom, again specify WSS3 (the only selection in the drop-down) as the location of the Search server.

8. Click OK.

At this point, we have a web application, and anonymous access has been specified for it. The next steps create a top-level site:

1. You should now be looking at the Application Created page. In the center of it is a Create Site Collections link. Click it.

2. Give it a name (I used Anonymous website) and leave the web address (http://wss3:*<nnnn>* where *<nnnn>* is the randomly assigned port number given to this web application).

3. Select Team Site.

4. Specify Administrator as the Primary Site Collection administrator. (Note that the site collection administrator could be anyone. For a site created for the Personnel department, it would be useful if it were someone within the department and not you. In this case of a site for anonymous access, however, the administrator of the server is fine.)

5. Note in passing that each site collection has its own set of (different) quotas, but only if you've created a separate quota template. Here we have only one listed.

6. Click OK.

7. The site is created and can be accessed via http://wss3:<*portnumber*>. (Mine is 7595, so http://wss3:7595 is what I can see.)

Q. *How do I check the settings for anonymous access in IIS?*

A. To check the settings for anonymous access in IIS, follow these steps:

1. Start > Administrative Tools > Internet Information Services (IIS) Manager.

2. Select websites in the leftmost column, and then select SharePoint – 7595 (or whatever you have).

3. From the menu bar, select Action > Properties.

4. Select Directory Security.

5. In the Authentication and Access Control Section, select Edit.

6. Click Enable Anonymous Access, and then click OK.

7. Click OK again.

8. Select All, and then click OK.

9. Close the Internet Information Services (IIS) Manager.

Q. *I already have a web application and I didn't specify anonymous access when I created it. How can I do so now?*

A. Many people have difficulty finding the location because it bears little relation to the location specified in Question 1:

1. Go to Central Administration > Application Management.

2. Select Authentication Providers in the Application Security section.

3. Select the web application you want to set this for (top right).

4. Select the zone, and the Anonymous Access section should be visible on the page.

Q. *What happens if I, in a document library, give access rights to a user and make that user a member of the Team Site Owners SharePoint group?*

A. As you remember, the standard security rule is "no rights to a lower level of security that aren't there in a higher level."

In this case, that means that to give a user access rights to a document library, that user needs to have access rights to the site containing the document library. It also means that if the user has Contribute rights to the site, the most the user can have is Contribute rights to the document library.

Suppose we specify that the user with Contribute rights to the site becomes a member of Team Site Owners in the document library and thus has Administration rights there. That would mean that the user has higher rights in the document library than in the site.

The system allows you to specify this when giving the users rights in the document library because what the SharePoint coders decided to do was not to say "you can't do this," but to make it possible. The only way to make it possible given those security rules is to make the user a member of Team Site Owners *at the site level, too.*

The security rules have been followed. The user now has Administration rights to the site and Administration rights to the document library, but at the cost of you not being aware this has happened because it occurs behind the scene.

So you think you have given Alice Administrator access to one specific document library, whereas now she actually has access to everything in the entire site structure that isn't marked as being off-bounds to administrators. Depending on who Alice is, this could be a disaster in the making.

Workshop

Quiz

1. Name the couple of "special" sets of users discussed in this hour?

2. Do all users always see the same things when they access the same page?

3. Why when we grant a user rights to a document library (or list) should we specify the user permissions directly rather than assign the user to a SharePoint group?

Quiz Answers

1. Anonymous access and the All Authenticated Users group.

2. No, what they see depends on which rights they have.

3. Because if we assign the user to a SharePoint group, that group will either have no access rights to that document library or doing so may increase the rights of that user to the entire site structure.

HOUR 11

Using What We've Learned So Far in a Site

What You'll Learn in This Hour

- ▶ Collecting data to create a site
- ▶ Assigning data to appropriate SharePoint lists and libraries, and accepting when data isn't suitable for that
- ▶ Deciding what to place on the default site page
- ▶ How a user accesses desired information

Brainstorming What Information a Site Could Contain

Now that we've learned the concepts of building a website using WSS 3.0, let's put them into practice by setting up a site for a particular purpose.

Assume that we're building a site that will be used as a model for large teams investigating a serious crime. The first thing is to brainstorm what kinds of information the team is likely to have and need. So, just at random, a few things come to mind:

- ▶ Eyewitness reports
- ▶ Interviews with suspects
- ▶ Interviews with relatives
- ▶ Photographs of suspects
- ▶ Photographs of witnesses
- ▶ Soundtracks of interviews

- ▶ Videos of interviews

- ▶ Videos of the crime scene

- ▶ Photographs of the crime scene

- ▶ Fingerprints

- ▶ DNA samples

- ▶ Links to other computer systems

- ▶ General information to the team members

- ▶ Restaurant, hotel information for out-of-area members of the team

- ▶ Images of menus

- ▶ Recommendations from local members of the team

- ▶ Dates of press briefings

- ▶ Dates of internal meetings

- ▶ Method for the boss of the team to report to his superiors

That gives you the general idea. Include anything and everything that's connected with the issue related to the site, even if it later ends up being rejected.

Making Sense of the Mass of Data

Brainstorming should lead to a mass of hodge-podge ideas. The next step to starting a website is to collate this date and assign it to SharePoint "things." We'll start with the documents previously listed (but we could start anywhere).

Thinking About Documents

Our first attempt at a list of the documents we will have is the following.

- ▶ Eyewitness reports

- ▶ Interviews with suspects

- ▶ Interviews with relatives

At this point (and this is normal), we discover that we've forgotten that the team will produce various reports, so we add them to the list:

- ▶ Weekly summaries

- ▶ Progress reports

- ▶ Text of press releases

- ▶ Transcript of press briefing

- ▶ Reports from team boss to higher management

It's fairly clear that all these documents will go into SharePoint document libraries. What is not clear is how many, because we may think of some more documents later on in the process.

We need to think about whether we need a document library that includes all these documents, some (fewer than eight) document libraries to contain them, or eight different document libraries (one document library listed item).

In other words, think about consolidation. To do that, consider the names of the previously listed categories. Interviews with eyewitnesses, interviews with suspects, and interviews with relatives should go in the same document library because

- ▶ They are all interviews.

- ▶ There is a floating line between a suspect and an eyewitness (or relative): Being one doesn't exclude being the other.

We will put all three categories in an Interviews document library. Then we need something that makes it possible for us to mark someone as both an eyewitness and a suspect, for example.

I often do this by having three Yes/No fields:

- ▶ Suspect: Yes/No

- ▶ Eyewitness: Yes/No

- ▶ Relative: Yes/No

This makes it possible to easily create views, such as Suspect (condition is Suspect=Yes) or even a combined view, such as Suspect and Eyewitness (first condition is Suspect=Yes; second condition is Eye-Witness=Yes).

> **Note**
>
> As well as using premade views, you can also use (in real time) filters on one or more fields to get the same effect. The problem is that before moving on you have to spend time resetting the filters back to the All settings.

Another option is to have a Choice type field with three choices (Suspect, Eyewitness, and Relative) and make this Choice type field (unlike the one we used in Hour 8, "Creating and Using Views and Folders") have multiple choices.

Note

I don't like this because what is then stored in the Choice field is a string (Suspect; Relative, for instance), and it's more difficult to filter and sort on the field.

The Interviews document library reduces the list by three items. Five items are left! We can immediately cross another one off: reports from team boss to higher management. This won't be available to team members other than the boss, so it can't be located in the same document library as anything else.

So, we create a document library called Reports to Senior Management. We'll decide later what to do to keep it secure. Four items left.

Because two of the four items relate to the press, both of them can be in a document library called Press Documents. To keep the two kinds of documents apart but still within the same document library, we'll use the same technique as in Hour 8 and use a field of type Choice called, perhaps, Type of Document. In this, we'll have just two alternatives: Press Releases and Press Briefing Transcripts. Of course, we'll pre-prepare views for each of those two values (just as we did in Hour 8 for HP, IBM, and so on). Two left.

Both the two left, despite the completely different names in the list, are just reports made on a regular basis. They might just as well be put in the same document library using a Choice field (and views) to keep them apart.

Note

Perhaps you think that there will be a demand for the latest three weekly summaries *and* the latest three progress reports to be visible on the same page. In this case, you need two document libraries.

Go back to Hour 6, "Using Libraries and Lists," and you'll see that you can have two web parts on the same page that show content from the same document library and yet show different content.

In other words, these two setups solve the demand for the latest three summaries and the latest three progress reports: two document libraries, and a single document library with two non-overlapping views.

Finally, around this point, we discover that we've completely missed one set of documents. Regular team meetings will no doubt be written up. In fact, because of the size of the team, there will be probably be team meetings of subteams and team meetings of the entire squad.

So, we need one document library for team meetings with an extra field, Team Name, to categorize them and ease the use of views.

The end result (at least for now) is the following document libraries:

▶ Interviews

▶ Press documents

▶ Summaries and progress reports

▶ Team meetings

▶ Reports to senior management

The Reports to Senior Management document library needs to be separate.

Pictures

In the original list, we have four sets of pictures:

▶ Photographs of suspects

▶ Photographs of witnesses

▶ Photographs of the crime scene

▶ Images of menus

The first three involve solving the crime; the fourth does not.

The first two—following the ideas stated earlier—can go into a single picture library. In this picture library, there must be a way (as earlier, with the Yes/No fields) of deciding whether someone is a witness or a suspect or both.

In fact, we now realize that we will have photographs of relatives, too, so this picture library will include them and be the equivalent of a document library.

> My preference is to keep the crime scene pictures in their own picture library. It's only a preference, but it seems logical because they are a completely different set of pictures (from those of people).

Note

The images of menus need their own picture library. For the moment, we can't think of any other social usage for a picture library.

Also, it may prove useful if the out-of-town members of the squad (that is, those for whom the images of menus were conceived) can recognize the other members of the squad. In other words, we need a third picture library (with photographs of squad members). Let's also add descriptions to the photographs in the picture library.

Note

> You'll often find, when trying to making sense of your collection of things and deciding what to include in a site, that you want other things to appear in a site, too.

The end result is that we have four picture libraries:

▶ Suspects, Eyewitnesses, and Relatives

▶ Crime Scene

▶ Menu Images (and other social bric-a-brac)

▶ Squad Member Pictures (with brief descriptions)

Now let's look at some of the easier items to categorize.

Announcements

One item obviously goes in an Announcements list: general information to the team members. This could be used both for general information about how the investigation is proceeding and for information for out-of-town squad members about interesting things about to happen in the town. Given the seriousness of the investigation, it's best to keep them apart.

We'll have two Announcements lists:

▶ General investigation information announcements

▶ Announcements about interesting local events

Dates

Two date items were previously listed: dates of press briefings and dates of internal meetings.

These are obvious candidates for different Calendar lists.

Tip

> Make the date items different because they are of different priority to different people.

Note

> We'll see later in this hour how "personal views" can improve the visibility of something you are interested in.

At this point, there could be a third calendar—one giving the local events for the out-of-towners' free time.

Now, we have three different Calendar lists:

- ▶ Press Briefings
- ▶ Internal Meetings
- ▶ Local Events

Unformatted Information

A few items listed in our original list are both in the social category and haven't been covered:

- ▶ Restaurant, hotel information for out-of-area members of the team
- ▶ Recommendations from local members of the team

Both items are likely to be free format, with a title and a brief description from the local squad member, and so they are suitable for the Custom list format with a title Bob's café and a description.

I see no reason why we can't combine these items if they are strictly free-formatted information. If the restaurant/hotel information is official (and so probably laid out within a certain number of set fields) and the recommendations are strictly off-cuff ones, however, there should be two Custom lists (with different fields).

Again, it's a decision for the site designer based on the designer's sense of how this information is going to be provided.

So, we have (in my judgment) two different Custom lists:

- ▶ Local Hotel and Restaurant Details
- ▶ Local Tips

Other Information

Here's what's left from the original list:

- ▶ Soundtracks of interviews
- ▶ Videos of interviews
- ▶ Videos of the crime scene
- ▶ Fingerprints

▶ DNA samples

▶ Links to other computer systems

Links

Links to other computer systems may seem to be the only obvious Links library required. I suspect, however, that fingerprints will be stored in a national (perhaps) fingerprint system rather than in our SharePoint site. Therefore, there ought to be a link to the fingerprint system.

I obviously don't watch television enough, because I have no idea where DNA information is stored and accessed. Let's assume that the information is similar to fingerprints and thus requires us to access another system.

From this, we can calculate that we will have one Links library, which will contains several entries, such as the following:

▶ Links to various police-related organizations

▶ A link to the fingerprint system

▶ A link to the DNA system

Just because we have listed something (about what the site should provide) in our brainstorming, we need to remain flexible and remind ourselves constantly that not everything needs to be stored in our own system. What is important is that our team can access the information, not that it is stored in our system. Links lists are often the solution to this "problem."

Audio and Video

We're left with audio and video. There is no list or library specifically for audio and video as there was for pictures. So, the logical place to put these files is in a document library (or libraries).

That is, if we put them in a library at all. Whereas MP3 audio files are small and are not going to be a problem for a document library, video files are large and thus are a potential problem for (for instance) backups. One option, therefore, is to keep video files in the file system.

The other thing is that the SharePoint v3 systems do not as delivered provide any functionality for playing back video files in a window within the browser. Typically, either software additions are required (if third-party additions to the basic SharePoint software are available) or a video file will open a completely separate copy of software capable of playing back the video format we are using.

In addition, it might first be necessary to check which file formats can be uploaded to a document library. The first question in the "Q&A" section shows how to check the file formats allowed in document libraries and how to amend that list.

Otherwise, if MP3 (for instance) is on the list of file types that are "banned," any attempt to upload a single MP3 file (or a batch of files containing at least one MP3 file) will fail.

For the purpose of this site-creation exercise, let's just assume that we've covered all the bases and that both audio and video files will be added to document libraries.

To be as logical as possible, let's have three separate document libraries:

- ▶ Soundtracks of interviews
- ▶ Videos of interviews
- ▶ Videos of the scene of the crime

Summary of Lists/Libraries

So far, our final tally of lists and libraries is as follows:

- ▶ Document libraries (8)
- ▶ Picture libraries (4)
- ▶ Announcements lists (2)
- ▶ Calendar lists (3)
- ▶ Custom lists (2)
- ▶ Links lists (1)

Placing the Lists/Libraries into the Web Pages

We've brainstormed our lists and libraries, so now, we must create them and add fields (as appropriate) for each list. Then you must decide which lists/libraries should appear in the Quick Launch section and which lists/libraries need to appear in web part form in the main section of the page.

Deciding on One Site or Several Sites

First, consider whether one site is enough for your needs. If you look at our list, it is, because the only thing we have that is of restricted access is one single document library; we can assume that there is nothing to stop the top management having rights to access the rest of the site. Therefore, we can also give them rights to that one Reports to Senior Management document library (following the rules outlined in Hour 10, "Learning About Authentication and Access Rights."

However, although that approach is possible, I always expect to have missed something when doing the brainstorming and follow-up design sessions. This means that I could have missed some other piece of information needed for contacts between the senior management and the squad leader.

In fact, I've probably missed the fact that they need to communicate. These days, many in senior management feel able to communicate via a computer. Therefore, a Discussions list open only to senior management and the squad leader is certainly a possibility we should add to our design.

Note

I thought about a Discussions list for the squad team itself. In the end, however, I decided that they'll be in a big room and will hold their discussions in person.

So, now we have both a Discussions list and a document library that are restricted access. The obvious solution is to put them in a subsite that does *not* inherit permissions.

In that (sub)site, we have so few lists/libraries that we might as well put both web parts in the main section of the screen. We can place the Discussions list on the left, and on the right the document library, the web part for which should perhaps use a view that specifies something between 10 and 20 items.

Tip

Typically, the best sort order for the main page of a site is by the Modified field in descending order. (So, specifying an item limit of five in a view will show the *latest* five items.)

I find 5 to be a useful limit if the page is crowded and 10 to be more suitable if it isn't.

Note

When an item is created (or in this case a document is added to a document library), both the Created and the Modified fields contain the time and time it was created. When an item is changed, the Modified field is amended but the Created field stays the same.

Usually, you want to know both about the latest new and the latest amended articles. Therefore, you use the Modified field.

If you want to see in one part of the screen the latest New documents and in another part of the screen the latest Modified (but not New) documents, however, you need to use two web parts from the same document library with two different views.

You want one view just sorted on Created; that gives the latest New documents. You want a second view that is sorted on Modified to give all documents that have been modified but which includes a filter that keeps out newly added documents. (To do this you create a calculated field called NotMod whose value is "=Created-Modified" and then have a filter that is defined as NotMod not equal 0).

Allocating Lists/Web Parts to the Default Page

What about the main site? There, it's obvious that we have so many lists and libraries that we are not going to fit the web parts for all of them in the center section. So what we look for there are the lists/libraries that need to be "in your face."

This knocks out most of the document libraries because we expect people to regularly look through them without prompting. For instance, the meeting reports and so on will automatically be read by people who were away at the time (or missed most of the meeting because they were daydreaming). Therefore, they don't need to be in the main section. And, in any case, there's a technique called *alerts* (discussed a bit later in this hour). With alerts, you can tell people when something has been changed in a document library (or list).

For both these reasons, we'll use what little space we have in the main section of the screen for some other lists.

The first obvious candidates are one of the two Announcements lists and two of the three Calendar lists.

Note

Why not both the Announcement lists and all three Calendar lists? Because the ones I don't plan to include on the standard page are the ones intended only for out-of-towners, because those lists are almost entirely uninteresting for local squad members.

You can tweak the calendars to make sure they don't take up too much space.

Of the rest, only one list/library should be included in the main section of the page: the Links list. That is there because people will be using it often as a way to go directly to other systems, and they won't want to need to first open it from Quick Launch.

Specifying What Will Be Listed in the Quick Launch Section

As for the question of which items to list in Quick Launch, it very much depends on how many lists/libraries you have.

At a minimum, you should have a link there for every list/library that you have not included as a web part in the main section of the screen. If you have the space, however, there's nothing wrong with having even the list/libraries behind those web parts that are present in the main section of the page (or some of them) listed in the Quick Launch section.

To some extent, in a company environment this can be decided by the size of the monitors in use there, and the standard screen resolution of them. Just as an overfull screen looks a mess, so does a nearly empty one.

Positioning the Web Parts in the Web Page

So far, there's been no discussion about how to position those web parts that we selected for the main section of the page.

A good start is to get rid of the standard WSS logo! It does nothing useful and just fills up useful space. Follow that, if you have two Announcements lists, by placing (one each!) at the top of the two columns.

For some reason, it's a good standard to have the Links list on the rightmost side of the screen. (Because we want all the links that are in the list to be visible here, that should be the rightmost section completed.)

That leaves the two calendars, which can therefore be placed only in the leftmost screen section (with the more important one first).

Here the view called Calendar does look nice, I agree, but it does take up a lot of space. So, you should at least consider making one or both of your web parts use another more boring view.

Figure 11.1 and Figure 11.2 illustrate this point.

In Figure 11.2 (and only half of the calendar is actually on screen), the second calendar dominates the entire screen (even though it contains no more information than the first calendar). So, use full calendars with care. If you want them to dominate, fine. If you don't, use more minimal versions.

That's enough for setting up the site. Now let's look at the needs of the people who require access to a site's information.

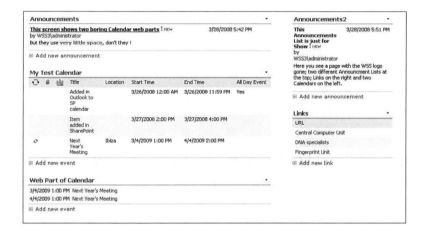

FIGURE 11.1
Using small-size calendars.

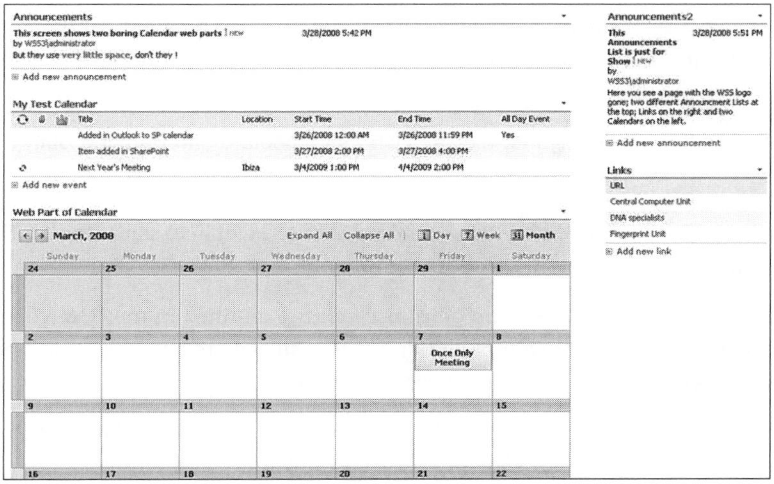

FIGURE 11.2
Using at least one "real" calendar.

Additional Functions for the Users of the Site

People tend to use a site in three different ways:

▶ They access the site regularly and check what's new there.

▶ They want to be told when things are new there.

▶ They want to be able to search for things from the site.

Note

> Of course, people might also want to do a combination of any of the things previously listed.

Let's look at these briefly, in order.

People Who Access the Site Regularly

People who access the site regularly want to see at-a-glance information. The information they see is what the site designer decides they are interested in.

People Who Want to Be Prompted for Updates

Another category of site users enjoy receiving alerts, which they can set themselves on lists and libraries to receive an email whenever something changes.

Note

> There are different settings for alerts, such as Immediate and Batched Daily.

For alerts to function, the SharePoint system needs to be able to send emails. This is something that our system hasn't been set to do.

The details of how to set this as an administrator are outlined in the "Q&A" section. Here, I assume that you are a user working with a site where outgoing email has been made possible. I show you how to set your alerts:

Open The Book Documents and select the Actions drop-down (see Figure 11.3). Choose Alert Me. Figure 11.4 shows the key part of what you then see.

Team Site
Team Site
Home
BookSite1
BookSite2
Web Parts Test
Team Site > The Book Documents
The Book Documents
View All Site Content
Pictures
My Own Photos
Documents
The Book Documents
Lists
Tasks
My Test Calendar
My Test Contacts
Discussions
Team Discussion
Sites
New
Upload
Actions
Edit
Type
Name
Edit in Datasheet
Bulk edit items using a datasheet format.
Open with Windows Explorer
Drag and drop files into this library.
Export to Spreadsheet
Analyze items with a spreadsheet application.
View RSS Feed
Syndicate items with an RSS reader.
Alert Me
Receive e-mail notifications when items change.
Book Text Test FileHP

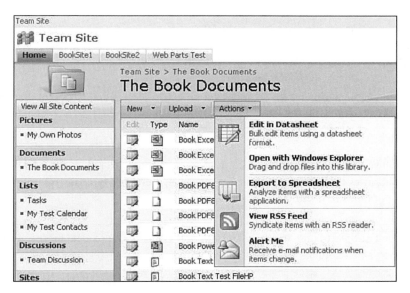

FIGURE 11.3 Choosing Alert Me.

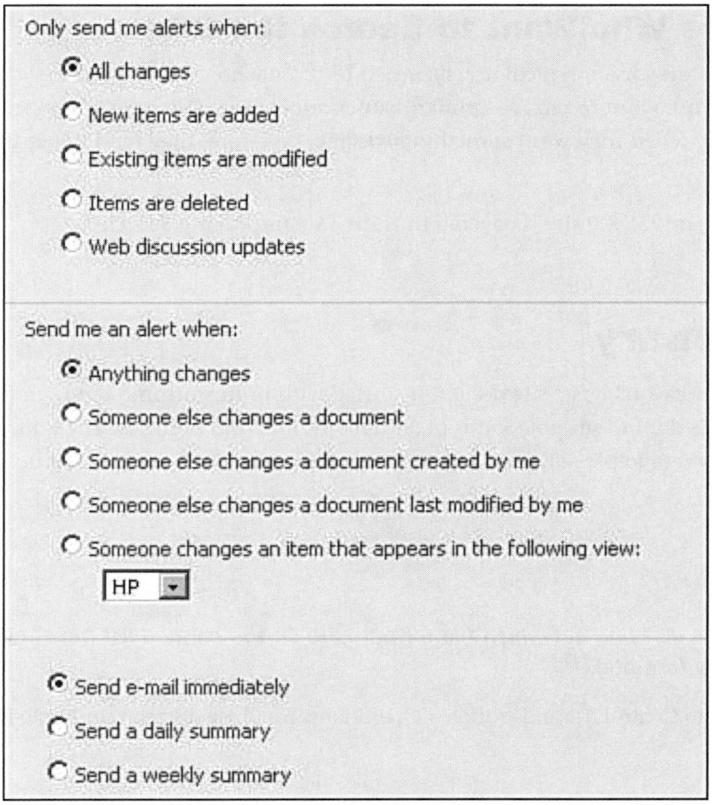

Only send me alerts when:
All changes
New items are added
Existing items are modified
Items are deleted
Web discussion updates
Send me an alert when:
Anything changes
Someone else changes a document
Someone else changes a document created by me
Someone else changes a document last modified by me
Someone changes an item that appears in the following view:
HP
Send e-mail immediately
Send a daily summary
Send a weekly summary

FIGURE 11.4 Specifying Alerts.

Note

> A common question: How do I set alerts for a single document or item? The answer is that you can't (unless that document is the only one in a view or the only one you created).
>
> In other words, alerts are for an entire list or library or for a subsection of that list or library as defined in the central section in Figure 11.4.

The top two sections of Figure 11.4 contain many options. To reduce the number of lists or libraries that can trigger an alert, however, alerts still typically occur for a number of items or documents, not just for one.

Tip

> You can't set alerts until the administrator has made them possible by specifying outgoing email settings in Central Administration.

People Who Want to Search the Site

The final category of typical users consists of those who neither want to visit a site regularly nor want to receive email about changes to it. These people typically access a site only when they want something specific; therefore, they tend to use the Search function.

Searching a WSS 3.0 site is covered in Hour 14, "Improving Searches."

Summary

This hour covered basic site design. It started with brainstorming data, and then assigned this data to suitable kinds of SharePoint lists and libraries. The hour then examined where to place the data in the site and how typical users might access the data.

Q&A

Q. *How do I find out which file formats are on the banned list (and how do I add new formats)?*

A. Go to Central Administration > Operations. You'll see a screen similar to Figure 11.5.

Select Blocked File Types (in the Security Configuration section).

Scroll down the list to see whether MP3 files are blocked. They are not, and neither are video file types such as AVI, MP4, and WMV. So, there's nothing to stop us from adding our audio and video files.

However, try to add a Microsoft help file (CHM). You won't be allowed to. So, let's just delete CHM from this list. Click OK to return to the screen shown in Figure 11.5.

Figure 11.6 tells us that "you must delete it from both the global and Web application lists."

All my tests with this function have shown that I *could* upload a file of a previously banned type to a WSS 3.0 document library after removing that file type *only* from the list in Figure 11.6.

This note from Microsoft is clearly beyond its sell-by date.

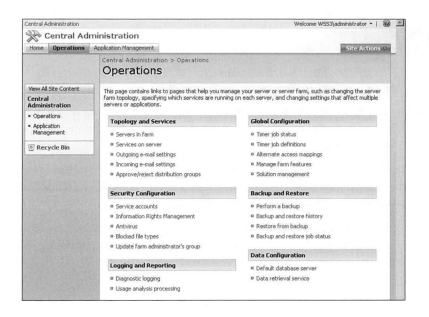

FIGURE 11.5
Operations in Central Administration.

FIGURE 11.6
List of Blocked
File Types.

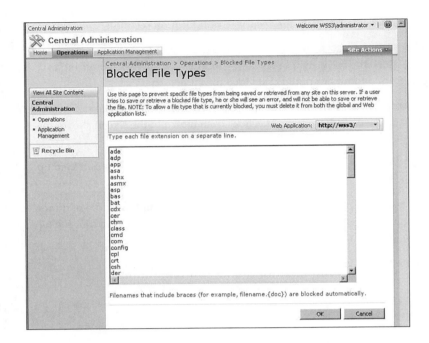

Q. *How can administrators make alerts operable?*

A. For alerts to work, the administrator needs to enable the SharePoint system to send email. This is done in Central Administration > Operations > Outgoing E-Mail Settings.

The main requirement is the need to have an SMTP server available. Typically, this is Exchange Server, but it could be any SMTP server (even a small free one installed on the same server as your WSS 3.0).

Getting the name of that SMTP server correct is the usual stumbling block in what otherwise is a relatively simple process (unlike setting incoming email settings).

Workshop

Quiz

1. Is the data we have gathered in the brainstorming phase the totality of data for the site?

2. If I only have a single document library that is of restricted access, should I locate it in the standard site and specify special access rights for it?

3. Can I specify that I get an email alert when a single item in a list or document in a document library changes?

Quiz Answers

1. It's not likely to be. The subsequent processes of assigning the data to lists and libraries and of then deciding what to include on the default page will all tend to throw up new data that was overlooked earlier.

2. It's one option you have. Unless you are 100 percent sure that you will not have any more lists or libraries with restricted access, however, it might be a better option to create a special site (with restricted access) for it.

3. Not as such. If the item in question is the only one in a view and you have specified alerts for a particular view, then yes, you can. But typically, the standard options, views, lists, and such will mean that an alert will act on several items or documents, not just one.

HOUR 12

Using Wikis and Blogs

What You'll Learn in This Hour

- ▶ Definition of wikis and blogs
- ▶ Installing and using wikis and blogs
- ▶ Improving the functionality of your wiki and blog

Wikis and Blogs in WSS 3.0

To most of you, the terms blogs and wikis are already familiar. *Blogs* are a way for people to write an open letter to (potentially) the world. Wikis don't get as much attention as blogs, so we discuss them first.

An example of a wiki is Wikipedia, which is an online encyclopedia that depends on the contributions of the masses to produce quality entries. For example, someone describes a pop artist's background and posts it. This description can then be amended and expanded on by anyone who knows more about the subject.

Wikipedia defines a wiki as follows (http://en.wikipedia.org/wiki/Wiki):

> A *wiki* is software that allows users to collaboratively create, edit, link, and organize the content of a website, usually for reference material. Wikis are often used to create collaborative websites and to power community websites.

I have my suspicions that wikis and blogs were added just so that a check mark will appear next to an itemized list of what the SharePoint v3 products contain. Even some Microsoft people acknowledge that what comes built in to the download provides only basic functionality. They advise that if you want more to go to third-party sites providing blogs and (to a less extent) wikis.

However, even the basic functionality included does provide some useful additional capabilities to the business sites that can be built using WSS 3.0 and MOSS 2007 products.

Note

Support for blogs and wikis in MOSS 2007 is identical to their support in WSS 3.0.

This chapter looks at that basic functionality. Then we'll look at a few free options to enhance that basic functionality and make it unnecessary to go to a third-party product or site.

Creating Wiki Support in Standard WSS 3.0

Let's start by creating a wiki site. For simplicity's sake, we'll make this a subsite of the default site:

1. Go to Home > Site Actions > Create > Sites and Workspaces.

2. Name the site **Wiki Test Site**, and specify the URL as http:<server TCP-IP>/WikiTest. Also specify a template of type (Collaboration) Wiki (see Figure 12.1). Accept all the defaults for the remaining fields.

FIGURE 12.1
Creating a wiki site.

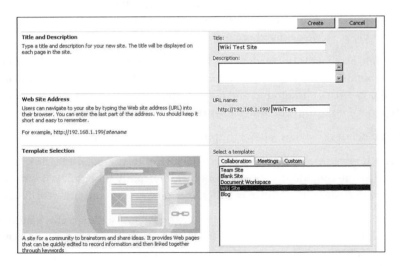

3. An "empty" site appears (see Figure 12.2). (This initial screen contains some guidelines as to what to do next.)

FIGURE 12.2
The Starter Page
of a wiki site.

At this point, you can click How to Use This Wiki Site to see a page with all the things you can do with your wiki (see Figure 12.3). (We'll only concentrate on a few basic things here.)

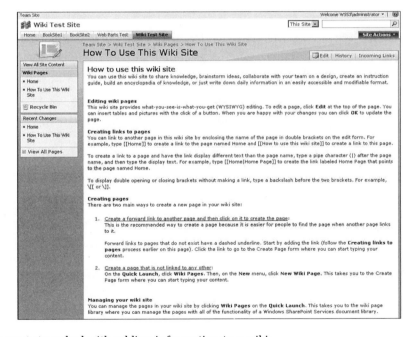

FIGURE 12.3
How to use a
wiki site.

The next steps deal with adding information to a wiki:

1. Go back in the browser or select Wiki Test Site in either of the horizontal menu lines.

The page suggests that you select Edit (refer to Figure 12.2). Before you do, however, read this page; you won't see this text again in this site.

Note

Here's the final paragraph in case you forget it: "Other example uses of wiki sites include brainstorming ideas, collaborating on designs, creating an instruction guide, gathering data from the field, tracking call-center knowledge, and building an encyclopedia of knowledge."

This is the site's top page, so you might want to write some information to your users describing how your company (or whatever) will use the wiki functionality.

Tip

If you use an English language version of WSS 3.0, but your users don't have English as their mother tongue, this is a good place to explain the wiki concept in their language (in addition to writing a translation of the same information suggested previously).

Assume that the wiki site will be used to share (internally) information about customer staff who work with us and the products installed at the customer company. Figure 12.4 is an example of a possible top-level page to start people off.

FIGURE 12.4
Creating a wiki home page.

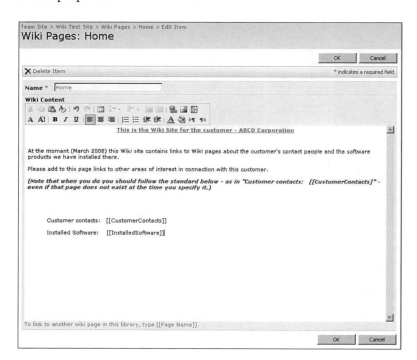

2. Click OK. Notice (see Figure 12.5) that—as shown in Figure 12.3—both links have a "dashed underline" because the pages that are linked to do not yet exist.

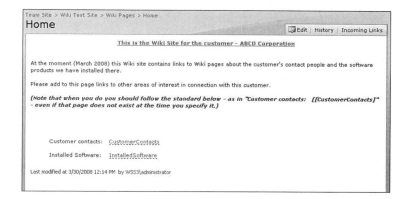

FIGURE 12.5
Dotted lines are nothing to worry about!

> Before you write in, there is a mistake in the explanatory text (a single closing bracket (]) where two are needed). Because this is a wiki, someone will probably fix it before you notice the error.

Note

3. Click the CustomerContacts link to get an empty version of Figure 12.6. Decide whether you want a title and explanatory text.

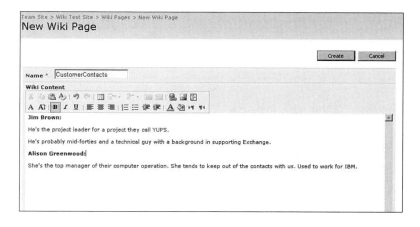

FIGURE 12.6
Starting to populate the CustomerContacts page.

Note

> You (or someone else) can always decide to add these things later.

Look at Figure 12.6 and refer to Figure 12.4. Information about other staff members will be added to the page by people coming to this page later.

Those people will probably follow the styling lead in the information already on the page so that information should be complete, but at the moment, it isn't. Whoever wrote the information about Jim Brown should have realized that people will need to know what the YUPS project is. That person doesn't need to write the information about YUPS himself but he needs to encourage other people to write something about YUPS on a different page by preparing a link to a YUPS page.

Even with that change the page is not yet optimal. In addition, we should remind people that they can add any information that they want to about the customer contacts.

FIGURE 12.7
A better Cus-
tomerContacts
page.

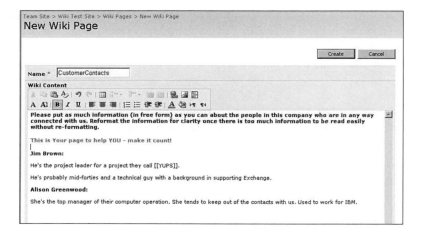

The final version of this page (before we click Create) might look like Figure 12.7.

4. Click Create. Your page now shows a "dashed underline" link to YUPS. This link encourages people to provide more information on YUPS within the YUPS page.

Note

We didn't put double square brackets around IBM, because everyone knows IBM. If this had been SysFred Inc., we would have used those double square brackets.

That's it for this introduction to the basic functionality that you get when creating a wiki site in your WSS 3.0 (or MOSS 2007) system.

Using the Wiki Library

Note

The wiki pages we have at the moment (Home, CustomerContacts, and the original version of How to Use This Wiki Site) are all stored in a wiki library. Apart from the Recycle Bin, the wiki library is the only thing automatically created when a wiki site is created.

Tip

To check what is provided by default when a site is created, click View All Site Content at the home page of the wiki site. To see the contents of this default wiki library (called Wiki Pages), click Wiki Pages at the home page of the wiki site.

There is no difference between this wiki library and a wiki library that you can create in a "normal" Team Site. In other words, at some point you must decide whether to use the wiki functionality within a normal (non-wiki) site or to have all wiki functionality within one or more wiki sites (or even to use both techniques).

I prefer having wiki functionality within wiki sites to using wiki libraries in normal sites. Having wiki sites means that it is possible to have special (probably less-restrictive, maybe even anonymous) permissions for the entire (wiki) site and thus automatically for all the wiki libraries it contains.

In some cases, however, a site might need its own set of restricted-access wiki pages. In that case, creating a wiki library within that site might be the correct decision.

WSS 3.0 provides both options and leaves the decision up to you (or your administrator).

Creating Blog Support in Standard WSS 3.0

This section looks at the standard functionality for blogs provided by WSS 3.0 out-of-the-box. I won't spend much time describing this standard functionality because the section which follows this section describes a way to improve on this standard functionality.

Let's create a blog site. Again, as with the wiki site, to keep it simple, make this a sub-site of the default site. To do this, follow these steps:

1. Go to Home > Site Actions > Create > Sites and Workspaces.

2. Name the site **Blog Test Site**, and specify the URL of it http://wss3>/BlogTest. In addition, specify a template of type (Collaboration) Blog. Accept all the defaults for the remaining fields.

FIGURE 12.8
Starting a blog.

3. Click Create a Post. Avoid the pitfalls new bloggers can fall into (in italic; see Figure 12.9).

FIGURE 12.9
Writing a blog item.

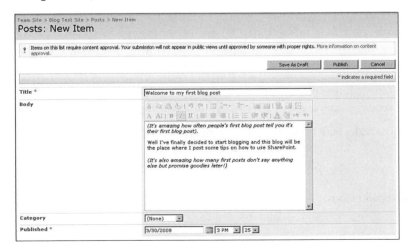

You can either *Save As Draft*, in which case you can't see it and will need to go to Manage Posts in Figure 12.8 to see what it looks like. Alternatively, you can go straight to Publish—you can, after all, correct it later.

It's a good idea to delete the Welcome to Your Blog post. It doesn't look professional (see Figure 12.10).

FIGURE 12.10
Your first blog post appears in the site.

4. Click the Set Blog Permissions link, which leads you to a Help screen with some good information about configuring your blog. One configuration example allows everyone in the organization to read all of your blogs but only members of your department to comment.

> If you try to select Launch Blog Program to Post on a client running, for instance, Office 2003, a message tells you that you require IE 6.0 and "a Windows SharePoint Services compatible blog editor such as...Word 2007" to do this. In the final section, we look at using an application to post a blog item to a blog.

Note

Instead of looking further at this standard basic blog function, I want to move on to an enhanced blog setup. This is a free application based on the standard WSS 3.0 blog functionality, but it adds a lot of improvements to it.

Adding Enhanced Blog Support

Codeplex is a site Microsoft provides for "community" (free) software. Many additions to WSS 3.0 are available there. The quality of these additions varies, but generally, products released under the umbrella title of "Community Kit for SharePoint" can be trusted. In this hour, we're interested in the subprojects of the Community Kit for wikis and blogs.

The wiki subproject (Enhanced Wiki Edition 2.0) at
www.codeplex.com/CKS/Release/ProjectReleases.aspx?ReleaseId=8087 is, at the time
of this writing, only at beta 2 level; it's not going to be covered here.

The blog subproject (Enhanced Blog Edition 2.0) at
www.codeplex.com/CKS/Release/ProjectReleases.aspx?ReleaseId=5134 is already at
final edition level. So, we will install it. The following instructions will be enough, in
most cases, although reading the Installation Guide first (from the URL just given) is
recommended.

Tip

> If you run your test server in a virtual machine, now is a good time to take a
> snapshot. (If you are running on a real server, back up!)

You are probably running a single-server version of WSS 3.0 using the basic installation, as suggested in Hour 2, "Installing Windows SharePoint Services 3.0." If so, you
must do one more thing: **Start the Windows SharePoint Services Administration
service**, which is not started by default in such an installation.

Tip

> To turn on the Windows SharePoint Services Administration service, go in the
> server to Start > Administrative Tools > Services and find the first service that
> starts with "Windows SharePoin" (not a misprint—that's all the text I can see).

Tip

> This should be the Windows SharePoint Services Administration service. Double-
> click it and change the start-up type to Automatic and click Start. When that
> finishes, click OK.

You will have extracted an install.bat file along with two other files from the downloaded zip file.

Now (and you did start the Windows SharePoint Services Administration service first,
didn't you?) is the time to run that Install.bat file to install the Extended Blog Edition.

One alternative when running this at the server is to run the update.bat from the
command line. When you do this make sure the command line is located at the directory to which you have extracted all three files. This is necessary as you will need
to specify the parameters indicated early on in the Installation guide. These are as
follows:

```
install.bat http://webapp http://webapp/blogsite
```

Therefore, in our case

`install.bat http://wss3 http://wss3/BlogTest`

The other alternative is to double-click the install.bat file in Windows Explorer. Doing so opens a command box. You are asked first for the name of the web application (http://wss3). It is *essential* that you have the preceding http://. You are then asked for the relative URL of the blog site (/BlogTest). Here, the forward slash is *essential*.

After you enter both, the batch job proceeds. If the install runs successfully, you'll see Figure 12.11.

FIGURE 12.11
The extended blog edition's home page.

At first glance, apart from a smarter look, there doesn't seem to be much difference. Most of the names in the Blog Admin section seem to be the same as those used in the standard blog that came with WSS 3.0. It's when you open these items that you start to see the difference.

You can also see that the blog post we wrote before we changed from the standard blog system to the enhanced blog system is still there. No existing blog posts are lost when you upgrade to the Extended Blog Edition because the technique used is of a feature (which retains content) rather than a template (which replaces everything with new base data).

| You can also move back later to the standard blog functionality by reversing the steps. That's a more complicated process, so you'll need to closely follow the steps in the Installation Guide. There too you won't lose any blog posts. | **Note** |

I like the look of that first blog when shown in the Extended edition (refer to Figure 12.11) more than I like the original version (refer to Figure 12.10). And did you see the "[Read More]" possibility, which means that you can fit more of your blogs onto a page?

Another benefit of this change is the addition of the RSS feed at the end of the Blog Admin section. Let's start by taking a brief look at that. Figure 12.12 shows the clean look of the RSS page.

FIGURE 12.12
Obtaining an
RSS feed to your
blog.

At the time of this writing, the best method here is to copy the URL of this RSS feed from the screen (http://wss3/BlogTest/rss.xml). Then open your RSS Reader and add this URL as a new RSS feed.

The link (in Figure 12.11) in the Blog Admin section to Blog Settings is also new in the extended version. It's behind this link that we can see most of the many new options that can be turned on or off. Figure 12.13 still only shows a few of the options.

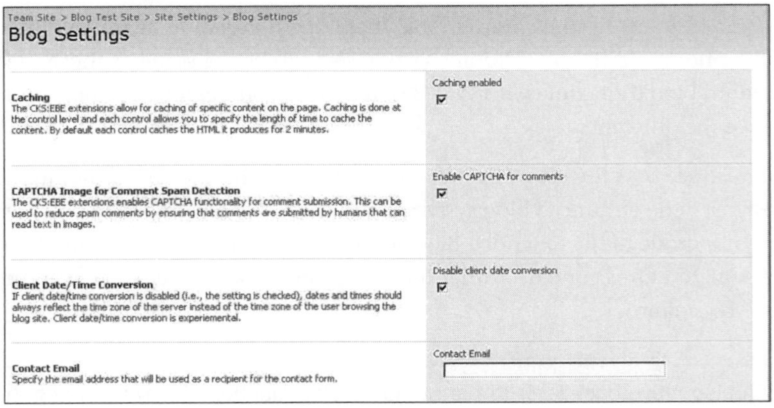

FIGURE 12.13
Specifying blog
settings.

The final new option I'd like to mention here is the support for *CAPTCHA*. This, in case you haven't come across the word before, is the technique of avoiding comments from automated systems by asking people who make comments to type in the letters and numbers that appear in a graphic.

CAPTCHA support is available only in the Wildlife and RoundedGreen themes.

If you click Comments when you're in one of those themes, you will see the typical CAPTCHA set of numbers and letters (and entry form for them) below the Comments field (see Figure 12.14).

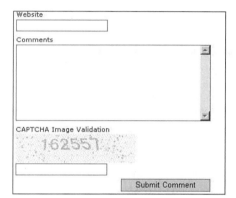

FIGURE 12.14
Using CAPTCHA image validation.

Another parameter that I turn off is Receive Trackbacks from Other Blogs (Yes/No); this parameter does not display in the part of the screen shown in Figure 12.13. I turn this off based on experience with my blogs (which are, however, not protected by CAPTCHA).

Complete the Contact Email field (see Figure 12.13). Receiving email every time someone comments may be a pain, but, provided you've managed to remove most of the spamby using CAPTCHA, it's not that much of a problem.

Further down the page is a parameter for Default Blog Theme. This parameter allows you to amend the standard look in Figure 12.11. There are five themes in addition to the default one. Use any theme besides the default, because most people will not bother to change the theme, so your blog will look different. Another reason to change from the default theme is that the default doesn't have CAPTCHA support.

If none of the themes suit you, and you feel like some guided coding work, the Designer Guide (accessible from www.codeplex.com/CKS/Release/ProjectReleases.aspx?ReleaseId=5134) contains instructions on how to create new themes.

Figure 12.17, shown later in the chapter, for instance, uses Summer.

The final section looks at using Windows Live Writer to create the text of blogs offline and then "publish" them to the WSS 3.0 site when you have a connection.

The other advantage of using Windows Live Writer is that you can easily include images. If instead you create blogs using the standard editor provided in both the standard version and in the Enhanced Blog Edition, the results are rather simple, mostly text-based blogs.

You can get similar results by using Word 2007. (You'll find brief details of how to use that in the Q&A section).

Installing Windows Live Writer

First, install Windows Live Writer using the following steps:

1. Download Windows Live Writer from www.microsoft.com/downloads/details.aspx?FamilyID=D2BAEDA0-AA9A-4080-9202-1F23902D1169&displaylang=en. That downloads WLinstaller.exe, which you need to run.

2. Remove the three settings because they have nothing to do with Windows Live Writer.

3. Figure 12.15 shows a list of products "you want to install." Select only Writer.

FIGURE 12.15
Choosing only Windows Live Writer.

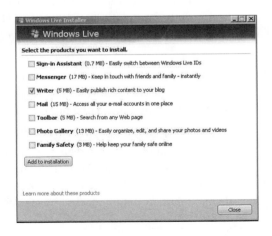

4. The next screen offers you even more products. Ignore it (or, even better, close it to move on when you get the chance).

If you have problems installing Live Writer, check a few things before you run the install again: ***Tip***

1. Make sure that you don't have any earlier "Live" programs installed. You confirm this by running the file you get in this zip file: http://download.microsoft.com/download/2/3/0/23036331-516d-4c7e-b9ac-31554a2fec06/WL-Beta-remove.zip.

2. Turn off (or pause) your firewall and virus checker.

3. Make sure you have enough disk space.

I suggest doing things in the order specified for two main reasons. One is that the application doesn't need much disk space. Therefore, it's unlikely that you don't have enough disk space (and so you check that last). The other reason is that, if you solve your problem with your first check, you won't have to turn off your firewall or virus checker even for a moment.

Now that Windows Live Writer is installed, follow these instructions to create the simpler standard connection to a SharePoint blog site:

1. Run Windows Live Writer.

2. In the Welcome screen, choose I Already Have a Weblog Set Up.

3. In the Choose Weblog Type screen, choose SharePoint Weblog.

4. In the next screen, enter **http://wss3/BlogTest**.

5. You can now create a new web post (see Figure 12.16). (Use some of the options in Windows Live Writer, such as Insert Picture.)

6. Select Publish, and it zooms off to the blog site, which now looks like Figure 12.17. (I switched to the Summer theme.)

FIGURE 12.16
Creating a blog
post in Windows
Live Writer.

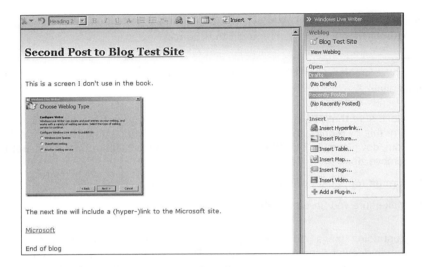

FIGURE 12.17
The blog post
has been pub-
lished in Win-
dows Live Writer.

Summary

This hour looked at the standard wiki and blog functions included in WSS 3.0. It then looked at extending the blog functionality by installing the free Extended Blog Edition. Finally, we went through how to install Windows Live Writer and how to use that offline (and online) to post blog items to a blog site.

Q&A

Q. *I have Word 2007. How do I use that to create offline blogs in the way you demonstrated for Windows Live Writer?*

A. The steps are similar:

1. Open Word 2007. Click the Office button at the top left of the screen.

2. Select New > New Blog Post.

3. You now see a Register screen. Select Register Now. (You gain no advantage by doing this later.)

4. A New Blog Account screen appears. In its Blog selection box, choose SharePoint Blog. Click Next.

5. The next screen wants to know about the blog account. Specify the blog site's URL (http://wss3/BlogTest).

Workshop

Quiz

1. Is it necessary to install the Extended Blog Edition if I want people to be able to read blogs that are located in my WSS 3.0 site structure?

2. Do I need to install Windows Live Writer to create a blog post offline and post it to a WSS 3.0 blog site?

Quiz Answers

1. No. You can use the standard version, too. The main problem you will have is that they will need to access your site to read your blogs. They cannot use RSS to read your blogs because only the Extended Blog Edition has RSS support.

2. No, you can also use Word 2007. However, if you don't have Word 2007, Windows Live Writer is a fine (and free) alternative that works well, for instance, alongside Office 2003 applications on the client.

Using WSS 3.0 Search and Installing Search Server 2008 Express

What You'll Learn in This Hour

▶ Bulking transfer data from one site to another using list templates

▶ How WSS 3.0 Search works and how it compares to Search in MOSS 2007

▶ Adding Search Server 2008 Express to the WSS 3.0 server

Bulking Transfer Data Using List Templates

This section shows one method of transferring data in bulk. We need to do this because, to be able to use Search, we need some data in our site that the Search function can index and then search.

You can add whatever data you want (preferably to different lists in the default [home] site). I will take advantage of the fact that I already have data in a WSS 3.0 site (the WSS 3.0 copy of my WSS FAQ sites), and copy that data to this site.

In this section, I'll show you how to transfer entire lists from one WSS 3.0 server to another (or one site in a server to another site in the same server) by using list templates. You can follow most of it on your own test site using the lists you already created.

I'll use Save List as Template to transfer three lists (the WSS FAQ, a Custom list, and two Links lists [for articles and KB articles]).

1. First, I open the WSSv3 FAQ list (a Custom list) in my other WSS 3.0 site and select Settings and List Settings (see Figure 13.1).

2. In Figure 13.2, select Save List as Template.

3. In Figure 13.3, select Include Content.

FIGURE 13.1
The first step in creating a list template.

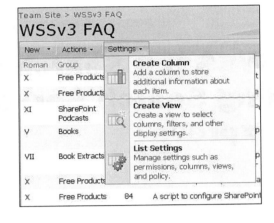

FIGURE 13.2
Select here "Save list as template."

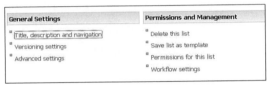

FIGURE 13.3
When saving the list as a template, specify Include Content.

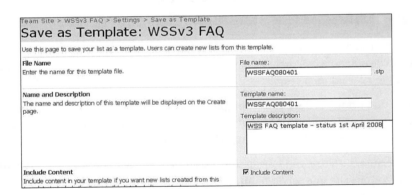

4. That gets the template in the List Template Gallery. Now I go to the List Template Gallery on the Operation Completed Successfully page. I now right-click the name WSSFAQ080401.

5. As Figure 13.4 shows, with Save Target As, I can save the template to my (client's) hard disk. I repeat this for Articles080401 and KBArticles080401, both of which were list templates from Links lists.

FIGURE 13.4
Right-clicking to
save the list
template to the
client's disk.

Now I have three list templates on my hard disk. The next step in this process is to
transfer them to the List Template Gallery of the other WSS 3.0 site (in this case, our
wss3 site):

1. Choose Home > Site Actions > Site Settings > List Templates > Upload
    Document (see Figure 13.5).

FIGURE 13.5
Uploading a tem-
plate (1).

2. Browse to find WSSFAQ080401.stp (see Figure 13.6).

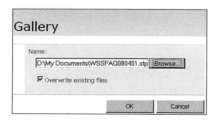

FIGURE 13.6
Uploading a tem-
plate (2).

3. Click OK, and click OK again. Repeat this process (upload document) f
    Articles080401.stp and KBArticles080401.stp.

The List Template Gallery will now look like Figure 13.7.

FIGURE 13.7
The List Template Gallery.

Now that the templates are in the gallery, they will be available in the Create function. To use them from the create function, follow these steps:

1. Choose Home > Site Actions > Create.

   In the Tracking section (see Figure 13.8), you can see two extra entries. In the Custom Lists section, there is one extra entry.

FIGURE 13.8
The Create function now including templates.

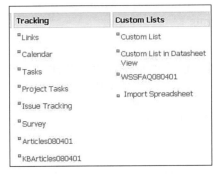

2. Select each entry in turn and specify a name (Articles, KB Articles, and WSS v3 FAQ).

Note

Each time you click OK, you'll see the newly created (copy of the) list. If no content appears, you forgot to select the Include Content option when saving the template (refer to Figure 13.3).

Now these three new lists are listed in the Quick Launch section of the page, and more important, we have enough data to be able to use the Search function.

Using the Standard Search Function

Tip

Make sure that SharePoint Timer Services are running by setting this service to Automatic and then clicking Start. (On the server, choose Start > Administrative Tools > Services.)

After a few minutes, a search on "Excel" gave me 145 hits, as shown in Figure 13.9. (Before the new lists were added, this search yielded only 3 hits).

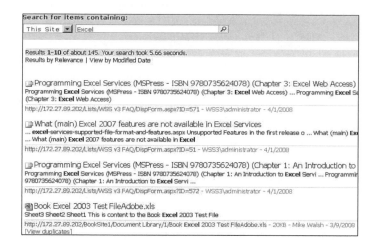

FIGURE 13.9
The results of searching the site.

In this example, I was at Home when I did the search. The search searched all the contents of the Home site. (In Figure 13.9, the drop-down contains just This Site.)

Now let's look at the options for Search in the standard WSS 3.0 product:

1. Open a newly added list. Many of the hits shown in Figure 13.9 were from the WSS v3 FAQ list. So, let's open that by clicking its link in the Quick Launch section.

2. Look at the Search section. You'll see that the drop-down now specifies This List and a This Site option (see Figure 13.10).

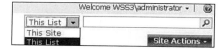

If we select This Site, we get the same result that we got when searching from the home page.

3. To illustrate the difference, I selected This List. Figure 13.11 shows the result.

FIGURE 13.11
Searching just a
list.

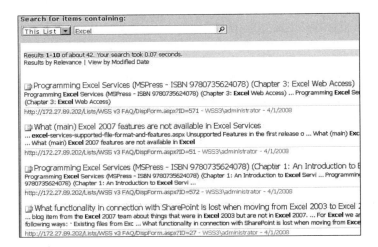

So, that's the first lesson to be learned: If you use WSS 3.0, you can either search the site (which are the site and its subsites) or a list. In addition, your options depend on where in the site you are.

The implementation of the MOSS 2007 Search function is more powerful than the WSS 3.0 implementation. This is one good reason for moving upward from WSS 3.0 to MOSS 2007 (even though the standard WSS 3.0 provides good searches within its limitations).

However, then Microsoft released a new product called Search Server 2008. The free version—Search Server 2008 Express—is perfect for a single-server WSS 3.0 installation.

What's more, at the present time, the combination of WSS 3.0 and Search Server 2008 Express offers a better search "experience" (as Microsoft people would say) than MOSS 2007 Search provides.

Therefore, the next section covers Search Server 2008 Express installation on the same server that runs WSS 3.0.

Note

Hour 14, "Improving Searches," details how to use Search Server 2008 Express both with our WSS 3.0 data and other data. It also identifies some restrictions that Microsoft puts on its use and potential workarounds.

Installing Search Server 2008 Express in a WSS 3.0 Installation

The present download link for the x86 version of Search Server 2008 Express is www.microsoft.com/downloads/details.aspx?FamilyID=ce0a29fe-e906-4767-b841-b41d7a31949f&DisplayLang=en.

Note

You can also just search for "Search Server" at www.microsoft.com/downloads or at http://www.wssv3faq.com (where it should be listed in the Articles section).

The installation is straightforward and is carried out in the VM—that is, on the server:

Note

Want to read the Installation Guide before doing the installation? Find it at http://technet.microsoft.com/en-us/library/bb905390.aspx. If you have the single-server installation from Hour 2, "Installing Windows SharePoint Services 3.0," however, you can just follow these instructions.

1. On whichever download page you use, select Download > Run (to run SearchServerExpress.exe). Then select Run again when a prompt asks whether you want to run this software. Finally, we get the Start screen (see Figure 13.12).

Note

The Microsoft Search Server 2008 forum at http://forums.microsoft.com/MSDN/default.aspx?ForumGroupID=533&SiteID=1 has some Microsoft people replying to questions.

We will use the basic installation because it matches the basic installation we used when installing WSS 3.0. It, too, uses a version of SQL Server 2005 Express for its databases.

FIGURE 13.12
The Search Server 2008 Start page.

Note

The advanced installation is used when there is a copy of SQL Server (2000 or 2005, and perhaps by the time you read this, 2008) in use. Typically, you would then also already be using that "full" SQL Server system for your WSS 3.0 databases.

2. Run Install Search Server. The server type is preconfigured as Standalone (see Figure 13.13).

FIGURE 13.13
Preconfigured and unchangeable Standalone installation.

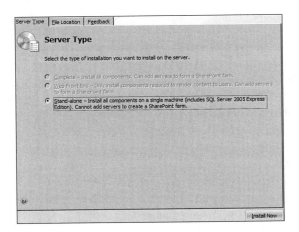

However, the File Location tab allows you to change the paths of both the Search Server 2008 Express installation and the index files (see Figure 13.14).

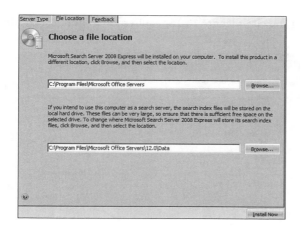

FIGURE 13.14
File locations ought to be changed in production.

In the VM I (and probably most of you) am running, there's only one drive. Therefore, accepting the default file locations is the way to go.

If you were running in production on a large server with several drives, however, you should specify that the index files will be stored in a different (and large and empty) drive.

Tip

3. Click Install Now. Then click Close. (Leave the check mark beside the Run the SharePoint Product and Technologies Wizard Now check box, as shown in Figure 13.15.)

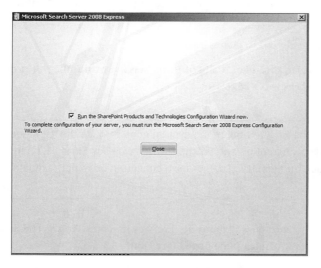

FIGURE 13.15
Close and run the wizard.

4. On the following screen, click Next and then click Yes to shut down a few services.

5. The screen shown in Figure 13.16 requires more than just clicking Next.

FIGURE 13.16
Creating a site.

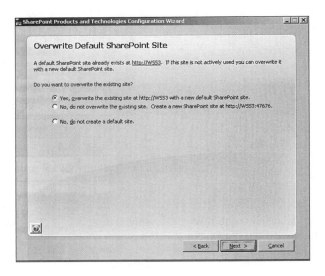

Instead, we must make a difficult decision: create a site and, if so, which.

We already have data at http://wss3, so we definitely don't want to use that default choice for Search Server 2008 Express. But, do we need a new site for Search Server (the second choice) or no site (the third choice)?

The Installation Guide (unless it's been updated in the meantime) gives no guidance.

In fact, we choose to create a new site.

6. Create a New SharePoint Site at http://wss3:<portnumber>. (In my case, <portnumber> was 47676.)

Note   If we choose the no site option, the system goes through the 12 stages of (SharePoint!) configuration and finishes. When we click Finish, it opens Central Administration and displays "server farm configuration is not complete" in bright red text.

7. After the wizard goes through its 12 steps, we click Finish. The Search Server 2008 (Admin) page opens (see Figure 13.17).

Look at the top line. You'll find that the URL isn't http://wss3:47676, but is http://wss3:17770/ssp/etc. (In my case, 17770 is the port number for the Central Administration site that WSS 3.0 created.)

FIGURE 13.17
Welcome to
Search Server.

The installation routine has created the Search Administration within a site
for Shared Services, which it has also created.

This is odd because WSS 3.0 doesn't have Shared Services. These only come with MOSS 2007!

Note

Now the standard Central Administration page (http://wss3:17770/default.
aspx) has in Quick Launch a Shared Services Administration heading,
under which is a Shared Services entry (see Figure 13.18)

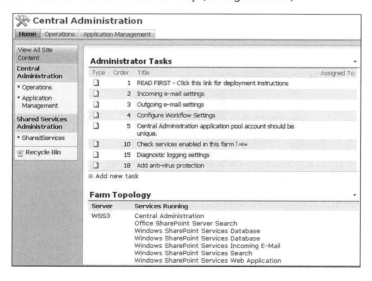

FIGURE 13.18
The revised
Quick Launch
section of the
Central Adminis-
tration site.

It also has an Office SharePoint Server Search service running and two Windows SharePoint Services Databases (one for WSS 3.0 and one for Search Server 2008 Express).

8. Click Shared Services to go to the Search Administration page (see Figure 13.19); Figure 13.17 also links to this page.

FIGURE 13.19
Search Adminis-
tration details.

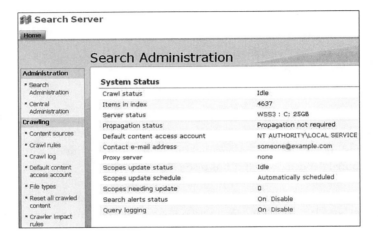

The next hour looks into the options shown in Figure 13.19. In that hour, you learn how to do searches using the indexes created by Search Server.

It might surprise you to know that doing a search at the home page for "Excel" will give exactly the same result as in Figure 13.9. So, obviously, a new technique is needed. That is covered in the next hour.

Summary

In this hour, we used the Save List as Template option to copy across lists complete with data from another WSS 3.0. This quickly gave us test data for the Search function. We also made sure that the Search provided with WSS 3.0 worked.

We also installed Search Server 2008 Express on the same server as WSS 3.0. The additional search functionality available in this free product (and the restrictions associated with it) are covered in the next hour.

Q&A

Q. *I heard that the WSS 3.0 Search routine is powerful, yet you don't indicate this. What's the real story?*

A. It depends what you are comparing. If you used the basic installation (= free database system) of Windows SharePoint Services 2.0, Search didn't work at all. To get Search, you had to either use SQL Server 2K (or later SQL Server 2005) and get only a simple Full-Text search or pay for a third-party search tool.

So, the fact that the WSS 3.0 Search routine also worked with even the free database version was one argument in favor of it.

The other reason in favor of it was that it was essentially the same search routine as used by MOSS 2007 and that search routine was a powerful one based on the technology developed by Microsoft for their www.live.com search portal. In the end, however, users of the WSS 3.0 Search were disappointed because MOSS 2007 actually uses most of the functions of that search technology and WSS 3.0 Search doesn't.

Workshop

Quiz

1. How do you get a list template onto your own hard disk?

2. What's the usual recommendation about how long to wait after adding content to a site and doing a search, and is this wait really necessary?

3. If you are located in your browser at a list, which two search scope options do you have?

Quiz Answers

1. You open the List Template Gallery and right-click the name of the template file and then select Save Target As to copy the template file to your hard disk.

2. About 24 hours. In most cases, it isn't necessary to wait that long.

3. This List and This Site.

HOUR 14

Improving Searches

What You'll Learn in This Hour

▶ Three main aspects of searching
▶ Adding IFilters
▶ Customizing Search Server 2008 Express
▶ Improving *all* of your searches

Searching Aspects

There are three main aspects to searching:

▶ **Crawling**. Looking for documents, files, and data. A site—like Google, who lives by providing information from everywhere—wants to crawl as many locations as possible. If you have a site on the Internet that you don't want crawled, specify that in some way.

In the case of a crawl of a company site, the intention is usually to crawl only meaningful locations for data. In that case, restrict what is crawled. As discussed in this hour, you want to define what you want to be crawled and what shouldn't be crawled.

▶ **Indexing**. Before you can index all the files that the crawl process finds, you need to "translate" the contents of file formats into words that the indexer can understand.

▶ **Searching**. Making sense of what you have indexed so that you have quality links high on the results listing.

Using IFilters to Translate the Contents of Files

This section looks at IFilters; how they are used and how new IFilters can be added.

What Are IFilters?

Microsoft uses pieces of code, called *IFilters*, to make sense of files that its search routines find. Some IFilters are built in to Microsoft's search products. For instance, WSS 3.0 and Search Server 2008 Express both include IFilters for many common file formats out of the box.

Figure 14.1 shows a few of the file formats that Search Server 2008 Express will crawl.

FIGURE 14.1
The list of file types included in the content index.

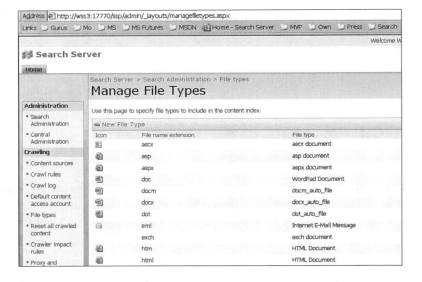

Note

In Figure 14.1, I include the address of the page so you can see that it is located in the Central Administration site's subsite called ssp (short for Shared Services Provider). You can access it via the File Types link.

The equivalent list for the WSS 3.0 is similar, but excludes the Office 2007 file types, such as DOCX.

Do not assume this list represents the file formats for which IFilters are included. A Microsoft document at http://technet.microsoft.com/en-us/library/cc280343.aspx

(version as of April 2008) includes a list of file types with two columns: IFilter support, and included in the default list (that is, Figure 14.1). Many formats in the default list have no IFilter support, including all Visio formats.

> Lucky for us, support for these formats is included in the freely downloadable filter pack, which is discussed in the section, "Adding an IFilter for Other File Types."

Note

The list covers most common formats such as the main Office formats (for both Office 2007 and earlier) and other common formats, such as HTM and TXT. However, several equally popular file formats are not included in Figure 14.1.

> The Adobe Acrobat format for PDF files is not supported by a built-in IFilter.

Note

The next sections show you how to add IFilters for PDF files to your server, which can then be used by both WSS 3.0 and Search Server 2008 Express.

> There are two different filters and two different methods of installation. One applies to Adobe Acrobat versions up to and including versions 6.x. The other applies to later Adobe Acrobat versions (which, at the moment of writing, is versions 7.x and 8.x). The 6.x installation is easier, but the 8.x version covers more documents. Both installations are shown in this hour.

Note

Adding a IFilter for Adobe Acrobat Files Up to Version 6.x

The IFilter for Adobe Acrobat files up to and including version 6.x can be installed by following the instructions on this page on the Adobe site: www.adobe.com/support/downloads/detail.jsp?ftpID=2611.

The web page (Adobe PDF IFilter v6.0) is an old one dating from the time when version 6.x was the latest version. Therefore, the page states that this IFilter works with SharePoint products only up to SharePoint Portal Server 2003. However, it works well with WSS 3.0, MOSS 2007, and Search Server 2008 Express.

Note

> To download the file ifilter60.exe, use the link halfway down the main section of text. Don't use the download links in the rightmost column.

The installation procedure is straightforward. (Just click the file and let it go.)

One key aspect of the installation process follows the installation of the IFilter itself. PDF needs to be added as a file type in the content index. This is done for Search Server 2008 Express by going to Figure 14.1 and selecting New File Type. Then specify both PDF and ONE (see Figure 14.2). (ONE is added because we will later need Search Server support for OneNote 2007 files [file format, .one]).

FIGURE 14.2
Adding file types to the list of indexable file types.

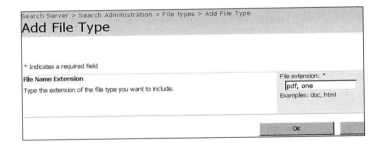

Note

> ONE (OneNote files) is not in the original list despite being the file format of a Microsoft Office 2007 (and 2003) product, and no IFilter is provided with them in either of the two products we discuss here. We add a ONE IFilter later in this hour.

This step isn't necessary for WSS 3.0 Search because WSS 3.0 doesn't have a place where you can set such restrictions.

Adding an IFilter for Adobe Acrobat Files That Works for Versions 7.x and Later

Starting with version 7.0 of Adobe Acrobat, Adobe included the IFilter functionality within the Acrobat product itself. This was fine for people who wanted to search in Acrobat documents when they were loaded into a Acrobat Reader, but it was useless to those who wanted, for instance, a SharePoint application to index the contents of Acrobat version 7.0 (and later) documents.

The solution is to install a copy of Acrobat Reader 8.0 on your WSS 3.0 Server. If you do, the IFilter built in to that version of Acrobat Reader becomes available to your WSS 3.0 and Search Server 2008 Express search routines. (Adobe is careful about not guaranteeing that it will work while intimating that it will.)

After installing Acrobat Reader on the server, you will also need to make some registry changes on the server. These required registry changes are included in a Filter Central (semi-official Microsoft) blog at http://blogs.msdn.com/ifilter/archive/2007/03/29/indexing-pdf-documents-with-adobe-reader-v-8-and-moss-2007.aspx.

Tip

If you are running a 64-bit version of WSS 3.0, read "PDF iFilter 8 - 64-bit Support" (http://labs.adobe.com/wiki/index.php/PDF_iFilter_8_-_64-bit_Support). Here, you learn how to adjust the working 32-bit IFilter included in Acrobat Reader 8.x so that it will work in 64-bit SharePoint (version 3) systems.

Another alternative is the commercial 64-bit Acrobat Reader 8.x IFilter from Foxit Software (who also have a 32-bit version). You can get this at www.foxitsoftware.com/pdf/ifilter/. These Foxit IFilters cost (mid 2008) $130 per server. They are reputedly faster than the Adobe ones, so are still worth considering.

Adding an IFilter for OneNote Files

OneNote (2003 and 2007) includes its IFilter in its own code to provide search functionality when you are in OneNote.

We have the same problem with OneNote files as with Acrobat 7.x files, and we have the same solution: Install OneNote 2007 on your server.

Tip

Alternatively, install the new filter pack. See the section, "Adding an IFilter for Other File Types."

There's a problem. No, installing OneNote won't break anything on the server. The problem: OneNote 2007 isn't free. That's annoying, but at least Microsoft officially says this solution works.

Note

Microsoft Knowledge Base article number 925765 (http://support.microsoft.com/?kbid=925765) contains the details of how to do this. It's essential that you read this article because you need after installing OneNote 2007 on the server to register the IFilter by changing three registry keys.

Adding an IFilter for Other File Types

IFilters of varying quality for other file types are available from various commercial and noncommercial companies. Just search for them.

The best-quality ones tend to come from companies whose main product uses their own proprietary file format. If these companies want their applications to be used, they need to provide working IFilters for them, so they do.

Tip

Follow the (Microsoft) Filter Central blog; it occasionally mentions newly available IFilters. The RSS feed for it is http://blogs.msdn.com/ifilter/rss.xml.

Microsoft has extended the range of IFilters for WSS 3.0 / MOSS 2007 and Search Server 2008 (Express) with a filter pack. The filter pack includes zip files, which was an omission to the standard list. That filter pack is available at www.microsoft.com/downloads/details.aspx?FamilyId=60C92A37-719C-4077-B5C6-CAC34F4227CC&displaylang=en (2007 Office System Converter: Microsoft Filter Pack). According to a Microsoft Filter Central blog item, the filter pack includes filters for the following file formats:

▶ Office 2007 (.docx, .docm, .pptx, .pptm, .xlsx, .xlsm, .xlsb)

▶ Zip (.zip)

▶ OneNote (.one)

▶ Visio (.vdx, .vsd, .vss, .vst, .vsx, .vtx)

Note

IFilters for Office 2007 were already included in Search Server 2008 Express. However, they were not included originally in WSS 3.0.

Because of these additional IFilters, you should install this filter pack. At the least, you gain the ability to index (and thus search on) OneNote files without installing on a server what is, after all, a client application.

Actions Needed After Installing Any IFilters

After installing one or more IFilters and carrying out the additional steps, restart the server and do a completely new crawl for documents (and new indexing); this ensures that these document types are included in the indexes.

Next, we discuss how to specify crawls in WSS 3.0 and Search Server 2008.

Crawling and Indexing in WSS 3.0 and Search Server 2008 Express

This section compares the methods used to crawl WSS 3.0, MOSS 2007, and Search Server 2008. (Re-)Crawling is necessary if an IFilter has been added.

Crawling WSS 3.0

Crawling in WSS 3.0 can be done at the command line. Open a command prompt and go to C:\Program Files\Common Files\Microsoft Shared\web server extensions\12\BIN. Run the following command:

```
stsadm -o spsearch -action fullcrawlstart
```

Crawling MOSS 2007

To crawl in MOSS 2007, do the following:

1. Go to Start > Administrative Tools > Central Administration.

2. Select Shared Services1 > Search Settings > Content Sources and Crawl Schedules.

3. In the Manage Content Sources page, click each content source and choose Start Full Crawl.

Note

For both WSS 3.0 and MOSS 2007, these (manual) crawls are typically done only after installing a new IFilter to create a completely new index. The first crawls are done automatically when the Search function starts.

Crawling Search Server 2008

To crawl in Search Server 2008, do the following:

1. At Figure 14.1, click Content Sources, and right-click Local Office SharePoint Server Sites. (Yes, despite this being WSS 3.0, we now have SharePoint Server sites!)

2. Choose Start Full Crawl (see Figure 14.3).

FIGURE 14.3
Starting a new crawl after adding an IFilter.

Using Other Search Server 2008 Express Options

Search Server 2008 Express allows more flexibility than WSS 3.0 in determining what exactly we want to search. Let's look at some of those additional functions.

The following steps show which locations we can search using Search Server 2008 Express:

1. Start in Figure 14.1 and select Content Sources. This time, look at what we can add as locations to be searched.

2. Select Content Sources, and (in the menu line) New Content Sources.

3. As you can see in Figure 14.4, we can crawl (and index) with Search Server 2008 Express more than we could in WSS 3.0.

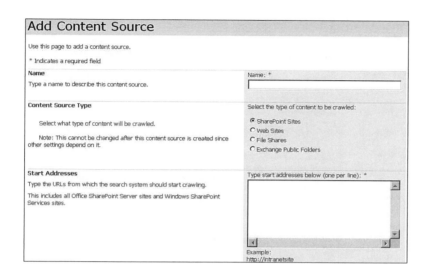

FIGURE 14.4
Adding content sources to Search Server 2008 Express.

The second sentence of the Start Addresses section changes with the selection of which content type is to be crawled (as does the example, under the multiline text field).	***Tip***

Normally, three main problems exist when you crawl "foreign" websites:

► You might need rights to access them.

► The sites' administrators might have blocked crawling.

► You have no control over the amount of data to be crawled.

The first of these (provided you know an appropriate name and password) is handled by selecting crawl rules (see Figure 14.5). As well as selecting paths that are *not* to be crawled, there's also the possibility of giving name and password access information (or alternative access information) for paths you want to be crawled.

We can't do much about the second bullet! If an information provider wants to block his sites from crawlers, he can.

The third bullet can be the most problematic, because at least in the first two cases, the crawl will stop almost immediately if it isn't allowed to crawl. However, a crawl that crawls many levels of a site just keeps on going until no disk space remains for the growing index file.

Search Server 2008 Express covers this with a set of options for how deep a search can go and whether it can hop from one server to another and so on. (Figure 14.6 is on the Contents Source page below the part of the screen shown in Figure 14.4.)

FIGURE 14.5
Account informa-
tion for crawling
a path.

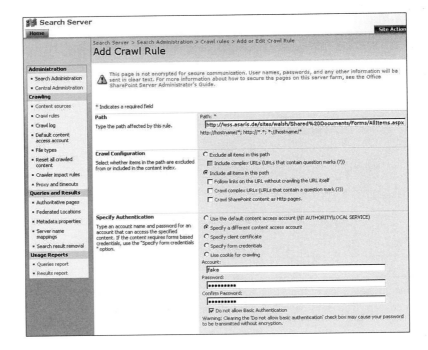

FIGURE 14.6
Specifying the
depth of a crawl.

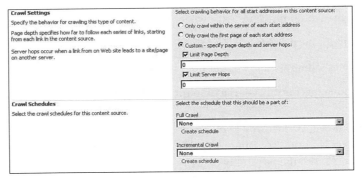

The main thing is that all these options are there, and they are especially valuable
with data stored in your own network (where you have set up file shares and are
aware of the names).

Note　You can also crawl (and index and search) Lotus Notes sources if you install and
configure some additional software. For full information, visit http://technet.
microsoft.com/en-us/library/cc160647.aspx.

Next, we'll look at how to do searches using the data we will have indexed in the crawling/indexing phases.

Ensuring Your WSS 3.0 Searches Use the Search Server Search Function

If we now use the Search function in the WSS 3.0 default site, we get the results that were given by the WSS 3.0 search.

To get better results, go to the newly created Search page—which is the default page of the new site we created in Hour 13. When we go to that page, we see a simple entry form for searches (see Figure 14.7).

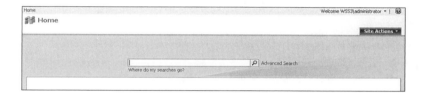

FIGURE 14.7
A simple entry form for Search Server searches.

Entering a search term here gives us a different (and probably slightly better) search than we would get from the standard WSS 3.0 search. However, we didn't go to the trouble of installing Search Server 2008 Express just to get the standard search; we already had something that looked similar in WSS 3.0, so let's look instead at the Advanced Search (see Figure 14.8).

That's more like it. We've all used search (and probably Google's Advanced Search), so I won't bother any more with this one.

However, it seems strange that to search the content that has been indexed by Search Server you need to go to a special search page. Obviously, we need to let WSS 3.0 know that it needs to use this Super Search rather than its normal Search function.

The following steps show how to make amendments in Central Administration so that we end up with a "Super Search" located where we usually have our standard WSS 3.0 search:

   1. Go to Central Administration > Application Management > Manage Web Application Features (see Figure 14.9). Doing so results in something that looks like Figure 14.10.

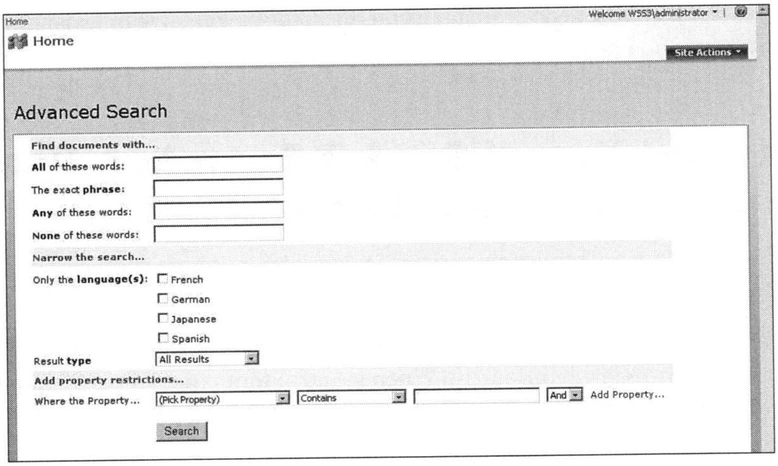

FIGURE 14.8
The Advanced
Search.

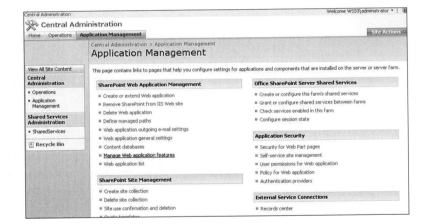

FIGURE 14.9
Selecting Man-
age Web Applica-
tion Features.

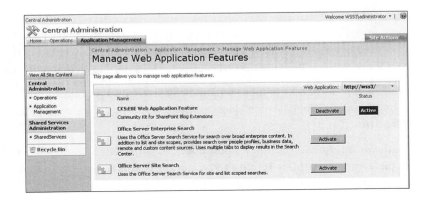

FIGURE 14.10
Activating fea-
tures.

> **Tip**
> Change the web application (at the top right) to point to http://wss3. At the moment, it's probably pointing to your search site (http://wss3:47676, in my case).

2. Activate both the Search features. Then, leave Central Administration and go back to the home page. Choose Access Site Actions > Site Settings. You'll see many new options in the Site Collection Administration section on the far right (see Figure 14.11).

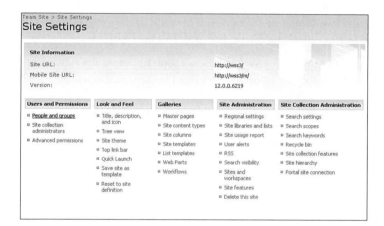

FIGURE 14.11
New options for site collection administrators.

3. Select search settings and fill in the screen that displays exactly as I did in Figure 14.12 (except use your own port number). The example in that screen under the Entry box is probably incorrect and certainly misleading.

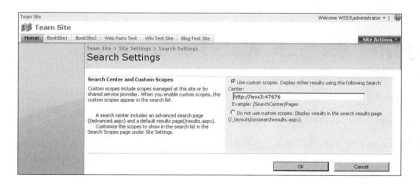

FIGURE 14.12
Specifying that the Search Center is used for searches.

4. After clicking OK, open a different browser copy and go to the default home page (http://wss3). Look at the upper-right side of the screen. You'll

see that in place of the normal search we had before there is a different looking search function with two options for the normal search, whereas we had only one option (Team Site) before (see Figure 14.13).

FIGURE 14.13
New options for site collection administrators.

In other words, we now have full Search Server 2008 Express search functionality available from the normal location of the WSS 3.0 search in each page in this set of sites that starts at the address http://wss3.

Unfortunately, there's a snag. We get a better search, but on the rightmost side of the result screen, Microsoft insists on giving us its Live Search suggestions (see Figure 14.14).

FIGURE 14.14
No such thing as a free lunch—Live Search.

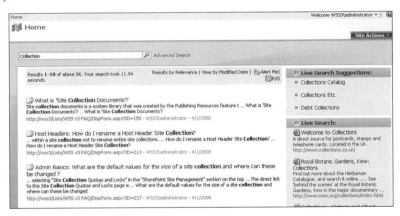

Adding Search Web Parts

Search Server also offers a selection of Search web parts that can be used in your sites. This final section shows you how to make these available for use.

(In the first browser copy, you should still be at Figure 14.11.)

The fifth entry in the Site Collection Administration section is Site Collection features. Select it. There is a new feature that will upload "all web parts required for Search Center" (see Figure 14.15). Activate it!

Now when we try to add a web part to a page (see Hour 9, "Looking at List Types and the Included Web Parts"), we have an additional Search section with 11 web parts (see Figure 14.16) that we can choose from.

FIGURE 14.15
Activating
Search web
parts.

> Read the section, "Q&A." It has some useful information about the limitations of Search Server 2008 Express.

Tip

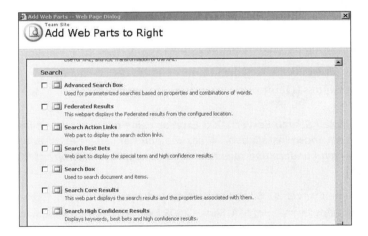

FIGURE 14.16
Some of the
available new
search parts.

Summary

In this hour, you learned that searching actually means deciding where to look for data; grabbing, interpreting, and indexing all the files that are within the scope we set; and finally having a search function to find suitable data for our needs from the mass of base data provided by the indexing stage.

You also learned both how to restrict your search by specifying only particular places to look for information and how to extend your search by adding IFilters to enable your indexing software to be able to extract sensible data from more file formats.

Finally, you learned how to make searching using Search Server 2008 the obvious choice for your searches when using WSS 3.0 (rather than WSS 3.0's own search software).

Q&A

Q. Is WSS 3.0 plus Search Server 2008 Express better than the search provided by the much more expensive MOSS 2007?

A. To get the same search functionality in MOSS that Search Server 2008 Express provides to a single-server WSS 3.0 installation, you need to install the Enterprise Server feature pack (which at the time of this writing is not out).

Without the Enterprise Server Pack, MOSS 2007 has lower search functionality than Search Server 2008 (Full and Express).

Q. Search Server 2008 Express is free and seems to be powerful. Why should I bother paying for Search Server 2008?

A. Search Server 2008 and Search Server 2008 Express are identical in functionality, but Express is limited to running on a single machine.

Q. I can install Search Server 2008 Express using either the basic installation or the advanced installation. What's the point of using the advanced installation, which I understand requires me to have a licensed copy of SQL Server 2005?

A. The Search Server 2008 Express Basic Installation installs SQL Express. This is an embedded version of SQL Server 2005 Express. Unlike the version (Windows Internal Database, WID) installed by a WSS 3.0 basic installation (which has no maximum database size), this version *does* have a 4GB maximum database size.

If you use the advanced installation of Search Server 2008 Express and thus use SQL Server 2005, there is no such 4GB database limit.

Q. I already have WSS 3.0 and it's using WID, so that I have no database size limit. Why can't I tell Search Server 2008 Express to use that?

A. You can't. The Search databases can only be stored in the standard SQL Express and therefore cannot be greater than 4GB in size.

Any content databases created in WSS 3.0 after installing Search Server 2008 Express will be created using SQL Express and so will also be restricted to 4GB in size.

But you can amend this by going to the configuration page in WSS 3.0 Central Administration *every time* you create a new content database and there change the SQL Express instance to the WID instance and then there will be no limit.

Workshop

Quiz

1. What are the three main aspects of searching?

2. What is the purpose of an IFilter?

3. What five content sources can Search Server 2008 Express search?

Quiz Answers

1. Crawling, indexing, and searching.

2. An IFilter is needed so that contents of a file in a particular file format can be understood by the indexing program. Without it, the indexing program usually can't extract meaningful data from a file.

3. SharePoint sites, websites, file shares, Exchange public folders, *and* Lotus Notes. (Yes, it was a partly unfair question, because only the first four are listed in Search Server 2008 Express as delivered.)

HOUR 15

Using Different Versions of the Main Office Products with WSS 3.0

What You'll Learn in This Hour

▶ Stating the rules for the interaction of Office products with SharePoint products

▶ Storing documents in document libraries

▶ Creating document workspaces in Office 2003 and 2007

▶ Differentiating between the workspaces in Office 2003 and 2007

▶ How files attached to Outlook 2003/2007 email messages can be stored in a WSS 3.0 site

Office Products and WSS 3.0: The Rules

The interaction between an Office product and a SharePoint site varies depending on which version of Office is being used in connection with which version of SharePoint. In this section, I define the "rules."

The standard "rule" is that the full functionality available in each Office version works only with the equivalent SharePoint version. So, to get the most out of SharePoint Team Services (STS) 2001, you need to run Office XP on your client. To get the most out of WSS 2.0, you need to be run Office 2003. To get the most out of WSS 3.0, you need to run Office 2007.

The second "rule" is that all the Office versions are backward compatible. So, if you have STS and Office 2007 or Office 2003, you'll get the same functionality you got with Office XP, but no more. Whereas if you have WSS 2.0 and Office 2007, you'll get the same functionality you got with Office 2003, but no more.

There are also a couple of exceptions to the preceding rules: The first exception is that any one particular Office application may offer no more functionality when used with SharePoint than an earlier version of that particular Office application. The second—and perhaps less-expected—exception is that a later Office application may offer less functionality with SharePoint than did an earlier version.

This hour looks at Word, Excel, and PowerPoint. Despite being principal Office applications, their functionality, when used with WSS 3.0, has hardly changed since Office 2003.

Let's investigate three main interaction areas of these Office products with WSS 3.0:

- ▶ Storing documents in document libraries
- ▶ Creating document workspaces
- ▶ Adding attachments to Outlook messages

Storing Documents in Document Libraries

You may ask yourself, "It's obvious that you can store Word (and so on) documents in a document library, so why discuss that?" The answer is that when these documents are stored in a document library, some differences exist as compared to the way other document types are stored in document libraries.

These differences are

- ▶ Edit available in Microsoft Word/Excel/PowerPoint, but not in Acrobat (for example)
- ▶ Standard Word/Excel/PowerPoint templates available for use
- ▶ WSS 3.0 column information included with the Word/Excel/PowerPoint file

Different Editing Options

The most obvious difference is that there is an Edit in Microsoft *XXX* (where *XXX* is Word, Excel, or PowerPoint) entry in the drop-down when you click the area to the right of a Word, Excel, or PowerPoint document's name in a view (see Figure 15.1).

When selecting an Acrobat file in the same library, there is no equivalent Edit in Acrobat option (see Figure 15.2). This is true even if you have the commercial version of Acrobat that allows changes and saving.

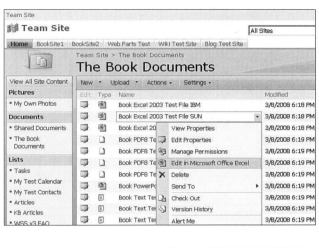

FIGURE 15.1
Edit in Microsoft Excel.

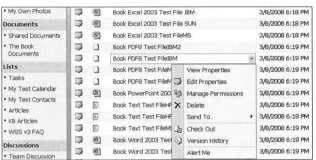

FIGURE 15.2
No edit capability in Adobe Acrobat.

Note

There is no PDF icon in Figure 15.2. To add it, first get a suitable icon from www. adobe.com/images/pdficon.gif and scale it to 16x16 pixels. Then save it to the server at C:\Program Files\Common Files\Microsoft Shared\web server extensions\12\TEMPLATE\IMAGES.

Open C:\Program Files\Common Files\Microsoft Shared\web server extensions\12\TEMPLATE\XML\DOCICON.XML in Notebook; copy the PNG row and change (twice) PNG to PDF. Save. Finally, run iisreset in the command line.

Available Templates

With these Office products, when you decide to use a new template for a document library, you already have a standard (for instance) Excel template that you can use.

Note

In fact, two Excel templates are listed: one for Excel 2007 and one for earlier versions.

Create a new document library by going from the default home page to Site Actions > Create > Document Library. Look at the options at the bottom of the New page (see Figure 15.3). Save the document library as **PropertiesTest**.

FIGURE 15.3
The Templates drop-down.

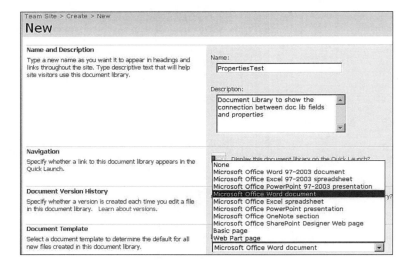

WSS 3.0 Column Information

There is a relationship between additional fields/columns in a document library and the properties of a Word/Excel/PowerPoint document that doesn't exist with a non-Office document.

Here's the situation in brief: A non-Office document (perhaps a PDF) has its own properties that are part of the document. When you add an Acrobat file to a document library, that document library might have extra columns/fields, and you will give those fields values. So, you might have a Company field and give it the value HP.

Now let's take that document offline so that we can edit it. The file is copied to our hard disk, and that Acrobat file includes both the document and the document's properties. However, the (WSS 3.0 document library) Company field no longer exists, so it no longer has a value. The information is lost.

Note

> If you are moving documents from a document library in one site to an identical document library in another site, you need—in the case of PDF files—to copy both the files themselves (typically from Explorer view to Explorer view) *and* the columns and their data (typically from Datasheet view to Datasheet view). Doing so is the only way to get the file, the file's own properties, and the WSS 3.0 column information across.

Compare this with an Office document. The first difference is that an Office document can be edited and then copied back to the SharePoint site without any of the column data being lost.

The main difference is that, when you make a copy of the document to your hard disk, the file you have on the hard disk contains the data from those WSS 3.0 columns. They are not lost.

Here, things vary between Office 2007 and Office 2003:

▶ **Office 2007**. If the column name is the same as an Office document property, the value entered into the column is transferred to the document property with the same name (accessed via Document Properties).

   If the column name is not the same as an Office property, the value entered is retained as a server property (accessed via Document Properties—Server).

▶ **Office 2003**. If the column name is the same as an Office document property, the value entered into the column is transferred to the document property with the same name. (There are a few standard document properties for which this doesn't apply, but we won't go into them here.)

   If the column name is not the same as an Office property, a document property is automatically created with that value.

Note

> If you are moving Office documents from a document library in one site to an identical document library in another site, you need *only* to copy the files themselves (typically from Explorer view to Explorer view). After all, those files contain the file, the file's own properties, and the WSS 3.0 column information.

To understand how this relates to Office 2007, look at Figures 15.4, 15.5, and 15.6.

FIGURE 15.4
Two additional columns in PropertiesTest.

Figure 15.4 shows a document library with one Word 2007 document. Two columns have been added to the document library. The first, Formula 1 Cars, is in the document list only. The second, Subject, is (also) the name of a document property.

Figure 15.5 shows the document with the Property section when Document Properties—Server is specified. This shows all three WSS 3.0 columns/fields (the entry fields that are visible when you upload a document).

FIGURE 15.5
Document Properties—Server.

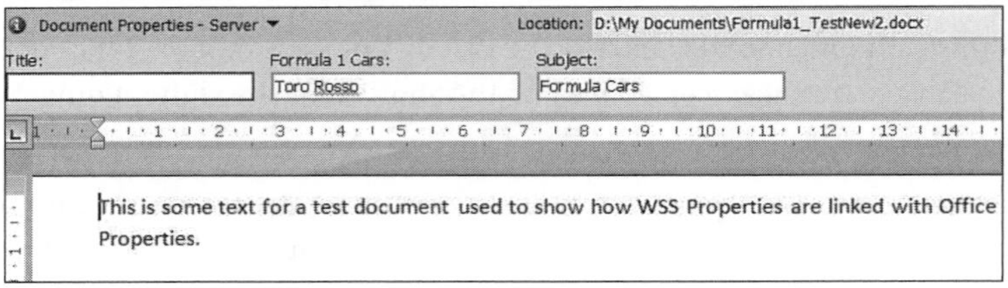

Figure 15.6 shows the document with the Property section when Document Properties is specified. The Subject property now contains the value Formula Cars that was actually input to WSS 3.0.

FIGURE 15.6
Document Properties.

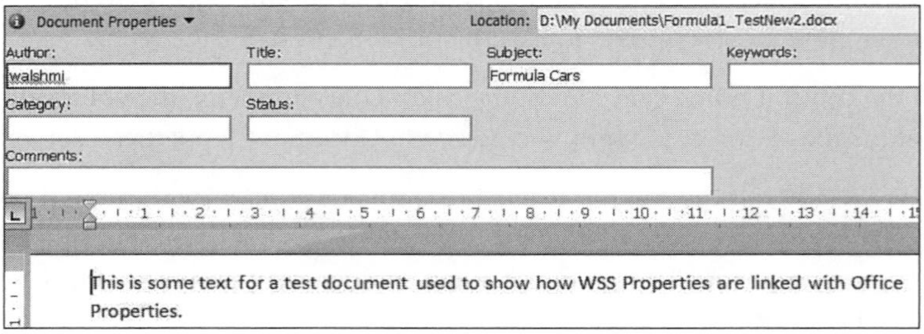

One main function that is restricted to Office products is the ability to create websites to discuss a particular document. And that's exactly what we do in the next sections. (First, we create a document workspace in Word 2007, and then we create one in Word 2003. In essence, it's the same procedure, but the details are different.)

Creating Document Workspaces in Office 2007

A document workspace is essentially a team site that's set up purely to discuss a particular document. The best way to see a document workspace is to create one.

To create a document workspace in Office 2007, follow these steps:

1. Open Word and create a document. I use the text "Test document for a document workspace."

2. When in Word 2007, click the (Office) icon at the top-left corner of the page; select Publish, and then select Create Document Workspace (see Figure 15.7).

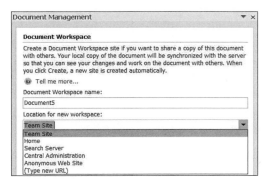

FIGURE 15.7
Selecting a location and name for the document workspace.

Figure 15.7 appears on the rightmost side of the screen. As you can see, you have two choices:

▶ You can specify a name for the document workspace. (We'll call it Book-DocWS1.) Currently, it has the name of the document (which hadn't been saved and was thus Document5).

▶ You can say where the document workspace should be created.

You can see how useful it is to have called our websites something recognizable. The only one in this list that is recognizable is our Anonymous Web Site; the others are too general.	*Tip*

All the sites listed are top-level sites (the default site of a site collection). Remember that we created a web application especially for the Anonymous Web Site, and the Central Administration and Search Server sites were also sites that used their own port numbers.	*Note*

3. Accept the offered Team Site. (Home would be the same in this case).

4. If you haven't saved the document, you'll be asked to. Then, you'll be asked for authorization with the typical Name/Password box.

Don't be worried if the authorization process happens twice.	*Note*

5. The document workspace is created. You'll see Figure 15.8 in the rightmost panel.

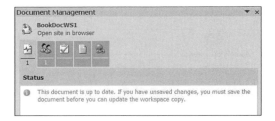

6. Select Open Site in Browser to see what we have.

Figure 15.9 shows the site that has been created. The breadcrumbs show that it is located under the Team Site. But unlike the subsites we created earlier, this did *not* inherit by default permissions from the Team Site, and instead the only user at the moment is the administrator.

Creating Document Workspaces in Office 2003

To create a document workspace using Word 2003, follow these steps:

1. Create and save a document. Access Tools on the menu line and select Shared Workspace.

2. Team Site is selected (see Figure 15.10). The drop-down shows various SharePoint *servers* that this workstation running Office 2003 has been connected to in the past.

Never mix Office 2007 and Office 2003 applications on the same client system!

Tip

---

3. The default name of the document workspace comes from the document name, but it can be changed. We'll change it to BookDoc2003WS1.

4. Accept the default value TeamSite. The result (shown in Figure 15.11) is similar to the Word 2007 equivalent. If we click Open Site in Browser, the website looks similar to Figure 15.9.

FIGURE 15.10
Selecting the site and document name in Office 2003.

FIGURE 15.11
The Shared Workspace panel.

Differentiating Between Office 2007 and Office 2003 Document Workspaces

Although creating a document workspace is a similar process in both 2003 and 2007, there are several differences. The main difference is that, in the Word 2003 version of the Shared Workspace panel, there is an extra icon.

If you click any icon and look at the bottom of the Shared Workspace panel, you'll see that it's possible to do administration tasks directly from Word with this new (document workspace) site.

That missing icon on the right for Word 2007 means that these options are no longer available in Word 2007. The unavailable options are

▶ Restrict Permissions

▶ Alert Me About This Document

▶ Version History

All are however—like all the other options here—available when accessing the document workspace in a browser (as administrator).

To summarize, there is little difference between Office 2003 and 2007 when creating document workspaces. The main differences are

▶ The creation of a document workspace failed often from Office 2003; it works better from Office 2007.

▶ In Office 2007, you don't have to rely entirely on the list of sites given you in the drop-down of where the document workspace is to be created; you can also specify a URL of a site or subsite.

Otherwise, the end result is the same. A site is especially created for a document, and it is possible to administer it from with the Office product or by using a browser and accessing the site itself.

Tip

> Several users could have the document open at the same time, and some of them could have it open for editing. (Only one person at a time can have it open for editing if the file is accessed from the WSS 3.0 document library. However, several people *using Word* could have the linked Word copy open for editing.)
>
> To avoid possible conflicts among competing edits, use the possibility of checking the document out so that only one person can have it open for editing at a time; the others can still read it.

The defaults in both Word 2003 and 2007 were to be asked if changes had been made in either the website version of the document or the Word "version" of the document. It's wise to at least leave the "ask" specified, although there is a case to be made for automatic updates.

Although these new document workspaces are not listed in our default site (in the Sites section of the Quick Launch), you can select View All Site Content at the top of Quick Launch. You'll then see a Sites and Workspaces section where they are listed (see Figure 15.12).

Sites and Workspaces		
Blog Test Site		8 days ago
BookDoc2003WS1		55 minutes ago
BookDocWS1		18 minutes ago
BookSite1	This is the first site created for the in 24 hours book	4 weeks ago
BookSite2	Uses the Basic Meeting template but wiith the Cardinal theme	5 weeks ago
Web Parts Test	This is a sub-site created to show how you can use the built-in web parts that aren't just representations of Lists/Libraries	2 weeks ago
Wiki Test Site		9 days ago

FIGURE 15.12
Sites and Work-spaces section.

> There's a second way to display these two workspaces listed on the default page. Go to the Q&A section if you want to know how to do this.

Tip

Adding Attachments to Outlook Messages

In Outlook 2007, when you add an attachment, if you just do Include File, the attachment is sent with the email. If the recipient opens the email, say, a few weeks later, the recipient may see an old version of the document because, in the meantime, you've updated it. There are, however, alternative ways to attach.

Click that strange icon to the right of Include. You get a new pane on the rightmost side of the screen (see Figure 15.13). This Attachment Options pane looks familiar. It's exactly the same list of sites as in Figure 15.7. However, Central Administration has moved two places up the list (see Figure 15.14).

The point is that it's the same technique. The attachment will now be stored in its own subsite of the Team Site, so the issue with the recipient opening the message two weeks after you sent is resolved. The recipient always sees the latest version upon opening the message.

FIGURE 15.13
Attachment Options pane in Outlook 2007.

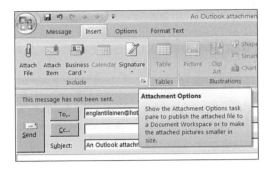

FIGURE 15.14
Specifying attachment options.

At the same time, anyone who receives the email including the message will see the info panel shown in Figure 15.15.

FIGURE 15.15
An email invitation to the document workspace.

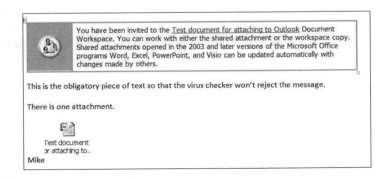

All the email recipients that can be are added to the list of users for the workspace that contains the document.

Note

This list usually contains domain users. In this case, my Hotmail address couldn't be recognized by the SharePoint site, and the sender got a message to that effect.

The workspace has already been created, as you can see by again clicking View All Site Content.

Summary

In this hour, we looked at the various ways in which Office 2003 and 2007 documents combine with WSS 3.0 systems, and especially at the differences when non-Office document formats are used.

We concentrated on three main areas: storing and editing documents that are stored in document libraries; creating document workspaces, which are sites created for discussing a document; and adding attachments to Outlook emails so that the attachment is not just the version that was available at the time the message was sent, but is (through being stored on a server) the latest version.

Q&A

Q. How can I have both sites and workspaces listed on the default page?

A. To do this, all you have to do is add a tree view to the leftmost column (or perhaps better still, replace Quick Launch with it).

  1. Go to the default site. Select Site Actions > Site Settings.

  2. The second option in the second column is Tree View. Select it.

     In Figure 15.16, notice that I have unselected Quick Launch and selected Enable Tree View. They are check boxes, so you can of course have both (or none) selected.

Note

Did you notice the option for Quick Launch in the Site Settings? A common question in the newsgroups has been how to remove the Quick Launch section from the page.

People saw the Quick Launch option (which enables you to change the order of items in Quick Launch) and expected a Remove Quick Launch option. It's not obvious that, to get to that option, you need to select Tree View.

Now the leftmost side does include all the subsites of Team Site, including the two document workspaces (see Figure 15.17). I don't know about you, but I think it's much messier than Quick Launch.

FIGURE 15.16
Specifying Tree View.

FIGURE 15.17
Quick Launch replaced by tree view (site hierarchy).

Tree View, which lists the entire structure of the site, is, however, more powerful (you can go directly from this page to a library/list that's in a subsite or workspace). So, it's up to the site designer or the customer requirements to decide what is chosen.

Workshop

Quiz

1. Are there any major differences between the interaction of Office 2003 applications and the interaction of Office 2007 applications with WSS 3.0?

2. Why is adding attachments to an Outlook email a SharePoint issue?

3. If you want to remove Quick Launch, do you go to the Quick Launch item in Central Administration?

Quiz Answers

1. There are no major differences so far as the products (Word, Excel, PowerPoint) are concerned. There is a major difference in the usage of PowerPoint 2007 with MOSS 2007 (Slide Library, which isn't in WSS 3.0) and there are major differences when using Outlook 2007 and Access 2007 with WSS 3.0 compared to using their 2003 versions.

2. Because one option is to store the attachment in its own document workspace.

3. No, you go to Tree View.

HOUR 16

Using Different Versions of Outlook with WSS 3.0

What You'll Learn in This Hour

▶ Combining WSS 3.0 sites and Outlook 2007

▶ Combining with WSS 3.0 sites and Outlook 2003

Because there are major differences between combining WSS 3.0 with Outlook 2007 and Outlook 2003, this hour discusses each version in separate sections.

Combining Outlook 2007 with WSS 3.0

This section looks at combining Outlook 2007 with WSS 3.0.

Linking Document Libraries to Outlook 2007

With Outlook 2007, it is possible to link a WSS 3.0 document library to Outlook. There are a couple of reasons to do this:

▶ It allows you to take the files offline to work with them (using standard Outlook 2007 functionality).

▶ It allows you to use Outlook 2007's built-in viewer to see inside your documents (only for document formats supported by the Outlook 2007 viewer).

Follow these steps to link a document library to Outlook 2007:

1. Open the document library and select Connect to Outlook in the Actions menu item. I choose The Book Documents (see Figure 16.1).

   Don't be surprised when control is transferred to an Outlook window that has a warning box on top of it (see Figure 16.2).

2. Select Advanced. In Figure 16.3, change the default name and write a description. (I use wss3—The Book Documents.)

FIGURE 16.1
Connecting a
document library
to Outlook
2007.

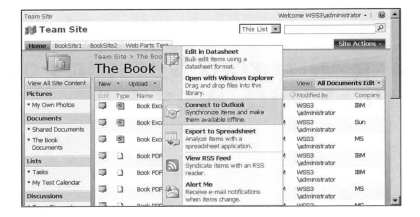

FIGURE 16.2
Starting to con-
nect the docu-
ment library to
Outlook 2007.

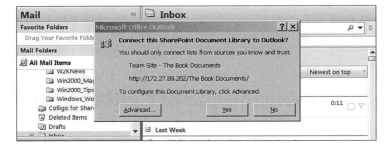

FIGURE 16.3
Changing the
folder name for
the listing in Out-
look 2007.

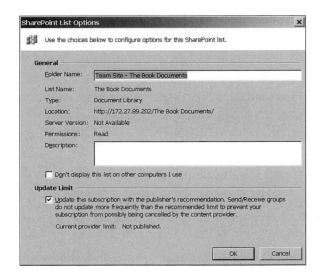

3. Click OK. This takes us back to Figure 16.2. Click Yes.

At this point, you are still under the control of Outlook 2007.

You need to specify the login information for that document library before the process is complete.

4. Complete the login box and click OK.

172.27.89.202 was the TCP/IP address of the WSS3 server at the time, and I had logged in using that address rather than wss3.

Note

---

5. Click the newly created WSS3—The Book Documents entry in Outlook 2007.

After a while, you will see something like Figure 16.5.

In Figures 16.6 and 16.7, I've chosen one of those earlier listed document libraries (Team Site—DocLib) to show you what different kinds of documents (stored in a WSS 3.0 document library) look like in the Outlook 2007 viewer frame when the document library is linked to Outlook 2007.

Figure 16.6 is a simple file in Adobe Acrobat format. Figure 16.7 is a PowerPoint file.

Expect a long wait for PowerPoint files to open.

Tip

FIGURE 16.5
Listing the document library in Outlook 2007.

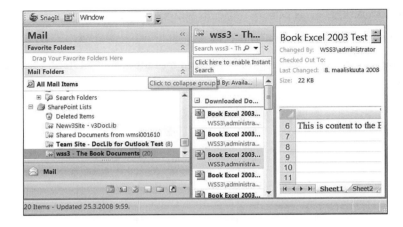

FIGURE 16.6
Viewing a PDF file in the Outlook 2007 viewer frame.

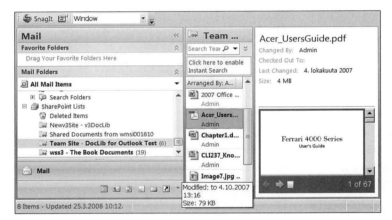

FIGURE 16.7
Viewing a Power-Point file in the Outlook 2007 viewer frame.

Deleting Connections to Old Servers

At some stage, you will want to delete some of your connections to old and fading test servers. To do this, follow these steps:

1. Select the name of the link and right-click (see Figure 16.8). (Here, I remove

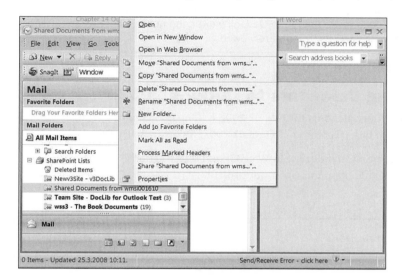

FIGURE 16.8
Deleting existing
document library
to Outlook 2007
links.

the one starting "Shared Documents.")

2. Select Delete Shared Documents. This gives you Figure 16.9.

FIGURE 16.9
Ignoring the
scary warning.

The text is a bit scarier than it ought to be. The key sentence is the last one—namely, that you are *not* deleting the list on the (SharePoint) server.

These SharePoint Lists in Outlook are synchronized according to a standard schedule and they are listed in the usual Outlook 2007 leftmost panel under a SharePoint List heading.

Note

In Figure 16.8, it is possible to change the name used there. So not specifying a name change when we added the new document library to Outlook 2007 wasn't a major problem, even if it resulted in two entries with similar names.

Finally, the link in Outlook appears in bold if new documents haven't been viewed in Outlook. So, in the present case, when we looked at some documents in the Shared Documents list in the Outlook viewer, the number in brackets after the name went down as items were viewed.

Linking Calendars to Outlook 2007

Linking your calendars to Outlook 2007 is done in a similar way to document libraries. To link a calendar to Outlook 2007, follow these steps:

1. Open a Calendar list in WSS 3.0 and select Actions. You have the Connect to Outlook option (see Figure 16.10).

FIGURE 16.10
Starting to connect a calendar to Outlook 2007.

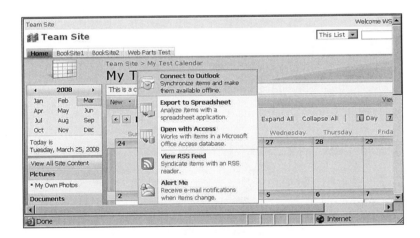

2. Select Connect to Outlook. Choose Advanced to change the name and add a description.

3. Click Create and OK. You must log in to the SharePoint site to complete the addition of a copy of the calendar to Outlook 2007.

Note

If you are using the same browser instance within a reasonable time period (following the addition of a document library, for instance), you might not need to log in.

As you can see from Figure 16.11, you get your normal Outlook calendar (on the left of the rightmost frame) and your SharePoint site's Calendar (list) on the right of the rightmost frame.

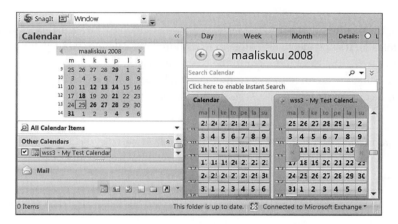

FIGURE 16.11
Seeing both the Outlook and the SharePoint Calendar.

Note

Calendar linking only works if Exchange Server is being used. Here the Exchange Server being used was the Finnish version.

Outlook 2007 treats the SharePoint calendar as just another calendar. Therefore, you can decide to show both alongside each other or even overlap them.

Tip

Overlapping two or more SharePoint calendars with your own calendar is a perfect way to solve the problem of being a member of several different projects, each of which has its own calendar located in SharePoint sites.

If you've added a calendar, look at the leftmost section of Outlook 2007. If you are in a work environment, you will probably see three sections, each with a calendar:

- ▶ My Calendars
- ▶ People's Calendars
- ▶ Other Calendars

This SharePoint Calendar is, of course, in the Other Calendars section.

For viewing in the rightmost pane, you can select any number (within reason) of calendars from one, some, or all the sections.

Tip

> If you prefer to use Overlay mode in Outlook 2007, choose that option in the View menu.

When the combination of products is WSS 3.0 and Outlook 2007, synchronization is two-fold. So, it's possible to add an item to a SharePoint calendar while you are in Outlook 2007 and have it appear in the calendar copy in the SharePoint site. It is also possible to add an item to the SharePoint calendar while accessing the WSS 3.0 site that contains it.

Note

> Synchronization occurs at the frequency specified. To see the synchronization, you need (in the SharePoint site) to re-access or refresh the page containing the Calendar list (or its web part).

Figure 16.12 is a SharePoint page containing two different web parts of the Calendar list that was refreshed soon after the meeting was added in Outlook.

FIGURE 16.12
Viewing a date in WSS 3.0 that was created in Outlook 2007.

Linking Contacts to Outlook 2007

At the moment, we don't have a Contacts list in our site. Before we can test functionality with Outlook 2007, we need to create a Contacts list. To do this, follow these steps:

1. Go to Home and select Site Actions > Create > Contacts. Call the Contacts list **My Test Contacts**, and allow it to appear in the Quick Launch section. Populate it with a couple of uniquely named people. Then select Actions > Connect to Outlook (see Figure 16.13).

FIGURE 16.13
Starting to connect a contact list to Outlook 2007.

2. Choose Advanced to change the name and add a description. Then click Create and OK.

As you see in Figure 16.14, whereas with calendars there were three different groups, there are here only two different groups of contacts: My Contacts and Other Contacts.

Just as with calendars, the link between the listing in the Other Contacts group and the SharePoint Contacts list is synchronized in both directions.

Unlike with calendars, however, you cannot overlay both Contacts lists to see a totality of contacts. Instead, you can either select one Contacts list (in Figure 16.14, the My Test Contacts list) or the other for display in the rightmost frame.

FIGURE 16.14
Looking at the two different Contacts lists in Outlook 2007.

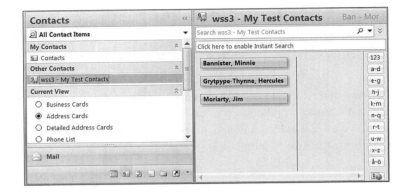

Note
The choice of which current view to use is available to both kinds of contacts. Once specified for a particular list, that setting is retained for that list even if the other Contacts list has been opened with a different current view setting.

The final thing that Outlook 2007 can do with WSS 3.0 is to create a meeting workspace (which is a site for a project that begins with a meeting). This is so similar to creating a document workspace that I don't discuss it here. (Refer to Hour 15, "Using Different Versions of the Main Office Products with WSS 3.0.")

Now that we've looked at how Outlook 2007 works with WSS 3.0, let's turn our attention to how Outlook 2003 works with WSS 3.0.

Combining Outlook 2003 with WSS 3.0

Compared to using Outlook 2007, you lose a lot of functionality when using Outlook 2003 with WSS 3.0.

Linking Document Libraries to Outlook 2003

Outlook 2007 was developed at the same time as WSS 3.0, and it's a standard Microsoft practice (and quite a sensible one) to ensure backward compatibility yet at the same time make sure that new functionality in a client product is available only with a new server product.

When using an Outlook 2003 client with WSS 3.0, no Connect to Outlook option appears in the Actions drop-down. (This option is available with Outlook 2007; compare Figure 16.1 to Figure 16.15).

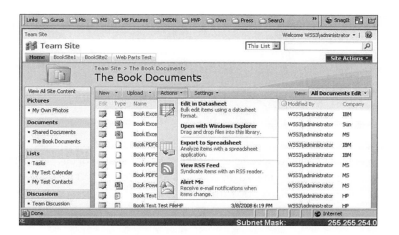

FIGURE 16.15
The Action drop-down for document libraries with Outlook 2003.

You cannot add a copy of a SharePoint document library to Outlook in the same way you can with Outlook 2007.

Linking Calendars to Outlook 2003

You can connect a WSS 3.0 Calendar list to Outlook 2003 (see Figure 16.16). What is missing in that list of alternatives—compared to the equivalent drop-down shown in Figure 16.10—is Open with Access.

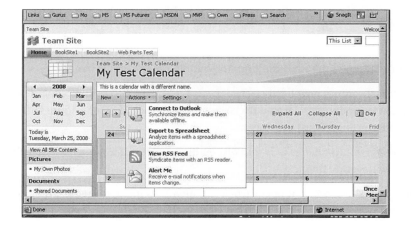

FIGURE 16.16
The Action drop-down for calendars with Outlook 2003.

If we choose the Connect to Outlook section here, you'll first see the warning message shown in Figure 16.17. You probably will remember that this isn't the same kind of warning message that was seen when doing the same operation with Outlook 2007.

FIGURE 16.17
The warning window when adding a WSS 3.0 calendar to Outlook 2003.

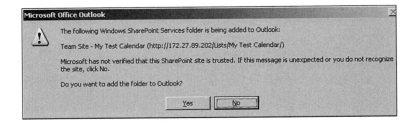

Note

There's no equivalent figure specifically for the calendar scenario, but Figure 16.2 is the same kind of warning message. Whereas the Outlook 2003 message is about "adding" to, the Outlook 2007 message is about "connecting to."

FIGURE 16.18
Side-by-side calendars is still possible with Outlook 2003.

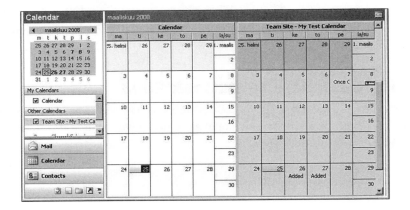

Figure 16.18 shows the situation after the addition of My Test Calendar.

The leftmost column now has only two groups of calendars, because Other Calendars now includes both other domain users' calendars (removed before Figure 16.18 was shot) and any SharePoint calendars.

However, the main difference is that although you can still lay calendars side by side, you cannot overlay them.

Figure 16.19 shows what happens when an attempt is made to create a new entry in the SharePoint calendar when working with Outlook 2003. It isn't possible, thus

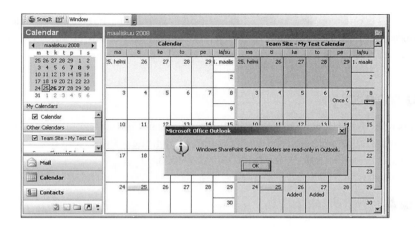

FIGURE 16.19
Meetings cannot be added in a SharePoint calendar while in Outlook 2003.

confirming that this is not the two-way synchronization that was possible with a SharePoint calendar and Outlook 2007.

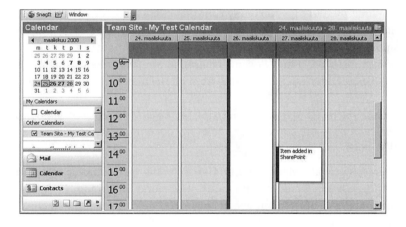

FIGURE 16.20
Meetings added to a calendar while in WSS 3.0 are visible in Outlook 2003.

One-way synchronization is still possible. Off-screen, I created a meeting while in SharePoint. Figure 16.20 shows that this (new) meeting is visible in Outlook 2003.

Linking Contacts to Outlook 2003

Contacts and Outlook 2003 is similar to calendars and Outlook 2003. There is a similar drop-down (similar to that shown in Figure 16.16) for calendars. However, an Edit in Datasheet option has been added because people are more likely (in SharePoint) to bulk-transfer contacts from one Contacts library to another than they are to move meetings.

Again this is one-way synchronization only, and attempts to add contacts while in Outlook produce the same kind of "are read-only" information window as we saw for calendars.

Summary

In this hour, we've looked at document libraries, calendars, and contacts, and have seen what additional functionality is available when these SharePoint lists are used in connection with Outlook 2007 and Outlook 2003.

Q&A

Q. *I am trying and failing to bulk-copy contacts from an Outlook Contacts list to a WSS 3.0 Contacts list. Do you have an explanation for this?*

A. There are a couple of reasons for this (and there are fixes).

You are trying to copy too many contacts at one time. Although there is no maximum number, copying in smaller batches works fine. Try to transfer only small batches of contacts at a time, and make sure that those contacts have been transferred. If they haven't, determine whether some key fields, such as valid email addresses, are missing from all the nontransferred contacts.

Q. *I made my document library available as a list in my copy of Outlook 2007, but I can't see the contents of one of my documents in the viewer pane. Why not?*

A. Microsoft provides viewers (for this pane) for all the common Office formats, PDF files (Adobe Acrobat), and many other standard formats. If you can't see the contents of one of your documents in the viewing frame, it means that no viewer has been installed for that particular file type.

Check the main Office page at www.microsoft.com/office to see if it has links to additional viewers.

Workshop

Quiz

1. How can you use Outlook to view the contents of a document that is stored in a WSS 3.0 document library?

2. What is the main difference between using WSS 3.0 Calendar and Contacts lists with Outlook 2003 and Outlook 2007?

3. Which possibility does the Actions drop-down for contacts when using Outlook 2003 offer that the similar Calendar drop-down doesn't offer?

Quiz Answers

1. Outlook 2007 has a viewing frame with built-in viewers for many standard applications. If a WSS 3.0 document library is listed in Outlook 2007, use this viewing frame to view the documents contained in that document library.

2. With Outlook 2003, there is one-way synchronization, whereas with Outlook 2007 there is two-way synchronization.

3. Edit in Datasheet View.

Sharing OneNote 2007 Notebooks and Access 2007 Tables with WSS 3.0

What You'll Learn in This Hour

▶ Sharing a OneNote 2007 notebook with WSS 3.0

▶ Setting up a relationship between a SharePoint list and an Access 2007 table (and vice versa)

Sharing a OneNote 2007 Notebook with WSS 3.0

OneNote 2007 is the modern equivalent of the Borland product Sidekick that in the early days of DOS ran in the background and you could use for quickly copying text to. I use OneNote as a structured location for keeping copies of important sections of web pages and articles. Other people use it as a storage location for videos; slide shows, etc. It's main strengths are the fact that you can paste almost anything to it and that you don't need to explicitly save what you have copied to it.

The information that people have stored in OneNote is typically very important to them and they need access to it wherever they are. Storing the OneNote 2007 "notebooks" in WSS 3.0 allows access to them from any PC running its own copy of OneNote 2007.

The user interface for getting OneNote 2007 to work with WSS 3.0 is not the best. Here are a few pointers:

▶ In OneNote 2007, always create a new notebook to share. You can not share an existing notebook.

▶ Always specify an existing document library within a site as the place in WSS 3.0 where the notebook will be located.

▶ The notebook you choose is irrelevant. All that's affected is the number and type of existing pages included with it. (Normally, choose Blank type.)

These "rules" will make the choices in the following figures more understandable.

Note

The section, "Q&A," discusses why you should have your OneNote notebooks available in WSS 3.0.

Here we go through the process of creating a Shared Notebook in OneNote 2007, adding it to WSS 3.0, and using the notebook from WSS 3.0:

1. Open OneNote 2007 and select Share > Create Shared Notebook (see Figure 17.1).

FIGURE 17.1
Creating a shared notebook.

2. In Figure 17.2, I chose the Personal Notebook style to give it some properties.

FIGURE 17.2
Specifying the notebook's properties.

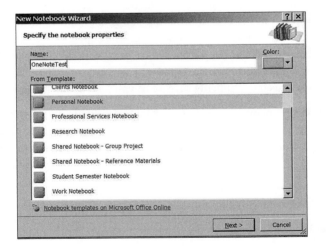

3. Figure 17.3 shows the available options for sharing a notebook. Choose the default options.

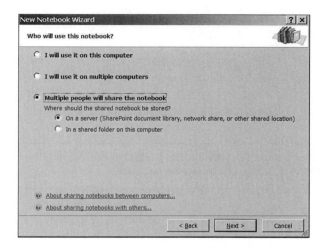

FIGURE 17.3
Sharing a note-
book.

4. In the Confirm Notebook screen that follows, section http://wss3, click Create to display the screen shown in Figure 17.4. Here we'll need to specify an existing document library. This creates a folder called OneNoteTest in

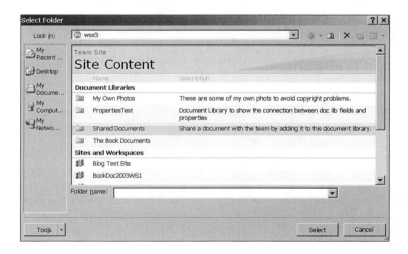

FIGURE 17.4
Specifying the
document library
for the note-
book.

the Shared Documents document library, but first we need to confirm our choice of document library (see Figure 17.5).

5. Select Shared Documents.

FIGURE 17.5
Confirming the
location.

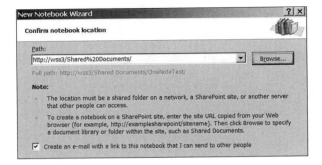

> **Note**
>
> It could be either Shared Documents, The Book Documents, or Properties Test.
> My Own Photos is an image library, so it's not suitable.

6. Having confirmed our library, we get a draft of the email that we can send (see Figure 17.6). Unlike many such emails in WSS 3.0 itself, we can edit the text each time we add a new shared OneNote notebook to our WSS 3.0 site and, of course, before we send it.

FIGURE 17.6
Being able to
edit the email
text.

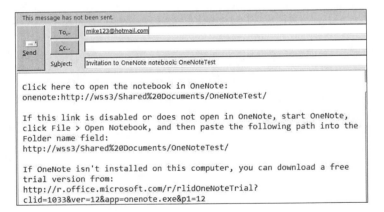

7. We'll see something similar to Figure 17.7. The new notebook has been added to OneNote, and it's marked with a checkmark icon to show it is shared.

8. Because we sent the email to our own address, we can click the link in that email to go to the website. We'll see that in Figure 17.8.

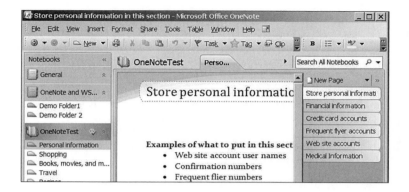

FIGURE 17.7
Identifying a
shared notebook
in OneNote.

FIGURE 17.8
The shared note-
book in the doc-
ument library.

9. The notebook has been created in Shared Documents as a folder. Open the folder (see Figure 17.9), and you see the sections and items that came standard with the Personal Notebook we selected in Figure 17.2.

FIGURE 17.9
Inside the
Shared Note-
book folder.

10. If you click Books, Movies, and Music, OneNote opens in your browser at that section (after a warning message is okay'd).

If that notebook had been closed earlier (in OneNote 2007), however, you are asked whether you want to open the entire notebook or just the section (see Figure 17.10).

FIGURE 17.10
Open a notebook
or open a sec-
tion?

Normally, you open the entire notebook. If all you want is to make a quick amendment to (or read something in) a section, just open that section.

11. If you choose to open the entire notebook, Figure 17.11 appears.

FIGURE 17.11
Opening the
shared notebook
in the document
library.

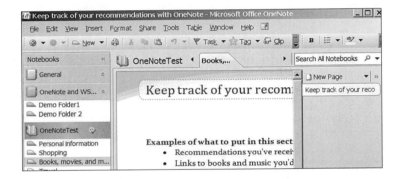

Note the difference between this and Figure 17.7, where the notebook was opened at the Personal Information section in the (OneNote) list.

Note

> The order of sections in Figure 17.11 differs from the sections' order in the listing from WSS 3.0 in Figure 17.9. The WSS 3.0 listing is sorted in name order, whereas the OneNote order is either the order in which these sections were created or the order in which the sections have been manually moved later.

Storing a SharePoint List as an Access 2007 Table

New with Access 2007 and WSS 3.0 is the possibility to store any SharePoint list (except surveys and discussions) as a table in Access 2007. The main reason for doing this, as we see in Hour 18, is to use the reporting facilities in Access 2007 on Share-Point lists. It's also useful for people who want to do all their work while in Access, because they can edit the SharePoint list in Access. A few restrictions apply, however, and some fixes are needed; Table 17.1 shows the least obvious ones.

TABLE 17.1   Restrictions and Fixes When Creating a Database Table from a List

All column types	Only the first 256 list columns are transferred to an Access 2007 table because Access 2007 supports only a maximum of 256 fields.
Calculated columns	The results of a calculated column are displayed in the Access 2007 table, but the formula can neither be seen nor edited in Access 2007.
Lookup columns	If the lists referred to in a Lookup field (in the list from which a linked table is being created) aren't already in the (same) Access 2007 database, Access 2007 automatically creates linked tables for those lists.

> These restrictions and fixes also apply when a SharePoint list is imported (the first option in Figure 17.13).

Note

(The reverse can also happen and most Access 2007 tables—depending on how they were designed—can be stored as a SharePoint list.)

To store a SharePoint list as an Access 2007 table, follow these steps:

1. Open Access 2007 and create a new database, BookDatabase1 (see Figure 17.12).

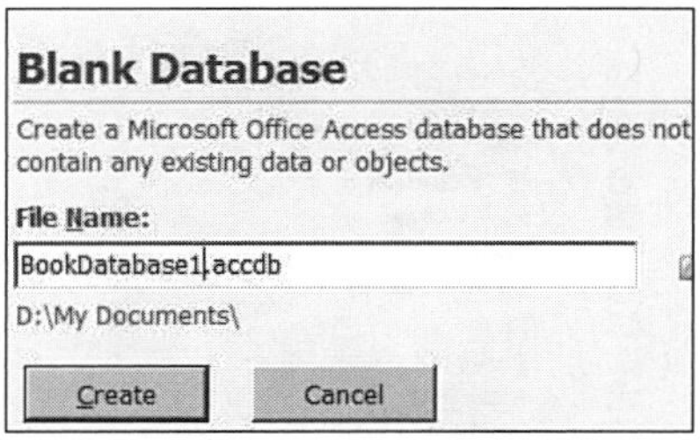

Blank Database

Create a Microsoft Office Access database that does not contain any existing data or objects.

File Name:

BookDatabase1.accdb

D:\My Documents\

[Create]   [Cancel]

FIGURE 17.12
Creating a database.

2. Select External Data (see Figure 17.13).

3. Select SharePoint List *from the Import section*, and specify http://wss3 as the site (see Figure 17.14). Choose the default value, Link to the Data Source by Creating a Linked Table. This sets up the two-way link.

FIGURE 17.13
Selecting External Data.

FIGURE 17.14
Specifying the site to import a list from.

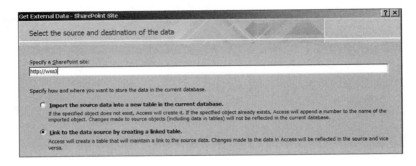

4. Click Next. First you'll be asked to sign in to the WSS 3.0 site, and then you'll be shown the available SharePoint lists for this operation (see Figure 17.15).

FIGURE 17.15
Selecting one or more SharePoint lists.

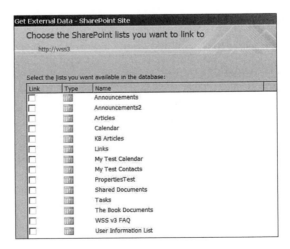

5. Because the options are check boxes, you can select more than one. For this test, we'll choose just one. Select the Links list, which has three entries in it.

Tip

> If the Links list you have doesn't contain any entries, add a few random items after you access it by clicking Links (on the right side of the screen) over the same-named web part. (www.ibm.com and www.hp.com are quick to write.)

6. Click OK. You are still in Access 2007, and you will see that two tables have been created. Click the "extra" one (User Information List). It contains a list of the standard user groups and the users that were given access rights to the site in Hour 3 (see Figure 17.16).

FIGURE 17.16
The contents of the User Information List table.

The Links table naturally contains our Links list (see Figure 17.17).

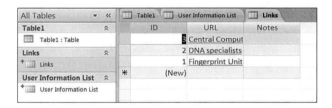

FIGURE 17.17
The contents of Links in Access 2007.

At the moment, the Synchronize item in the menu line shows gray and is nonaccessible. Let's add a value to this table (see Figure 17.18).

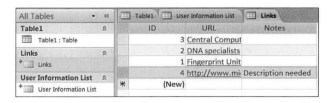

FIGURE 17.18
Adding a URL to links while in Access 2007.

Note

> The main drawback with the Links list is that we can only add a URL in the URL field, not a description. To add an equivalent description, we must amend the row in the Links list in WSS 3.0. This makes a Links List less suitable for being amended while in Access 2007, but still a good candidate for creating a report from.

There's a list of options that can be done to that *SharePoint* list while in Access 2007. Near the end of that list is the Refresh List option (see Figure 17.19). You can see this

FIGURE 17.19
SharePoint list options.

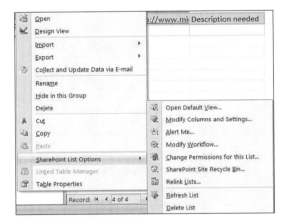

option if you position your cursor on top of Links, right-click, and select SharePoint List Options. However, you don't need to use this option. In fact, to synchronize the Access version and the list in WSS 3.0, you don't need to do anything except to (re)open the page containing the list.

Tip

> In WSS 3.0 (after a change in Access), you only need to refresh the list if it is open. In Access (after a change in WSS 3.0), if the database is open, you need to close it and open it again (when you select Links, in our example) to have the latest version. In this case, Refresh List may be a faster approach.

Refresh List *is* needed if you have changed the *structure* of the list while in Access 2007.

Tip

> Search the Access Help for "Import from or link to a SharePoint list" if you want a detailed list of how the WSS data types are mapped to Access data types when an Access table is created from a SharePoint list.

The next section discusses creating a SharePoint list from an Access table.

> The section "Q&A" explains why you would want to have a list synchronized in Access 2007 or an Access table synchronized in WSS 3.0.

Note

Adding an Access Table as a WSS 3.0 List

Sometimes there is a need to make information stored in Access 2007 available to people using browsers. In that case, an Access table can be added to a WSS 3.0 site as a list.

There are three alternatives: You can create a copy of an existing Access table in WSS 3.0; you can create a new WSS 3.0 list when in Access; and you can move an existing Access 2007 list to WSS 3.0.

Creating a Copy of an Existing Access Table in WSS 3.0

To create an existing Access table as a WSS 3.0 list, follow these steps:

1. Create in Access 2007 an AccessToWSSTest database.

2. Create four columns: Company, Location, Purpose, and Number of Staff.

3. Populate these columns with (for instance) HP, Las Vegas, Sales, 30 / HP, Boston, Research, 250 / HP, Boston, Sales, 50, and so on with varying companies (HP, IBM, MS, Sun). Also populate these columns with locations, purposes, and staff numbers.

   In Figure 17.20 notice that the only option when in Access 2007 is to put the HP, IBM, and so forth data in a text field. To do this in a WSS 3.0 list, use a custom field with those values prespecified.

4. Close the database when you have filled in some more rows, and then save the design as Company Staff Numbers.

5. Reopen the database. Table 1 is now Company Staff Numbers. Now we can copy it to our WSS 3.0 site.

6. Again select the menu item External Data. This time, click the SharePoint List link, which is in the Export part of the menu area.

FIGURE 17.20
The Access
2007 field
types.

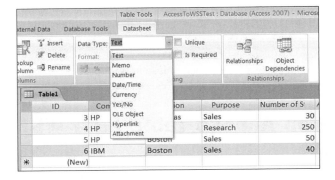

7. Figure 17.21 appears. Here you enter the address of the WSS 3.0 site you want to export this table to.

FIGURE 17.21
Exporting a table
to WSS 3.0.

8. Accept all the defaults and click OK. The wizard goes through several steps, after which the list is created in WSS 3.0.

9. A final screen asks if you want to save the steps the wizard has just done to speed things up next time you do this. Save them.

The process itself is now complete, and we can go to the WSS 3.0 site to see what the Access table looks like there.

When we go to Home in the WSS 3.0 website, we don't see a link to Company Staff Numbers. Didn't it work?

In fact, it did work, but—unlike when you create a list in WSS 3.0 itself—the default is to not create a link to the list in the Quick Launch section. The following steps create that link:

1. Select (in Home) Lists, and you'll find Company Staff Numbers.

2. Open this and you'll see that the default view of the list as created from Access 2007 is the Datasheet view (see Figure 17.22).

ID	Company	Location	Purpose	Number of Staff
1	HP	Las Vegas	Sales	30
2	HP	Boston	Research	250
3	HP	Boston	Sales	50
4	IBM	Boston	Sales	40

Team Site > Company Staff Numbers

Company Staff Numbers

New ▾ Actions ▾ Settings ▾

FIGURE 17.22
The default view is the Datasheet view.

> The ID numbers have been changed (from 3–6 to 1–4). In Firefox, which can't display the Datasheet view, it's a Standard view.

Note

3. In both cases, we can make sure the list appears in the Quick Launch section via Settings > List Settings > Title, Description and Navigation, and by clicking the radio button for Yes in the Display This List on the Quick Launch section.

Here we test whether synchronization will work without needing to specify synchronization:

1. Add another row (IBM, New York, Production; 500) while in the WSS 3.0 version of the list.

2. Go back to Access 2007. Again if the database is already open, close it and open it again. You see exactly the same content as before. Synchronization does not take place.

> When we created an Access 2007 table from a WSS 3.0 list, Figure 17.15 offered us the alternative of "importing" or "linking to." When we created a WSS 3.0 list from an Access 2007 table, however, Figure 17.22 offered us no choice—all we had was "exporting."

Note

Creating a WSS 3.0 List When in Access 2007

To create a WSS 3.0 list when in Access 2007, select Create > SharePoint List (see Figure 17.23).

FIGURE 17.23
Creating a shared WSS 3.0 list when in Access 2007.

Moving an Existing Access Table to WSS 3.0

The final option is to move an Access table permanently to WSS 3.0. Here are the steps to do that:

1. Click the Move to SharePoint icon on the far right of the External Data menu.

2. Specify http://wss3 as the site to move to (see Figure 17.24).

FIGURE 17.24
Moving to a SharePoint site.

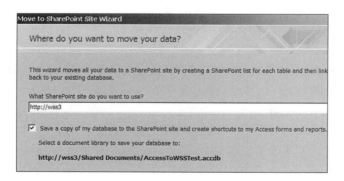

3. Select Browse in order to specify the document library to save this data to.

4. Select Shared Documents and click OK.

5. We see Shared Documents with the OneNote folder. Click OK.

6. Click Next.

Now the database is stored in the WSS 3.0 document library. It's also stored in your local My Documents directory in the file system of the client (see Figure 17.25).

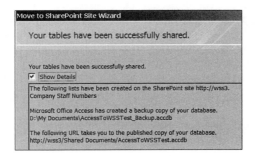

FIGURE 17.25
Showing where the database is stored in the client.

Now we can go to the WSS 3.0 site and access Shared Documents to see the database listed there.

This allows us to read (or edit) the database in our local copy of Access by a double-click on the name (and even set alerts on it). Because this is a database and not a table that looks like a SharePoint list, however, the only editing we can do with it outside Access is to change its name in the document library and add a description (and add, or change, values for document library columns).

In order that a different client computer sees the latest version, you'll see in Access that a new row (Publish Changes) has been added (see Figure 17.26) where you can specify that changes you have made locally can be published to the SharePoint site version of the database.

Publish Changes	Save your changes to the server.	Publish to SharePoint Site

All Tables	▼	«	Company Staff Numbers		
Company Staff Numb...	☆		ID	Company	Locatio
Company Staff Numbers			1	HP	Las Vegas
User Information List	☆		2	HP	Boston
User Information List			3	HP	Boston

FIGURE 17.26
Creating a shared notebook.

Full synchronization is achieved only if you start with an existing WSS 3.0 list and make an Access 2007 table from it (or create a new SharePoint list while in Access 2007, which has the same effect).

Note

> If you start at the Access end with an existing table, you can either transfer the contents (which creates each time an additional list if you don't first delete the previous version), or you can physically move the Access database containing the table so that the database is stored in a WSS 3.0 document library. The database, even if it is stored in WSS 3.0, is still a database and needs a local copy of Access 2007 in order to be able to open it.

Summary

In this hour, you connected a OneNote 2007 notebook with a document library in WSS 3.0. You also created an Access 2007 (database) table from a WSS 3.0 list and learned how to synchronize the table and the list. You learned that you can achieve the same effect by creating a SharePoint list when in Access 2007. You exported an Access 2007 table to WSS 3.0 and repeated this action. Finally, you moved an Access 2007 database to a WSS 3.0 document library.

Q&A

Q. *Why should I have my OneNote files accessible from WSS 3.0?*

A. If the working methods you use mean that you use OneNote a lot and you want to continue to use it to collect information that others should see, put those OneNote notebooks in a WSS 3.0 list.

Q. *Why should I put a synchronized copy of my SharePoint list in Access 2007?*

A. This is the subject of Hour 18.

Q. *Why should I put a copy of my Access 2007 table/database in a SharePoint list?*

A. Exporting the table to WSS 3.0 is like the situation with Excel. You can create a SharePoint list from a database table, but there is then no connection between the two. Changes made to one will not be synchronized to the other. You do it to make the (static) data regularly available to a wider group of users (perhaps on a monthly basis).

Moving the database is similar to the situation with OneNote. You do it so that your Access 2007 information is stored in a server so that it is available via a browser. Users can then add, edit, and delete information (if they have sufficient rights), but only if they have a full copy of Access 2007 on their clients.

Workshop

Quiz

1. We stored the OneNote notebook and the Access database to the document library called Shared Documents. Was it necessary to use this particular document library because we wanted to be able to share the information?

2. What was the reason (in one word) why it was good to have a synchronized copy of a SharePoint list stored as a table in Access 2007?

3. Can you create a synchronized list in WSS 3.0 from an existing table in Access 2007?

Quiz Answers

1. No. All document libraries can be shared. The fact that Microsoft decided to use the name Shared Documents for their default document library doesn't make it any more or less shareable than any other document library.

2. Reporting, which we cover in detail in the next chapter.

3. No. You can create a unique copy, but it isn't synchronized.

Using Access 2007 Tables to Produce Reports from WSS 3.0 Lists

---

What You'll Learn in This Hour

- ▶ Creating a simple report from a single WSS 3.0 list
- ▶ Creating complex reports combining data from several WSS 3.0 lists

The Evolution of Making Reports of SharePoint Lists

WSS 3.0 lists are designed to be viewed onscreen. They usually don't print well, so you must use a help program if you want quality reports from lists.

With WSS 2.0 and Office 2003, this was done by transferring the contents of a list to Excel 2003 and creating a report there. This took work.

Now with the Office 2007 products, Microsoft allows you to have SharePoint lists synchronized with Access tables. Therefore, you can use Access 2007 to produce reports on those SharePoint lists.

> It's impossible to use the Excel technique with Excel 2007 because Microsoft removed functionality in Excel 2007 that is needed for this.

Note

Hour 17, "Sharing OneNote 2007 Notebooks and Access 2007 Tables with WSS 3.0," covered how to get a synchronized copy of a WSS 3.0 list in an Access 2007 table. This hour concentrates on the reporting aspects.

We'll start with a basic report that uses a single WSS 3.0 list / single Access 2007 table.

Creating a Simple Report from a Single WSS 3.0 List

This section is closely linked to Hour 17. To create a simple report from a single WSS 3.0 list, follow these steps:

1. Create an Access 2007 table from a WSS 3.0 list (using import and linking, as in Hour 17's "Storing a SharePoint List as an Access (2007) Table" section).

2. This time, call it BookDatabase2 and select the Company Staff Numbers list. The Company Staff Numbers table in Access 2007 should look like Figure 18.1.

FIGURE 18.1
A synchronized WSS 3.0 list in Access 2007.

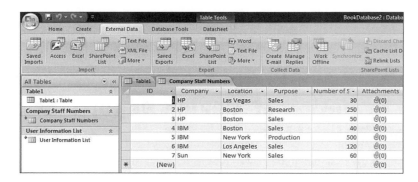

The next step is to create a report from this list. Note that the Company Staff Numbers table is open.

3. Click Create in the menu line. You'll see a Reports section with a number of options that look promising (see Figure 18.2).

FIGURE 18.2
The Reports section.

Let's start with the Reports Wizard.

4. Clicking Reports Wizard gives us a pop-up window. Select the fields we
   want to include from the Company Staff Numbers table (see Figure 18.3).

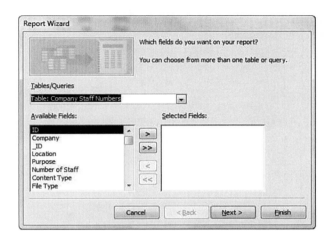

FIGURE 18.3
Using the Report
Wizard.

> We could select Table1 (which is empty) or the User Information list, which just
> lists the SharePoint site's users with their rights, but this table is better.

Note

> The wizard allows only a single table to be used on the report. We'll have to use
> something else for the next section.

Tip

5. We want the Company, Purpose, Location, and Number of Staff columns.
   Move them from left to right (in Figure 18.3). Click Next.

   Now, we need to configure group levels. For this report, let's group on
   Company and Purpose (see Figure 18.4).

6. Click Grouping Options. This allows you to amend the group intervals
   (Normal and 1st–5th Initial Letter). Click Cancel (leaving the interval at
   Normal), and click Next.

   Now we can decide on the fields to be sorted at the detail level. Here we
   have two fields left (because we are already grouping by the other two
   fields), so it's logical to sort on the Location field (see Figure 18.5).

   It might be useful to click Summary Options. In Figure 18.6, I specified the
   Sum and that the percent of the total should be calculated for sums.

FIGURE 18.4
Specifying grouping in the Report Wizard.

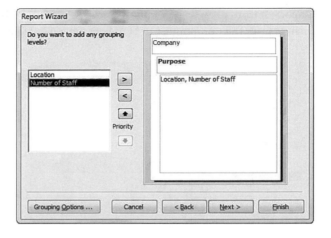

FIGURE 18.5
Specifying sorting in the Report Wizard.

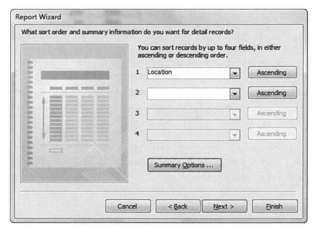

FIGURE 18.6
Specifying summarizing in the Report Wizard.

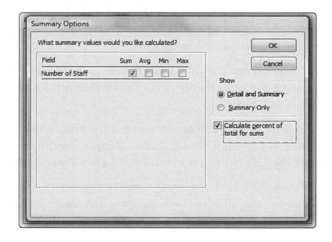

7. Click Next. The next screen lets you choose the layout from three options (see Figure 18.7). The graphic shows what each layout will look like. Just to be different, I chose Outline layout (although you'll probably use the default, Stepped).

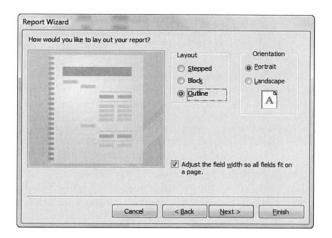

FIGURE 18.7
Specifying layouts in the Report Wizard.

8. Figure 18.8 offers a list of standard "styles." I chose Flow, which looks better than a basic look and has legible text.

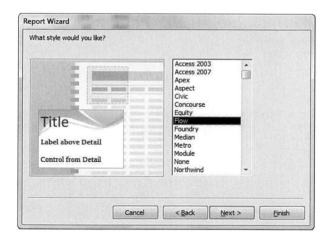

FIGURE 18.8
Specifying styles in the Report Wizard.

9. The lower half of the next screen offers us a chance to modify the report, which seems pointless because we haven't seen it yet. Just click Finish (see Figure 18.9).

FIGURE 18.9
Specifying a title
for the report.

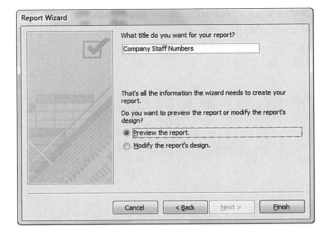

Figure 18.10 shows part of the completed report. It looks fine, but the per-centage figure I asked for looks like overkill. In addition, the flowing blue doesn't flow.

FIGURE 18.10
Part of the final
report produced
by the Report
Wizard.

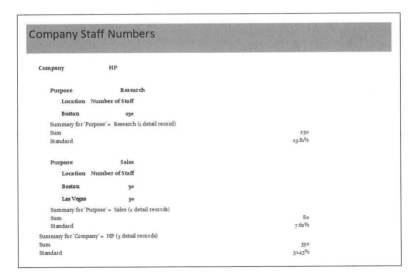

10. Now, we could print the report (and I have no objection if you do). For now, however, just close the print preview and view the report details that the Report Wizard created for us (see Figure 18.11).

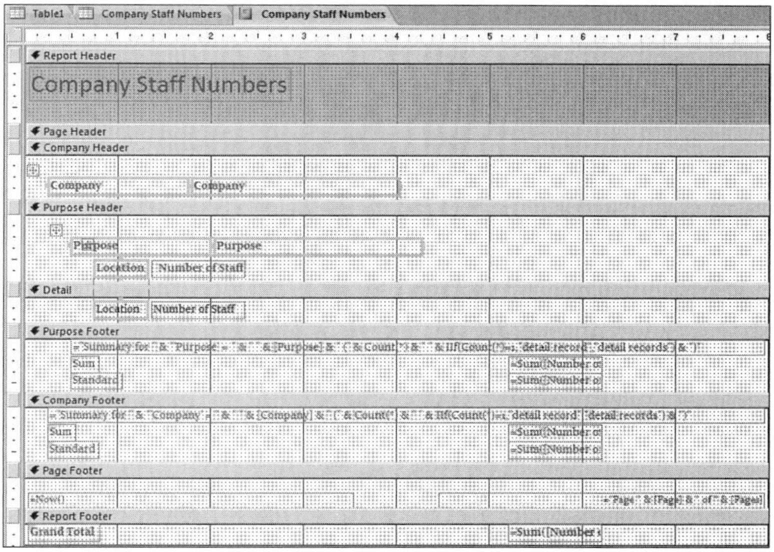

FIGURE 18.11
A report design we can edit in detail.

Here it's possible to do something to the title and get rid of those two Standard and = Sum (etc.) pairs that gave those percentages, so that's what we'll do in the next steps:

1. Select the title and then Property Sheet in the menu line. This gives us a list of choices for this field. Figure 18.12 shows the first few.

FIGURE 18.12
The Property Sheet for a field in a report.

For a report of a *single* list, use the Report Wizard to get an almost correct report quickly and then tidy it up by hand; don't create a new report from scratch.

Tip

Finally, what you now notice is that this report is listed in the All Tables section of the database (see Figure 18.13). It is thus available whenever the database is opened.

FIGURE 18.13
The report now belongs to the database.

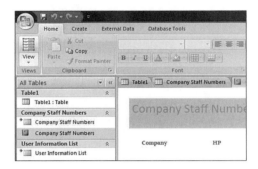

2. The final check is to see what happens if we add a few more entries to the original WSS 3.0 list. Add a few more entries for HP and IBM:

   ▶ HP, New York, Research, 45

   ▶ IBM, New York, Sales, 155

   ▶ IBM, Boston, Production, 240

3. Having made those changes in the WSS 3.0 list, go back and click again to open the Company Staff Numbers report.

   When we open this report, those additions to the WSS 3.0 are incorporated, as Figure 18.14 shows, where I earlier had—as promised—removed the two Standard/Sum rows.

This section showed how to quickly create a quality report from a single WSS 3.0 list, how the report is stored, and how a rerun report reflects all changes made to the WSS 3.0 list in the meantime.

The next section deals with the more complicated situation where the request is for a report that combines data from two or more different WSS 3.0 lists.

Creating a Report from Several Different WSS 3.0 Lists

To create a report from several different WSS 3.0 lists, the first thing we need is a list (preferably located in a different site to give a real test of this) that we can combine with the list we have in the Access database.

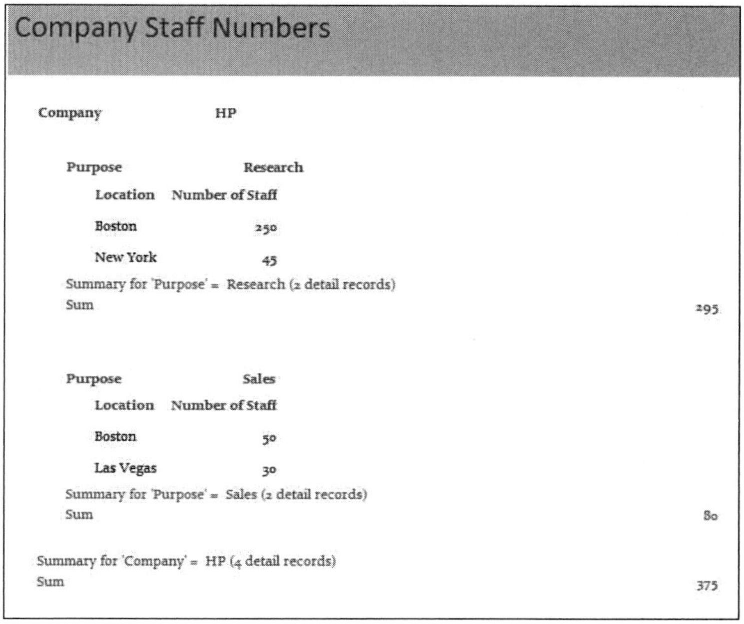

FIGURE 18.14
Part of the same report after data was added to the WSS 3.0 list.

As a first step, let's go in our WSS 3.0 system to the Web Parts Test site and create a simple list that provides corporate-level information about HP, IBM, Microsoft, and Sun. Follow these steps:

1. Go to the Web Parts Test site using the link in the menu line.

2. Select Site Actions > Create > Contacts > IT Companies (and choose No to it being in Quick Launch).

   Figure 18.15 shows that by using the Contacts list, we have all the columns

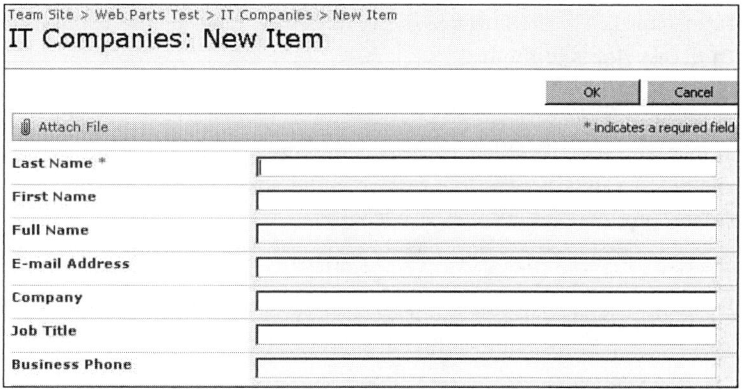

FIGURE 18.15
Creating the new Contacts item.

we need. However, we have one required column that we don't need (Last Name). It doesn't matter what values we enter in that field, but for simplicity, enter the same values you will enter in the Company field (that is HP, IBM, MS, and Sun).

3. I find the corporate addresses with Google Advanced Search (for instance, "Hewlett-Packard corporate address"). As I obtain the information, I fill in the information for each (see Figure 18.16).

FIGURE 18.16
Corporate infor-
mation in the IT
Companies list.

We can now use the standard technique from Hour 17 to import the list to Access 2007.

4. In Access 2007, open the same database we used earlier (BookDatabase2). Select External Data > SharePoint Lists (Import). This time we need to add a new site URL because we don't want to use the (http://wss3) site that is already there.

5. We created the Contacts list in the Web Parts Test site, so we need (in the equivalent of Figure 17.15) to import from http://wss3/WebPartsTest. Again, create a linked table.

6. In the equivalent of Figure 17.16 (the screen with lists), select =IT Companies, and then click OK.

    We now have two extra tables in Access 2007: IT Companies and User Information List1. The latter of these, as before, gives us the list of users with access rights to the list.

Note

Because this Web Parts Test site, and the Contacts list within it, inherits rights from the main site, this access information is the same as that contained in the existing User Information list.

Next—and before we start the report design—we need to set up a link between the two lists from which we want to make a joint report. To do this, follow these steps:

1. Select the IT Companies table (single-click). Select Database Tools > Relationships. The IT Companies table comes to the screen (see Figure 18.17).

FIGURE 18.17
The first table is listed in the Relationships panel.

2. Select Design > Show Table > Company Staff Numbers. Click OK.

3. Now we have two tables in the Relationships panel. Close the Show Table windows.

4. Go to the IT Company box (still in the Relationships panel) and scroll until you see Company.

5. Select Company (see Figure 18.18), and drag it across to the Company line in the Company Staff Numbers box (see Figure 18.19).

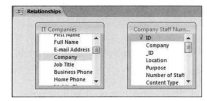

FIGURE 18.18
Starting the link between two tables in the Relationships panel.

6. Click Create.

7. That completes the relationship. Leave the two connected tables on the screen (see Figure 18.20). Go to Create in the menu line.

FIGURE 18.19
Completing the link between two tables in the Relationships panel.

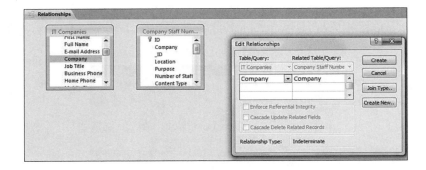

FIGURE 18.20
The two tables in connected state.

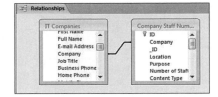

> ***Tip***
>
> If you want to create a report that uses two or more tables (that is, SharePoint lists), don't use the Report Wizard.
>
> It creates the kind of report that you typically don't want to see when combining tables, and trying to amend the report afterward is a nightmare.
>
> Instead, always use the Report Design option, which gives you the chance of adding your fields exactly where you want them.

8. After Create, select Report Design > Add Existing Fields (near the far right of the set of options).

9. If necessary (the first time you do this, it will be), specify that you want to see fields in other tables (see Figure 18.21).

FIGURE 18.21
Selecting fields from available tables.

10. Drag Company (from Company Staff Numbers) to the Page Header section. Remove (right-click/Delete) the leftmost box, which is only text, and align the rightmost box to the left margin.

11. Right-click that (Company) box and select Group On.

Now you'll have a Page Header section, a Company Header section, a Detail section, and a Page Footer section.

12. Reduce the size of the Detail section—it will contain only one row with a bit of space above and below—and increase the size of the Company Header section.

13. Move the Company field from the Page Header section to the Company Header section, and transfer all the Company data (Address, City, and so on) one by one from the IT Companies table (just visible at the lower-right corner of Figure 18.22) to the Company Header section. Again, remove the leftmost box and align the rightmost box.

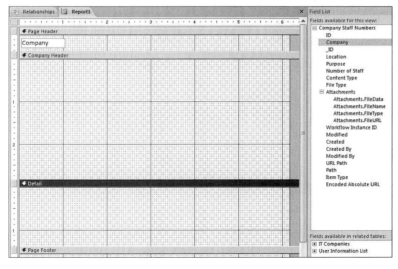

FIGURE 18.22
Preparing the report page.

14. Do something similar for the Location Purpose and Number of Staff fields from the Company Staff Numbers table. This time, copy them to the Detail section and put them all on the same row (data boxes only). You'll end up with something like Figure 18.23.

15. There's too much space around the Detail section, so reduce that space and then select the Company field.

16. In the set of options at the upper right of the page, select Property Sheet.

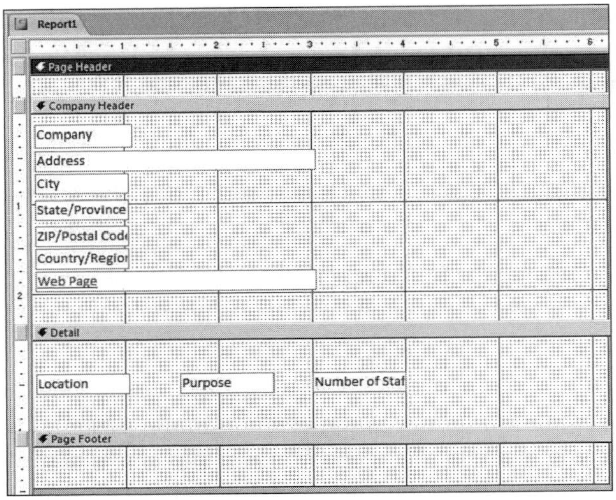

FIGURE 18.23
The Design view
is almost ready.

17. It's possible to make the Company Name bold by changing the font weight
in the Property Sheet to Bold or Extra Bold (see Figure 18.24).

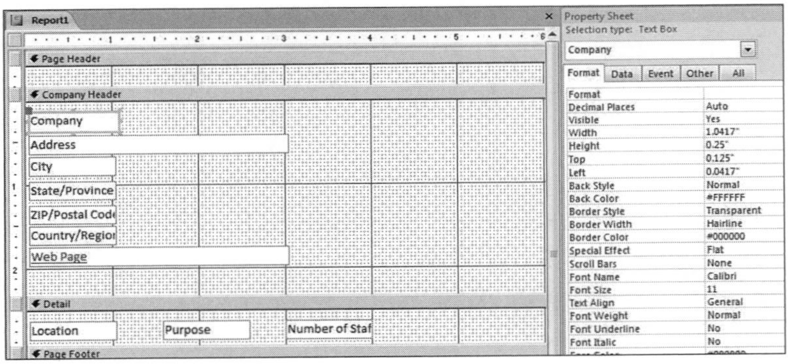

FIGURE 18.24
Amending a field
with the Property
Sheet.

18. Select Title (center of the list of options), and a Report Header section (and
Report Footer) is created with text you can amend. Make that text **Report
on IT Companies**.

19. Select Page Numbers (just under Title) and accept the default value. A page
number formula appears in the Page Header section.

20. Select View (top left) > Print Preview to see the report (see Figure 18.25).

21. Save the report as **IT Companies Report**. It is listed in both the Company
Staff Numbers section and the IT Companies section at the left of the screen
(see Figure 18.26).

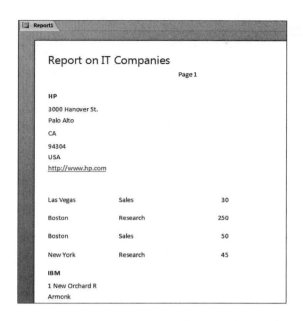

FIGURE 18.25
The almost final report.

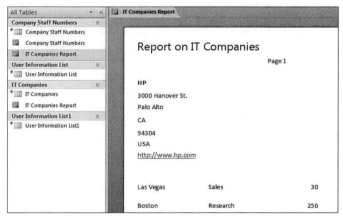

FIGURE 18.26
The final report.

It's not a brilliant report, and most bosses will want you to add some things, but it clearly shows how Access 2007 can help you create a single report that combines data from two (or more) WSS 3.0 lists.

Any change in either of the two lists involved in this report leads to a revised report the next time it's opened.

Note

Summary

In this hour, you used Access 2007 to create reports on data stored in WSS 3.0 lists. We created a simple report (on one list) using the Report Wizard and created a more complicated report (on two lists from two different sites) using the Report Design function.

Q&A

Q. *This all seems straightforward. Is it?*

A. If you have a single SharePoint list and want to create a report from it, using the Report Wizard is a straightforward method that produces quality reports in different looks.

But producing a report from several different SharePoint lists is not easy, and it requires skills that most SharePoint users and administrators don't have.

Using the Report Design tool, the report created in this hour was created smoothly and quickly. However, this report is a fairly simple report that uses only two different lists. When you have more than two lists involved, spend more time and thought on setting up their relationships before you start the Report Design process.

To create reports from several SharePoint lists, you will need to read some Access 2007 books and will also need to read up on connecting database tables.

Q. *How do I remove a table in a database that is connected to a SharePoint list? I don't want to delete in case the original list vanishes.*

A. It's actually not a problem. In Access, select the table that is synchronized with WSS 3.0. Then click Delete on the top of the page. You'll see Figure 18.27. Click Yes.

Delete removes just the Access copy. The WSS 3.0 list won't be affected at all (except that it will no longer be linked to Access).

FIGURE 18.27
Deleting means
only removing a
link.

Workshop

Quiz

1. Why do we use Access 2007 to provide reports on SharePoint lists?

2. Which technique is recommended to create a report from a single WSS 3.0 list?

3. Which technique is recommended to create a report from two or more WSS 3.0 lists?

Quiz Answers

1. WSS 3.0 (and MOSS 2007) does not provide any sensible alternative, and Access 2007 produces quality reports from SharePoint lists.

2. The Report Wizard.

3. The Report Design method.

Creating Workflows in WSS 3.0

What You'll Learn in This Hour

▶ What workflow options that you have as a WSS 3.0 (and MOSS 2007) user

▶ Creating a workflow using the three-state workflow included with WSS 3.0

Understanding the Main Workflow Options

Workflow has become one of the key functions of SharePoint 3 products. Workflow functionality is based on the Windows Workflow Foundation (WWF), which was released a bit earlier than WSS 3.0 and MOSS 2007, but the SharePoint team was obviously aware of this throughout its development.

You can use workflows in connection with SharePoint 3 products in six main ways:

▶ The single built-in workflow function included in WSS 3.0

▶ The five built-in workflow functions included in MOSS 2007

▶ Workflows created in SharePoint Designer 2007

▶ Workflows created in InfoPath 2007

▶ Workflows created in Visual Studio 2005 (and by now Visual Studio 2008)

▶ Workflows using third-party products

The single built-in workflow function (the "three-state workflow") in WSS 3.0 is the main topic of this hour. It is covered in detail later.

Predefined MOSS 2007 Workflows

The simple three-stage workflow type included in WSS 3.0 is also available in a MOSS 2007 installation. However, several other predefined workflow types come only

with MOSS 2007: Approval, Disposition Approval, Collect Feedback, Collect Signatures, and Translation Management workflows. These workflows pre-associated
with the Document content type. In other words, when you create a document
library in MOSS 2007, these workflows are automatically available in those
document libraries.

Tip

> I'd heard there were *three* built-in MOSS 2007 workflows. I suspect these were
> Approval (2 different types); Collect (2 different types); and Translation (1 type),
> which I count as *five*.

To see the status of these (and the three-state) workflows (when in a site), go to Site
Actions > Site Settings and click Workflows in the Galleries column. This displays the
status of the workflows in that site collection.

WSS 3.0 and MOSS 2007 built-in workflows are relatively simple workflows with limited capabilities.

SharePoint Designer 2007 Workflows

You can add more complicated workflows to both WSS 3.0 and MOSS 2007 and still
avoid programming by using SharePoint Designer 2007. This kind of workflow has
been allocated an entire chapter of this book. (See Hour 20, "Using SharePoint
Designer 2007 to Create Workflows.")

InfoPath 2007 Workflows

Despite the Microsoft paper that includes a "Design Custom Workflow Forms in Office InfoPath 2007" section (along with sections on creating forms in MOSS 2007 and
SPD 2007), you don't actually create a workflow in InfoPath 2007.

What you do is create InfoPath forms that display data from an existing workflow.
After doing so, you can make InfoPath rules that react on changes to that data.

In other words, there are no InfoPath 2007 workflows. There *are* standard (WSS 3.0,
MOSS 2007, SPD 2007) workflows (or workflows written in Visual Studio) and InfoPath 2007 forms that feed off them. This sort of workflow is second hand—a useful
technique that enables InfoPath 2007 specialists to use workflows in their forms, but
not a new workflow.

Visual Studio Workflows

The simplest explanation I have ever read about the benefits of workflows made with Visual Studio versus workflows made with SharePoint Designer 2007 is this: Workflows made with Visual Studio have loops, whereas SPD 2007 workflows don't.

I suspect it's somewhat more complicated than that, but writing workflows in Visual Studio certainly requires the kind of developer skills needed when writing code to provide new functionality in WSS 3.0 and MOSS 2007.

As such it's beyond the scope of this book. If you are interested in going further with it look for a SharePoint developer book that dedicates considerable space to workflows.

Third-Party Workflow Products

Third-party products provide functionality that you *could* write yourself if you had both the time and the Visual Studio–based development skills. Here are two companies I have heard good things about regarding their version 2 products. The version 3 products of both companies appear to be only for MOSS 2007 users, so ask the vendor if they work for WSS 3.0 if that's what you need:

▶ **Captaris**. At the time of this writing, Captaris Workflow 6.5 was available (www.captaris.com/workflow/index.html). Captaris also has a second workflow product called SharePoint Workflow Wizard (www.captaris.com/workflow/captaris_workflow_sharepoint_wizard/index.html).

▶ **Nintex**. Nintex had a product for WSS 2.0 called SmartLibrary. For SharePoint 3 products, the product is Nintex Workflow 2007 (www.nintex.com/Nproducts/Workflow.aspx).

Creating a Workflow Using the Three-State Workflow Method

> When reading this section, concentrate on the interchange between the two different list types during the workflow process.
>
> For people reading this book without the advantage of working with a company network running Exchange, regard the addition of an SMTP server and the emails that it should send to users in the workflow chain as a bonus.

Tip

I included enough detail for you to get the free SMTP server to work. These instructions worked for me until my local ISP (which was being used for DNS) decided that I was breaking the rules on not having a server connected to the Internet via a private subscription.

If this happens to you—or if you can't get it to work at all—don't worry. The workflow process doesn't rely on emails being sent. You can still follow this book without a working SMTP server.

Try the installation as described. If it works, great. If it doesn't, assume that the email arrives at the time I describe.

The three-stage workflow method is the sole workflow method that is built in to WSS 3.0. (It is also built in to MOSS 2007.) It is a simple but useful process to follow in a business environment.

The three stages are as follows:

1. Someone creates a job to be done.

2. Someone does the job.

3. Someone checks that the job has been done correctly and marks it as complete.

The principal components of the entire workflow process are

▶ A list based on the Issue Tracking list type

▶ A list based on the Tasks list type

▶ Outgoing email messages specified in Central Administration

▶ A built-in workflow service

▶ A working SMTP server

▶ A working email address (for the user)

Without these six components, workflow might work, but not properly.

Ensuring Your Users Have a Working Email Address

The sixth component is slightly different to the others: Make sure that all the people in the workflow chain can receive email. They can only do this if their correct email address is specified in their profile. Check this by (as administrator) going to Site Actions > Site Settings > People and Groups. Then, click the name of each user to check the email address. Figure 19.1 is an example of amending the default to an address at my own ISP in Finland.

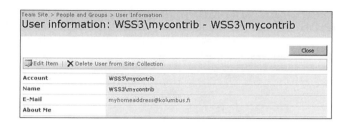

FIGURE 19.1
Making sure users have a good email address.

After checking that all the users have a valid email address, start at the bottom of principal-components list. (In this test case, use the users you use for workflow—I use MyContrib and the administrator. Also, for reasons revealed later, use one or more addresses at *your* local ISP unless you run Exchange in a work environment.)

Ensuring You Have a Working SMTP Server

Remember from Hour 11, "Using What We've Learned So Far in a Site," you learned that to get alerts to work, you must specify your outgoing email specifications and that the difficulty is writing the correct server name. That assumed you actually *had* an SMTP server. In a work setting, that is likely to be the case. If you try to follow this book at home, however, that probably won't be the case (until you install one).

A free SMTP server that works and has some good options is PostCast Server. (Be aware that it doesn't seem to work in the free version for Gmail and Hotmail addresses; so make sure you always use your local ISP email address for your test users.)

According to PostCast, the (nonfree) professional version can send messages to Gmail addresses (http://www.postcastserver.com/help/SMTP_Gateways.aspx). The Professional version costs $49. A free 30-day trial is available, so you can check it out.	*Tip*

The website for PostCast Server is www.postcastserver.com/download/. I installed version 2.6.0 and followed the defaults.

Note   It's a matter of choice whether you set the processing of messages to Immediately or Manually (the default). After you know everything works, switch to Immediately. While performing your first tests, however, it's easier to follow the process if
you can see when a message arrives in your SMTP system.

Using Manually means that you can follow the process (which means looking at
three different places, as you will see) *slowly*. That said, slowly is the only way (in
my opinion) to really understand what's going on behind the scenes.

FIGURE 19.2
Confirming that
the SMTP server
works.

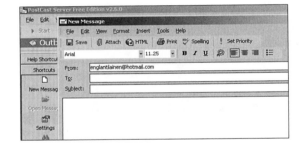

Having installed PostCast Server, the best thing to do is make sure that it will send
messages to your email addresses. Do this by creating a new message in the open
Outbox (see Figure 19.2).

When you receive that email, you know that everything is okay. You can now check
that you actually have a workflow system!

Tip   The email message will first appear in the Outbox. Then, assuming you have set
the PostCast Server to Manually, you need to click the Start button at the left of
the menu line that becomes available to you.

Don't worry if you get an odd small error message. Just click OK to accept it, and
your real message will be sent. This seems to happen once with a new installation of PostCast Server. (Be even less worried if you don't get such a message!)

Checking for a Built-in Workflow Service

To check that you have a working workflow system, go to Site Actions > Site Settings > Workflows (in Galleries). The Three-State workflow is listed and active (see Figure 19.3).

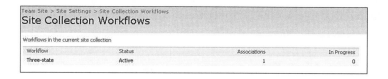

Team Site > Site Settings > Site Collection Workflows

Site Collection Workflows

Workflows in the current site collection

Workflow	Status		Associations	In Progress
Three-state	Active		1	0

FIGURE 19.3
Checking that the workflow is active.

Central Administration > Operations > Outgoing E-Mail Settings

Outgoing E-Mail Settings

Use the settings on this page to configure the default e-mail settings for all web applications. Learn about configuring e-mail settings.

Mail Settings

Specify the SMTP mail server to use for Windows SharePoint Services e-mail-based notifications for alerts, invitations, and administrator notifications. Personalize the **From address** and **Reply-to address**.

Outbound SMTP server:

    wss3

From address:

    englantilainen@gmail.com

Reply-to address:

    englantilainen@gmail.com

Character set:

    65001 (Unicode UTF-8)

    OK   Cancel

FIGURE 19.4
Specifying the outgoing email settings.

Checking That Outgoing Email Messages Are Specified

To check that you have specified working outgoing email parameters, go to Central Administration > Operations > Outgoing Email Settings (see Figure 19.4).

You need to fill in the values in Figure 19.4 if you are using the PostCast Server. If you are using Exchange, they are probably already specified.

Ensuring You Have a List Based on the Tasks List Type

The next principal component is to make sure you have a list based on the Tasks list type. Here it's possible to follow the usual method of Site Actions > Create > Tasks to create a new Tasks list, which will be used for the workflow tasks.

I strongly recommend you let the system handle this creation. When you specify the workflow settings for your Issue Tracking list, you are asked which Tasks list to use. You can ask for one to be created. In that case, the name that will be given for it is *<the name of the workflow>* Tasks.

The one snag with letting the system create the list (of type Tasks) is that this list will not appear in Quick Launch, which for our demonstration here is a nuisance. So, you will later need to enter the list and change the In Quick Launch setting.

Creating a List Based on the Issue Tracking List Type

Now you create a list of type Issue Tracking. To do this, follow these steps:

1. Go to Site Actions > Create > Issue Tracking and add the name **ThreeStateTest** (see Figure 19.5).

FIGURE 19.5
Creating a list of type Issue Tracking.

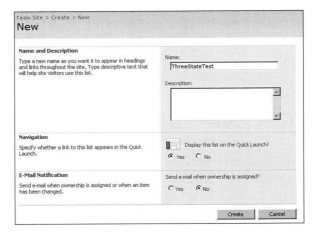

2. After creating this list, access the list's menu item Settings and choose List Settings from the drop-down. Remove attachments by going to Advanced Settings and setting attachments to No. After that, you'll return to the same List Settings screen. You can now select Workflow Settings, after which Figure 19.6 appears.

3. Name the workflow **FirstWorkflow**, and select New Task List from the drop-down. Also activate the box the arrow points at (which isn't default) and deactivate Allow This Workflow to be Manually Started. Click Next.

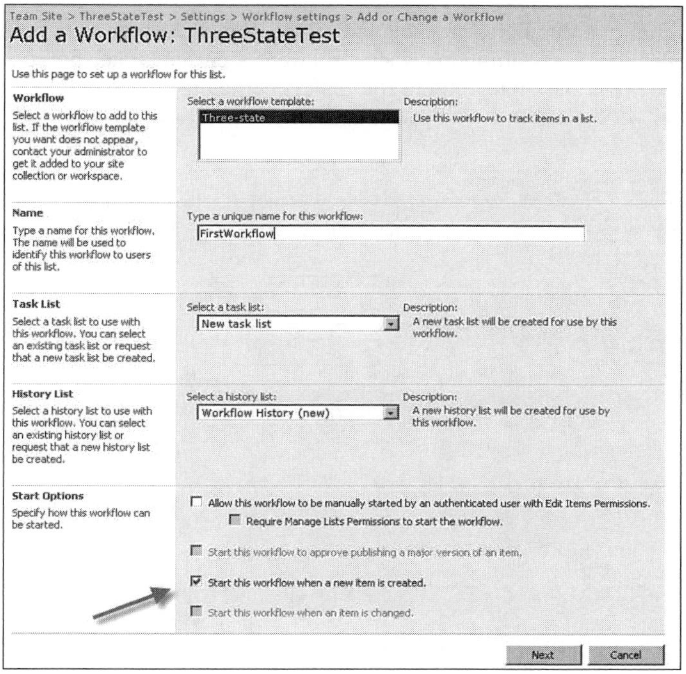

FIGURE 19.6
Amending the
workflow set-
tings.

4. Specify what happens when a workflow is started and what happens when the workflow changes to its middle state. (Changing the names of the three states is pointless—imagine changing the initial state to Complete!)

Figure 19.7 shows the settings for the initial state. (The middle state settings are similar.) This lets you change the messages that are issued and also let's you decide whether someone else (apart from the default person the task is assigned to) will get an email when the task starts.

Turn off the two places where Send Email Message is specified. All this does is send a pointless email that consists of a single link.

5. While still on the Task Details page, instead of having the task passed for review to the administrator (who will create this task), specify that MyAdmin will review the task (see Figure 19.8). (We'll use the administrator to create the task, so his name will be in the Created By field.)

Specifying a custom value for the Task Assigned To field is a less-flexible approach than using the contents of the Created By field because after this is set, *all* the

Note

> workflows that use this Issue Tracking list will be sent to MyAdmin for review. Use this approach for those situations where you want a particular key person or group to check off something before the task is complete.

FIGURE 19.7
Specifying the details of the workflow.

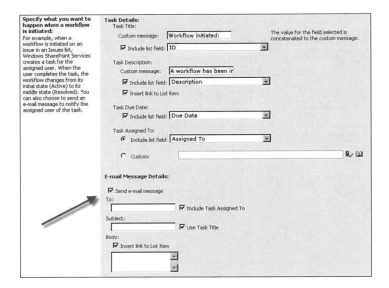

FIGURE 19.8
Changing who will review tasks in the workflows.

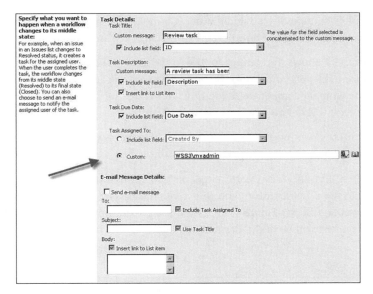

Creating the Workflow

Now that the six principal components are set, we can start the process of creating our workflow. First, however, let me explain why we have two lists: an Issue Tracking list and a Tasks list.

The Issue Tracking list is a high-level coordinator of numerous different jobs. Each job produces one entry in the Issue Tracking list, and it's possible in the Issue Tracking list to connect them to one another.

Each job in the Issue Tracking list generates a number of jobs in the Tasks list. Roughly speaking, each major step in the progress of that Issue produces a new entry in the Tasks list.

First, let's prepare for the rest of this hour by ensuring that the new FirstWorkflow Tasks tasks list appears in the Quick Launch:

1. Go to Lists > FirstWorkflow Tasks.

2. Open FirstWorkflow Tasks.

3. Go to Settings > List Settings > Title, Description and Navigation.

4. Specify there that the list appears in Quick Launch.

The final preparatory step is to use two browser copies as follows:

1. Open one browser copy at the ThreeStateTest list.

2. Open the second browser copy at the FirstWorkflow Tasks list.

3. Scale the browser copies to take up half the screen space; that way, you can see both.

Let's now create a new job in the Issue Tracking list.

Tip

Take this slowly. Create or change something in one of the two lists, and then go to the other list (perhaps with Refresh, although this isn't necessary) to see whether the other list changed.

If you have the PostCast Server, look at the Outbox to see if a message arrived. If it has, click Start to send it on its way.

Refresh your client's mail reader to see if an email has arrived. If it has, look at its contents.

1. Create a sample item in the ThreeTestState (Issue Tracking) list. Fill in the form as shown in Figure 19.9. (MyContrib was checked with the "head" to the right of that entry box, so it shows as wss3\mycontrib [underlined with no caps]).

FIGURE 19.9
Adding the new job in Three-StateTest.

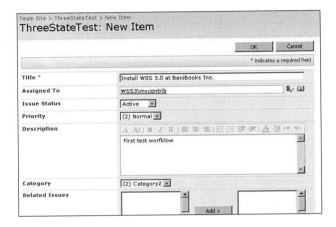

2. Click OK to display the ThreeStateTest list containing one item (see Figure 19.10).

FIGURE 19.10
ThreeStateTest list, with one item.

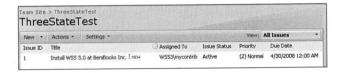

3. At this stage, nothing has happened at the SMTP server, so we have no new email. Go to the FirstWorkflow Tasks list and refresh the page, and there is a new entry (see Figure 19.11).

FIGURE 19.11
Tasks for Work-flow1, with one item.

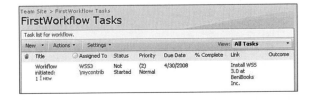

Figure 19.11 shows why nothing's happened: The status shows that the job hasn't started.

4. As administrator go to FirstWorkflow Tasks to get an email sent to MyContrib so that he's aware that he can start working.

5. Click OK (while still logged in as administrator) to send that email (with the text shown in Figure 19.12). Simultaneously, the status changes to In Progress (see Figure 19.13).

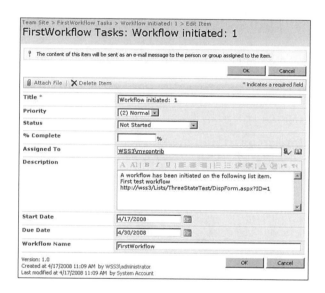

FIGURE 19.12
Telling mycontrib there's something for him.

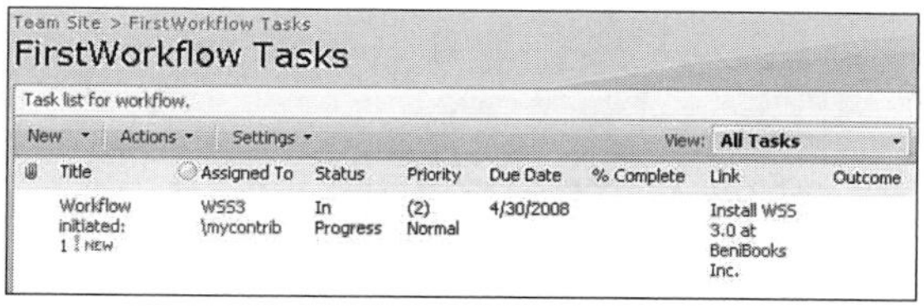

Meanwhile, the ThreeStateTest list also shows the workflow in progress (see Figure 19.14).

FIGURE 19.13
Task is in progress in First-Workflow Tasks.

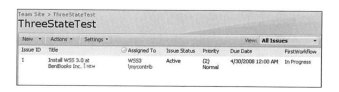

FIGURE 19.14
Issue is in progress in ThreeStateTest.

6. While in the browser at FirstWorkflow Tasks, change the user from Administrator to MyContrib (see Figure 19.15) and open the Workflow Initiated: 1 item.

FIGURE 19.15
Sign in as My-
Contrib.

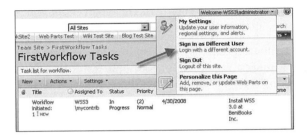

7. Edit the Workflow Initiated: 1 item so that the task is complete (and at 100 percent). Click OK.

8. Refresh the FirstWorkflow Tasks page. You'll see a second task in the list (see Figure 19.16).

FIGURE 19.16
Now the admin-
istrator's task is
in the Tasks list.

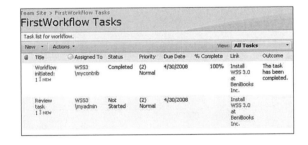

After a page refresh, ThreeStateTest looks like Figure 19.17.

FIGURE 19.17
The task is re-
solved but still in
progress.

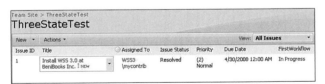

The apparent contradiction of having the task resolved but still in progress is because the task has been done but has not been checked!

The SMTP server now shows an email message that is ready to be sent to the email address of MyAdmin (see Figure 19.18).

9. Select the message and click the Start button. The message is sent to your email system. Figure 19.19 shows the type of message you see.

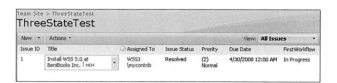

FIGURE 19.18
An email for
MyAdmin.

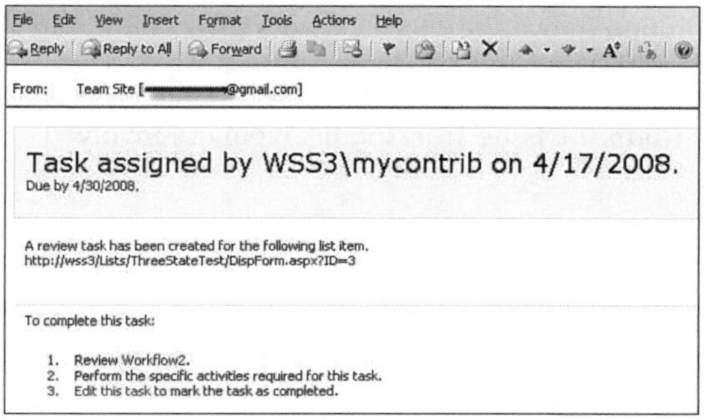

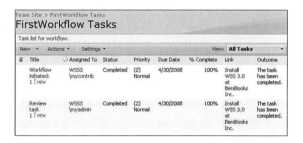

FIGURE 19.19
An email mes-
sage to tell
MyAdmin she
needs to review
a task.

10. Go again to the FirstWorkflow Tasks page and sign in as MyAdmin. Edit Review
Task 1 and mark it is Completed 100%. Now FirstWorkflow Tasks shows
Figure 19.20.

FIGURE 19.20
Two completed
tasks.

11. Open and refresh the ThreeStateTest page (see Figure 19.21).

With that, the workflow is completed.

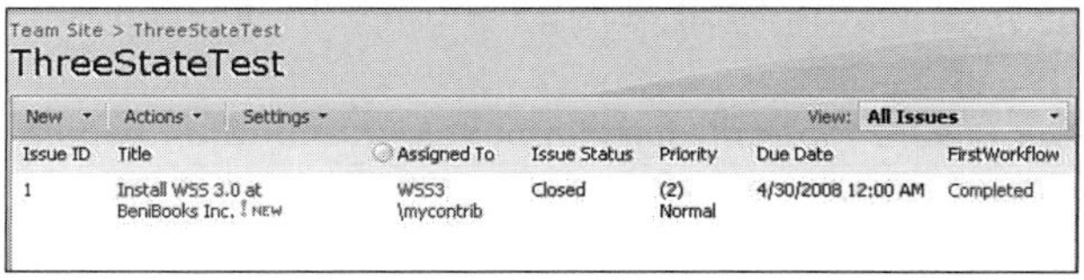

FIGURE 19.21
One closed and
completed
issue.

Summary

In this hour, you learned about the different kinds of workflows that can be created using various tools for SharePoint 2007 environments. The hour continued with a detailed run through of the three-stage workflow, which is the only workflow included in WSS 3.0. The example chosen used the Issue Tracking list type, a list type specially created for the handling at overview level of workflows.

The "Q&A" section contains a question about the requirements for workflow when other types of lists (than the Issue Tracking list type) are involved.

Q&A

Q. *A Workflow Settings option is available in most other types of lists, not just the Issue Tracking and Tasks list types. Are there any special requirements for these other list types?*

A. The main difference with using the Issue Tracking and Tasks lists is that those two list types are already set up for workflows, and so they already have the necessary columns.

The main column that is needed in other list types is a Status column, which needs to be of type Choice with three options. These don't have to have the same names as the equivalent column in Issue Tracking and Tasks, but must have three options to match the three-stage workflow, which is the only one available to WSS 3.0.

Other useful (and usually essential) columns are a Data and Time column for the due date and a column for the name of the person/group responsible for the work at a particular stage. Both of these columns, like the Status column, are already in the Issue Tracking and Tasks list types, and it's probably a good idea to use the same names when adding these columns in the other list types.

When that is done, the process is similar to the process we've gone through in this hour. The list is opened and workflow settings specified. Just as with Issue Tracking, it's best to select New Task List (and New History List) so that just as with Issue Tracking the detail work is done in a list of type Tasks.

Q. *How do we ensure that only certain people (rather than people with certain access rights) approve tasks?*

A. Because the process consists of a main list (Issue Tracking, document library, or whatever) and a Tasks list, it's possible to have different access rights for the two lists.

Workshop

Quiz

1. I listed six different ways to add workflows to WSS 3.0. Which method isn't really a way to create workflows?

2. Is it necessary to have an SMTP server available for workflows to work?

3. If I want emails to work, do I need to have an SMTP server installed on the WSS 3.0 server?

Quiz Answers

1. InfoPath 2007. You can write forms that use data from workflows, but you can't *create* workflows in InfoPath 2007.

2. No, the workflow works fine. The difference is that no alerts or email messages can be sent if there is no SMTP server available. In other words, the people expected to react to tasks in workflows would then need to monitor the Tasks list so that they would know when to react.

3. No, you need to have an SMTP server available and specified in the Outgoing Email section. The server can be anywhere that is accessible (typical, therefore, in the domain or network) from the WSS 3.0 server.

HOUR 20

Using SharePoint Designer 2007 to Create Workflows

What You'll Learn in This Hour

▶ Background of SharePoint Designer 2007
▶ Creating workflows using SharePoint Designer 2007

Introducing SharePoint Designer 2007

SharePoint Designer (SPD) 2007 is a follow-up product to FrontPage 2003, which is a tool for customizing non-SharePoint websites, WSS 2.0 websites, and SPS 2003 websites.

One common misconception about SPD 2007 is that it is a part of some Office 2007 package. This isn't true. SPD 2007 is "owned" by the Microsoft Office team, but it isn't bundled in the various Office 2007 packages.

If you want SPD 2007, you need to buy it. Luckily, it's not that expensive, and there are no confusing variants of it. Also you won't need many copies of it, even in a company environment.

But, if you're a SharePoint site administrator, you will need a copy. So if you are going to be a SharePoint site administrator, ask your boss for a copy of it now.

> *Tip*
>
> Don't let too many people have copies of SPD 2007. Your WSS 3.0 installation can be severely compromised if too many people can access it with SPD 2007.

Note

> You can use SPD 2007 with WSS 2.0 and SPS 2003 sites, too, but my advice is to use FrontPage 2003 with those sites if you already own a copy of FrontPage 2003. When using FrontPage 2003 all the functions will work with those sites. SPD 2007, by comparison, offers a lot of functionality that only works with WSS 3.0 and MOSS 2007. Using it with WSS 2.0 or SPS 2003 sites is frustrating for people who don't know which functions will not work with those version 2 sites. It is completely safe to use SPD 2007 with version 2 sites. However, NEVER use FrontPage 2003 with version 3 sites as those sites would be corrupted as a result.

This hour concentrates on creating workflows using SPD 2007. Two other SPD 2007 topics are covered in Hour 21, "Using SharePoint Designer 2007 to Create Data View Web Parts" and Hour 22, "Making Safety Copies of Your Data and Using Them."

Key Facts About SPD 2007 Workflows

These things are useful to know about SharePoint Designer 2007 before you install it:

▶ A SPD 2007 workflow, like the WSS 3.0 built-in workflow we looked at in Hour 19, can only be a workflow on a single list or library.

▶ All SPD 2007 workflows are created using a wizard. This makes them powerful, but at the same time, they are restricted to doing what the wizard makers thought you—the user—would want to do. (Although the wizard generates code and the code can be changed by hand later.)

▶ Through the wizard, SPD 2007 workflows are easy to create.

Where to Install SharePoint Designer 2007

The most common place to install SPD 2007 is on a client system (XP Pro or Vista) from which you will be accessing a server system (or a virtual machine [VM]) running WSS 3.0).

There is another alternative, but it's not recommended: Install SPD 2007 on the server (or VM) where you are running WSS 3.0. This might be handy for a testing environment on a portable (especially if that portable is not running XP Pro or Vista).

Tip

> The installation process for SharePoint Designer 2007 isn't discussed here because it is a guided installation typical of Microsoft commercial products.

Note

I used a copy of SPD 2007 running on my Vista portable (to access a VM running on a MacBook running OS X Tiger).

I also have a (different) VM on that Mac that is running both WSS 3.0 and SPD 2007. However, I chose to use SPD 2007 on a client because it is a more realistic environment.

Starting to Use SharePoint Designer

When you first open SPD 2007, it has a clean look (see Figure 20.1), even if it is a look that a Visual Basic user will feel more at home with than the typical user of Office products.

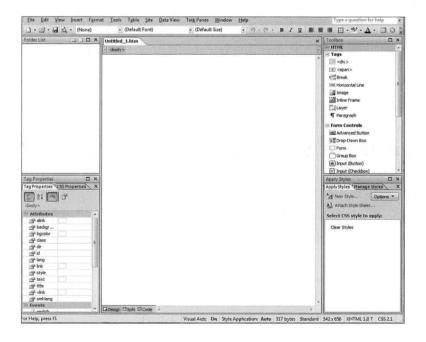

FIGURE 20.1
Opening SPD 2007 for the first time.

We want to access the site and do things there instead of using a generic Untitled_1.htm file. So, to open the site in SPD 2007, choose File > Open Site, and specify http://wss3 (once or twice; you may be asked for credentials, in which case, use administrator). (See Figure 20.2.)

FIGURE 20.2
Opening the
WSS 3.0 site.

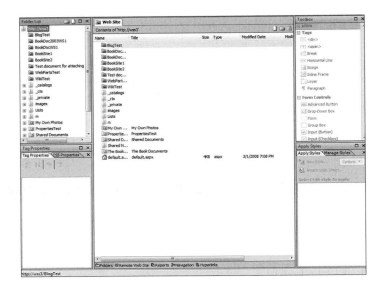

There's an interesting error (and this is SPD 2007 with SP1) at the lower-left corner. Despite the fact that the site is open at http://wss3, it says that we are at http://wss3/BlogTest, which as we can clearly see in the top of the central section is the first site *within* http://wss3 that is listed. It is *not* open, however, just selected.

Creating a Workflow Using SPD 2007

Now that SPD 2007 is open, we can create a workflow. To do this, select File > New > Workflow (see Figure 20.3).

FIGURE 20.3
Selecting Work-
flow.

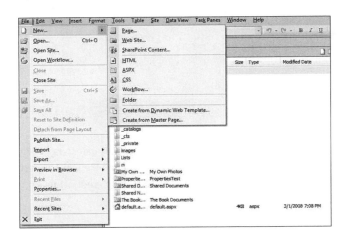

Don't worry if you see Figure 20.4 for a while after clicking Workflow. After a short delay, you see the more useful Figure 20.5.

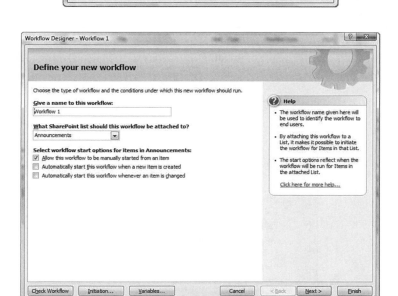

FIGURE 20.4
Waiting for data
from the server.

FIGURE 20.5
Defining the
workflow.

Here the important thing is the next section. It has three options for when to start a workflow:

► Manually started from an item

► Automatically started when a new item is created

► Automatically started when an item is changed

The first and the second items in this list are familiar to us from the three-stage workflow we created in Hour 19, but the third is new: the ability to start a workflow when something changes.

An example of this type of workflow can be something as simple as an administrator who wants to let people change the contents of documents within a document library, but he wants to stay informed about each change.

Let's see how this scenario plays out for a document in The Book Documents document library. To do this, follow these steps:

1. Change the workflow name to **SPD Workflow 1** and select The Book Documents document library. This time, have the workflow automatically started when an item is changed.

Note

> We could select all three options (or any two). But, let's suppose that only a changed item interests us.

Figure 20.6 shows the list of possible conditions that you can apply to this workflow.

FIGURE 20.6
A list of conditions.

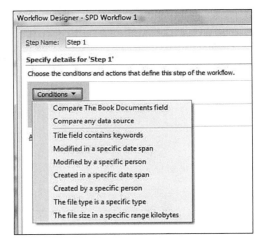

Note

> This illustrates both the advantages and the disadvantages of having SPD workflows created only via wizard. These options are useful ones (positive), but if we want some other condition, we can't have it (negative).

The Modified by a Specific Person option would be what our suspicious administrator is looking for.

In addition to conditions, there are actions (see Figure 20.7), with again a fixed list of options.

2. Unlike with conditions, however, this is not a list of all your options, it's just a list of the most common actions. Select More Actions in Figure 20.7. This gives you Figure 20.8, which has a longer list of options.

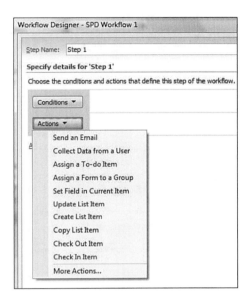

FIGURE 20.7
A list of common actions.

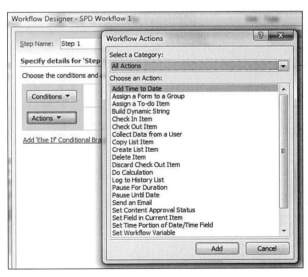

FIGURE 20.8
A longer list of possible actions.

The three possible actions that are not visible in Figure 20.8 are Stop Workflow (which seems a crazy alternative until you see that you can have Else If conditions), Update List Item, and Wait for Field Change in Current Item.

3. Here I select

▶ Condition = Modified by a Specific Person

▶ Action = Create List Item

Note

> Send an Email is probably the more likely option if the administrator is really worried. However, we had enough of sending emails in Hour 19, and what we're doing now is more interesting for what happens next. Later (in the Q&A section), we'll add a condition that will send an email.

Figure 20.9 shows what happens next.

FIGURE 20.9
One condition and one action set.

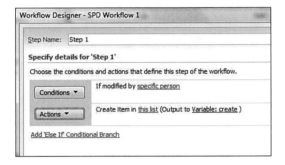

4. Specify the person we want to monitor for modifying documents in the list. Click a name, and there's a useful pop-up with a list of names to choose from (see Figure 20.10).

FIGURE 20.10
Choosing the user to monitor.

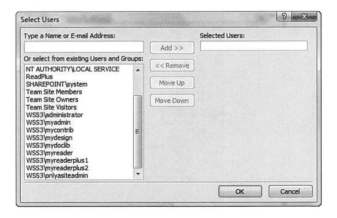

5. I'll select MyContrib. (There's no point in selecting someone with Read rights who can't modify anything.) Then click This List (see Figure 20.9) and select My Test Calendar (just to show that this will work with any kind of list). Then modify each of the fields (from My Test Calendar) listed, as shown in Figure 20.11.

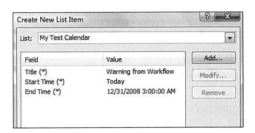

FIGURE 20.11
Creating a new list item in a workflow.

6. Click Finish. This particular workflow doesn't need any Else If conditions or further steps. You'll see Figure 20.12 for a while.

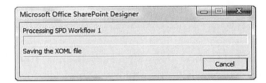

FIGURE 20.12
Processing the workflow.

Creating the workflow is now finished, and control in SPD 2007 is returned to the situation of Figure 20.2, with one difference: There is now a new entry (below default.aspx): Workflows. Figure 20.13 shows what happens if you double-click that.

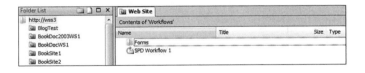

FIGURE 20.13
Seeing where the workflow is stored.

This first workflow created in SPD 2007 has both created a new site called Workflows, which will be used for all the workflows that are created in this site, and has also created an entry in the site that contains details of SPD Workflow 1. Clicking that shows the files created by the workflow (see Figure 20.14).

FIGURE 20.14
The files belonging to the workflow.

We can now abandon SPD 2007 for a while (leave it open, though—you need it in the "Q&A" section), because we want to determine whether the workflow we just generated actually works.

1. Go back to our browser. Open the site there. Open the My Book Documents library. Change the user to MyContrib, and then open a document. Amend it and save it back to the site.

   Figure 20.15 shows the document library after the change is made. There is a new column (which just appeared) called SPD Workflow 1, with Completed in the row of the amended document.

FIGURE 20.15
Checking the state of the document library.

2. Clicking Completed confirmed what we already knew: that the file Book Excel had been amended by MyContrib and when this happened. In addition, we can confirm that this had no effect on the Tasks list and that no events had been noted in the workflow (see Figure 20.16).

FIGURE 20.16
Details about the workflow.

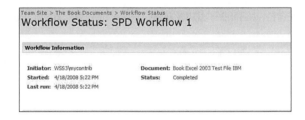

   Figure 20.17 confirms that such an item had indeed been added via the workflow to the calendar (just as we had specified in the workflow).

FIGURE 20.17
Checking the state of the Test Calendar.

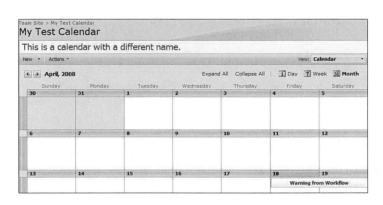

Now that we've clearly established that sending a message to a calendar (especially with that long period between start and end time) was not particularly a good way of informing the administrator that MyContrib had amended an item in My Book Documents, what have we learned from this hour?

We've learned that using SPD 2007 to create workflows is more powerful and yet much easier to do than using the so-called "simple" three-stage workflow included in WSS 3.0.

The SPD 2007 workflow wizards are powerful, relatively flexible, and will probably provide as much workflow as most people will want.

Even if you are a Visual Studio expert, don't discard the SPD 2007 option for workflows, but use it when you can and use Visual Studio for your workflows only when SPD 2007 workflows aren't flexible or powerful enough for your needs.

Summary

This hour compared SharePoint Designer (SPD) 2007 with FrontPage 2003 and showed how to buy it and where to install it. SPD 2007 was used to create workflows.

Q&A

Q. *Once I've written a workflow in SPD 2007, can I modify it?*

A. Yes, you can. Here's how you amend the workflow that was created above to send a message to the Announcements list instead of posting a message to a calendar:

1. Go back to SPD 2007 and select File > Open Workflow (see Figure 20.18).

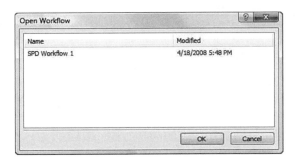

FIGURE 20.18
Starting to modify an existing workflow.

2. Select SPD Workflow 1 and click OK. You will get Figure 20.9 again (only with the person and the list specified).

3. We want to change the list that the message is sent to, but we still want the message to be sent when MyContrib amends something. So, we open the Actions box and choose Create a List item. This time, however, we select the Announcements list and give Title a value. We then select Add and get a list of fields from the Announcements list. We select Body and write some text in it. Clicking OK results in Figure 20.19.

FIGURE 20.19
Adding a second
action.

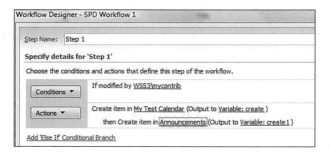

4. If we now click Finish, an item is created in the calendar and a (different) item is created in Announcements. So, we click the drop-down that appears to the right of the Create Item in My Test Calendar line and select Delete Action.

5. Now we have only one action. We click Finish to end the creation of the revised workflow. If MyContrib is so foolhardy as to amend anything in My Book Documents, the world will see (see Figure 20.20).

FIGURE 20.20
The workflow
has sent a mes-
sage to An-
nouncements.

Q. *How about Else If? How does that work?*

A. (See the first question in this section.) Go again to the present workflow, and select Add Else If conditional branch. Fill in the second pair of conditions and actions. You get Figure 20.21.

You can, of course, add a second step in a similar way.

FIGURE 20.21
An example of
Else/If.

Workshop

Quiz

1. Which product does SPD 2007 replace?

2. If you have a copy of Visual Studio (and development skills to match), why would you still use SPD 2007 for workflow?

3. Can you send messages to different people at the same stage in the workflow?

Quiz Answers

1. SPD 2007 is one of two replacement products for FrontPage 2003 (and the one of the two that is specifically for use with WSS 3.0 and MOSS 2007).

2. SPD 2007 could be used for prototyping or for workflows that don't require Visual Studio.

3. Yes. As you can see in Figure 20.20, it's possible to add a second action to the same step of a workflow. Both actions could be sending emails (see Figure 20.22 for an example of sending an email).

Using SharePoint Designer 2007 to Create Data View Web Parts

What You'll Learn in This Hour

- ► When to use Data View web parts
- ► Creating Data View web parts
- ► Customizing Data View web parts

Problem: Uploading the Same Document to Two Document Libraries

Some of the most common questions in the SharePoint newsgroups and forums are questions about how to upload documents to two different document libraries at the same time.

Another common question (and which is along the same lines) is how to show the same list content in two (or more) different sites.

Uploading documents to two different document libraries at the same time could be done with a mass of special coding. When one of the standard methods for upgrading a document is used, a set of code could grab the request and ask you to specify additional destinations for the document (other than just the document library where the user was located in the browser when the upload document function was accessed).

Apart from the fact that this special coding would require quality SharePoint programming skills, it also leads to two (or more) physical copies of the same document being stored in the SharePoint database. So, it requires more storage. Of course, the content of these two (or more) documents, once uploaded, could change over time (unless your special coding was extremely clever).

Solution: Using Data View Web Parts

Data View web part (DVWP) makes the same document available from two or more sites while it's stored only in one site. You decide in which site to store a list or library. That will also be the place where the contents of that list or library will be maintained. I often call this the "master" copy, but really, it is the only copy.

After you have such a "master" list or library, you can create read-only views of the information contained in that master copy.

Note

> The read-only copy won't look identical to the original. For some people, this is a major drawback (especially with document libraries). For others, it's an opportunity to present the data in a clearer way in the "slave" copy than how it was presented in the standard WSS 3.0 views.

That read-only view of the data is provided by using a DVWP, and it is created in the second (or third) site by using a standard function of SharePoint Designer (SPD) 2007.

Note

> DVWPs were also available in FrontPage 2003 where the list you were accessing needed to be in the same server. In SPD 2007 the list you are accessing needs to be in the same site collection, which is more restrictive.
>
> If we add a DVWP list to a subset of the Team Site we can now only select a ("master") list from another subsite of the default Team Site or from the default Team Site itself and not (for instance) a list from the anonymous website (which is a different site collection).

Tip

> Don't worry too much about this restriction. You can also use the DVWP part functionality to access the content of databases (and SharePoint lists that are in a different site collection **are** in a database).

In the next section, you create a DVWP that obtains its data from a different list in the same site collection (but not in the same site).

Creating a Data View Web Part from a List

This is a complicated process the first time it is done, so I split it into several small sections.

Starting to Create a DVWP from a List

To start the process of creating a DVWP from a list, follow these steps:

1. Go to the main page of a subsite of the Team Site and create a DVWP of one of the lists or libraries in the main Team Site.

2. Open SPD 2007 (SPD 2007). Choose Open Site and select http://wss3. You may be challenged for authentication. If so, log in as the administrator.

3. You will then see a list of subsites (and so on). Open Book Site1, but don't go any further.

Creating a New Page for the DVWPs

Once that is opened in SPD 2007, to create a new page into which we'll place our sample DVWPs, simply go to File > New > Page, and select ASPX (see Figure 21.1). That gives you an empty ASPX page called Untitled_1.aspx.

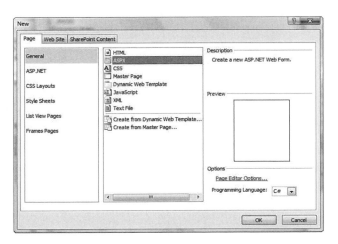

FIGURE 21.1
Creating an ASPX page.

Selecting the Source for the DVWP

Follow these steps to select the source ("master") for the DVWP:

1. Go in the menu line to Data View and select the first option, Insert Data View. You'll now see Figure 21.2.

FIGURE 21.2
Starting to create a DVWP.

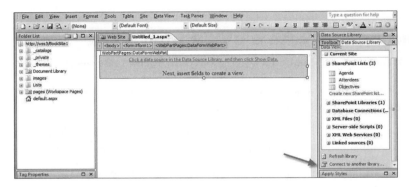

2. Select one of the lists from the top-level Team Site. Notice, however, that all the lists in the rightmost column are lists from the site where we are at the moment (BookSite1).

3. Scroll and choose Connect to Another Library (arrowed). You get a small box asking you which other library (and offering none) (see Figure 21.3).

FIGURE 21.3
Adding another site address.

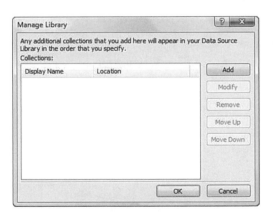

4. Select Add, and add http://wss3 (see Figure 21.4).

5. Click OK. It's now listed in the Manage Library page.

6. Click OK again. Now you see there is an additional entry at the bottom of the SharePoint Lists column (see Figure 21.5). You probably need to scroll to see it.

FIGURE 21.4
Specifying the
Team Site.

FIGURE 21.5
Team Site is
available in the
Data Source Li-
brary.

7. Open that entry by clicking the plus sign (+). The set of lists we can use from that site for our DVWP becomes available (see Figure 21.6). You can see that it is the same kind of sublist that was available for the site BookTest1.

FIGURE 21.6
A selection of
list, libraries,
and other
sources to
choose from.

8. Now we just need to open the SharePoint Lists section (+) to see which lists we can use for our read-only copy (left part of Figure 21.7). Alternatively, we can

FIGURE 21.7
Selecting a list
or a library.

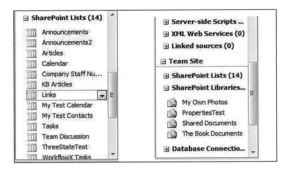

open the SharePoint Libraries section to see which libraries we can use for our read-only copy (right part of Figure 21.7).

Let's use a list, because that is usually the simplest, and we need to understand the concept. The "Q&A" section includes a solution to another problem that you have when using a document library.

9. Select the Company Staff Numbers list.

This ends the process of selecting the source; we'll be using the Company Staff list as our "master."

Aside: The Company Staff List in the Original Version

Figure 21.8 reminds us what the Company Staff List looked like when accessed in BookSite1.

FIGURE 21.8
The original ver-
sion of the Com-
pany Staff
Numbers list.

ID	Company	Location	Purpose	Number of Staff
1	HP	Las Vegas	Sales	30
2	HP	Boston	Research	250
3	HP	Boston	Sales	50
4	IBM	Boston	Sales	40
5	IBM	New York	Production	500
6	IBM	Los Angeles	Sales	120
7	Sun	New York	Sales	60
8	HP	New York	Research	45
9	IBM	New York	Sales	155
10	IBM	Boston	Production	240

Specifying the Data for the DVWP

After that aside, go back to the process of creating the DVWP. We previously selected the entry for Company Staff Numbers (in the leftmost column of Figure 21.7). We will now see Figure 21.9. Follow the steps that start with Select Show Data.

FIGURE 21.9
The Data View pop-up box.

1. Select Show Data and you'll see Figure 21.10. The center panel (Figure 21.10, left) knows that you will be using the Company Staff Numbers list.

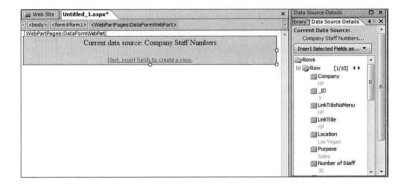

FIGURE 21.10
Starting to create the Data View.

The center panel guides you about what's next: Next insert fields to create a view. The fields we want are Company, Location, Purpose, and Number of Staff. So, let's do that:

2. Click once on Company. Then hold the Ctrl key and click once on Location, Purpose, and Number of Staff. Now that all four are selected, drag them to the center (Current Data Source) panel and release the Ctrl key.

3. You'll now see something like Figure 21.11, and notice that it's in the same order as Figure 21.8. That is, it is in ascending ID order.

Tip

> Save this page as DataViewTestPage.aspx, because the next section of work is fiddly. It's easy to make mistakes: In SPD 2007, save this page at the present location, but replace the Untitled_1.aspx name with DataViewTestPage.aspx.

The fiddly stuff starts.

Customizing the Look of the DVWP

The next steps customize the DVWP so it looks like this:

▶ Grouped in company order with the company name in bold.

▶ Subgrouped in purpose order.

▶ Has a total of the number of staff per company.

▶ None of the Sun records are listed.

1. To get the menu you need, select the small arrow at the upper right of the left-most section of Figure 21.11. (If you don't see it, make sure that you select the entire section rather than a single row; it should then appear.) A pop-up menu appears, allowing you to customize the DVWP (see Figure 21.12).

FIGURE 21.11
The Data View version of the Company Staff Numbers list.

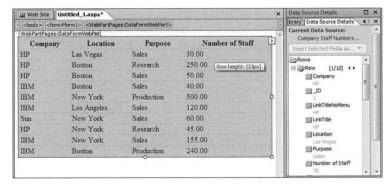

FIGURE 21.12
Starting to customize the Data View list.

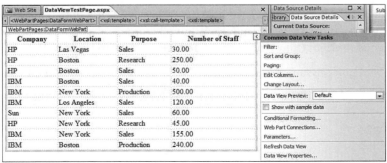

2. Let's start at the top with Filter. If you see any pop-up that says, "The list referenced here no longer exists," just specify (as a Filter) Company > Not Equal > Sun.

3. The list in the center changes to reflect this. There is no longer a line for Sun. Then, select Sort and Groups (see Figure 21.13).

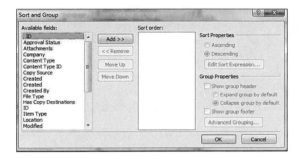

FIGURE 21.13
Adding sorting and grouping fields.

4. First, you'll see that you can't specify any group properties. You must first specify at least one sort field

5. Explicitly say that you want to sort a field. Having done that, you can then specify whether that field is a group field.

6. Add Company from the leftmost column to the Sort Order column.

7. Now group properties are available, so you can select that you want a group header and you want the group to be expanded by default. You also want a group footer (see Figure 21.14).

8. Do the same for purpose (without the group footer), and add Location to the Sort Order column. However, don't specify that it is to be used for grouping.

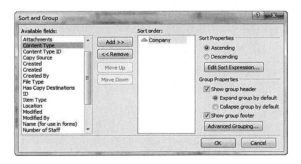

FIGURE 21.14
Company gets a grouping header and footer.

9. Click OK. Figure 21.15 appears (with no Sun lines). It is reasonable looking, but there's no need for the company names and the purposes to be repeated; let's get rid of those columns.

FIGURE 21.15
The Data View still has repeated names.

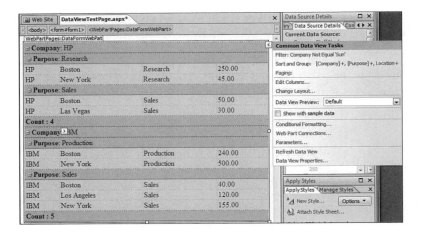

> **Tip**
>
> This is a good time to save a copy. Decide for yourself whether you want to save with the same name or with a new one.

10. Having saved the page, click the top-right arrow again to see Figure 21.15. Choose the fourth parameter (Edit Columns) to easily remove the company name and the location from each row.

This now is our final version (see Figure 21.16). I seem to have removed the column headings along the way. How about you?

FIGURE 21.16
No repeated names.

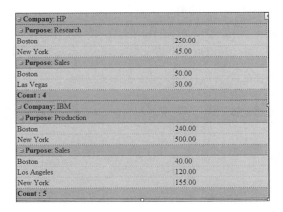

Getting the company header to be in a bold font is not done in the same way as with other Microsoft tools! By now, you're probably expecting to click or right-click something and then find a Format option from which you can select bold. In fact, all you do is go to HP in the list, select those two characters, and then go to the B in the second SPD 2007 menu line and click it.

> **Note**
>
> Don't worry. When you do this for HP, SPS 2007 realizes that you want to make all the company headers bold. So in this case, IBM also becomes a bold IBM.

Summarizing the DVWP We Created

If you go back to look at the list of things we wanted to see in this DVWP, you'll see that we have quickly and easily achieved three of the four things we specified:

The list is grouped by company (and the company name is bold); we have a subgroup as required and all the Sun rows have been removed.

We haven't yet got a sum of staff numbers after the rows of every company. At the moment, the information we have there is Count=4, or the number of rows, which isn't what we are looking for.

The process of getting this the way we want is long, complicated, and requires code, so I moved the text and diagrams (and code) explaining how to solve this to this book's website (www.informit.com/title/9780672330001).

The lesson to learn (and the reason for including that requirement in the list) is that you can do many things with a DVWP quickly and easily by using the user interface provided in SPD 2007. But, be aware that some requests can only be solved by code.

By all means go to the website to see what's involved; next time you read an article (or book) that shows how easy creating a DVWP is, you can smile to yourself.

Creating a Flashy DVWP

With that warning clearly given, let's move on to the more appealing, working, and (yes) flashy stuff that every teacher of DVWPs loves.

It's time to have different colors for the numbers of staff. Let's go for red for more than 200 per function and green for less than 50:

1. Go to the 250.00 in Figure 21.16. Select it and right-click. This can be tricky to get right, and you want to avoid the entire row being selected. Figure 21.17 shows what it looks like when you select the item.

FIGURE 21.17
Selecting the number correctly.

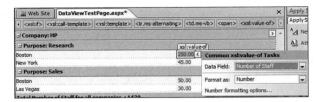

Figure 21.18 shows the result (top half) of doing a right-click (when the cursor is over the number).

FIGURE 21.18
Right-clicking correctly on the number.

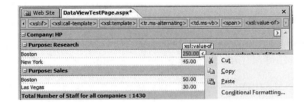

2. Select Conditional Formatting. A panel called Conditional Formatting appears in the rightmost column.

3. Now that you have the Conditional Formatting pane, select Create > Apply Formatting. This gives you Figure 21.19.

4. Click Click Here and fill in the first criteria (Number of Staff > 200), as shown in Figure 21.20.

FIGURE 21.19
The Conditional Criteria page.

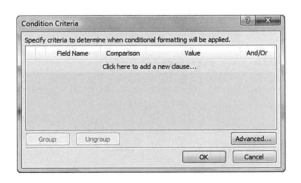

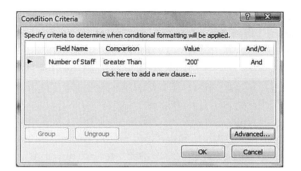

FIGURE 21.20
The first condition.

Note

Selecting Advanced gets you into the same kind of XPath/XSLT coding that caused problems in the earlier section.

5. Click OK. Fill in as much of the font information as you like (see Figure 21.21).

FIGURE 21.21
Specifying red for the high numbers.

6. Play around with some of the other options if you want. I'll just click OK and repeat the action for Number of Staff < 50 and green (which results in Figure 21.22).

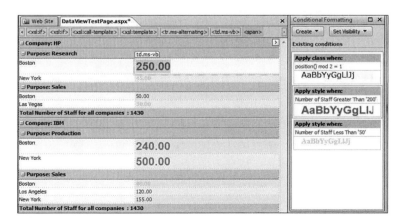

FIGURE 21.22
Red and green (and a large font) for large and small numbers, respectively.

In this book, you unfortunately can't see the colors that have been selected, so I made the font for the larger numbers large so that you can see (in Figure 21.22) that this kind of conditional formatting does work!

Summary

This hour looked at the roles of Data View web parts. It covered how to create them and how to customize them. It also noted that not all customization requirements can be easily solved by using the SPS 2007 user interface and that sometimes code will be required.

Q&A

Q. *You mentioned a problem with creating a view for a document library. What is it and how is it solved?*

A. In the DVWP for a library, the field with the address of the document is not a hyperlink, it's a text string. In other words, you always need to convert the contents of that field to Hyperlink (unless you are only using other data from the library, which seems unlikely).

There is, however, one problem. The file is usually in a different website. So, the filename, even if it includes the library name, isn't enough. Instead, we need to add the correct full path to the filenames. Figure 21.23 shows the top of a simple DVWP with a single field, URL Path (from My Book Documents).

FIGURE 21.23
The URL Path field in a DVWP.

Right-click the name and select Hyperlink. Fill in the address as shown in Figure 21.24.

Click OK. Now the Link in the DVWP will correctly open the document.

FIGURE 21.24
The formula for a hyperlink to a document in another site.

Q. *Can I use the web part connection between a standard web part and a Data View web part?*

A. Yes, provided they have a suitable matching field. You can also use the web part connection technique between two different Data View web parts.

Workshop

Quiz

1. Are you restricted to creating DVWPs from lists and libraries?

2. What is the main difference between creating a DVWP from a list or a library?

3. Can I do everything in a Data View by means of selection boxes?

Quiz Answers

1. It's easier to do that than most other things (provided the lists or libraries are in the same site collection). However, there are many other sources of information for DVWPs, such as databases (where it's best if these are SQL Server databases).

2. Libraries typically require hyperlinks, which usually require more effort to set up.

3. No. Some customization requires code.

Making Safety Copies of Your Data and Using Them

What You'll Learn in This Hour

▶ Saving your own copies of lists and sites

▶ Using different ways to save copies of your lists and sites

This hour identifies some of the different ways in which you can make copies of *your* key data and how you can use those copies to help *you*. There's still a need for that single backup specialist doing his stuff for the entire installation, but he has his own books. This hour makes *your* life easier and helps *you* sleep at night.

Using Colligo to Create a Copy to Use Offline

One idea to consider is to have a copy of the SharePoint data that is vital to you offline. Therefore, even if the server crashes and the server administrator uses all his skills to get the system back to what it was, you can still use (and, in some cases, work on) your data even though the server is down.

If you have Outlook 2007 on your client, you can use Outlook 2007 OST files as your offline copy of lists. However, I'm not going to go into detail about how to do that because there's a better way. This involves using a third-party product from a company called Colligo (www.colligo.com). Colligo had similar products for WSS 2.0.

I wouldn't recommend that you use a third-party product rather than a free method if it weren't for the fact that Colligo has a free product (Colligo Reader). As its name implies, Colligo Reader only allows you to read the contents of your SharePoint lists offline. If you want to be able to make changes offline and synchronize them back to the SharePoint site, you must pay $125 for a copy of Colligo Contributor.

If you already have Outlook 2007 installed on your clients, there *is* a case to be made for using the OST method of having offline copies of your lists, even though that method doesn't work as well.

Both Colligo products look identical after they are installed and a site is specified. Figure 22.1 shows how to specify a site you want to install within Colligo Reader (which is followed by a screen for selecting which lists and libraries you want to be included in the offline (but synchronized—in the Reader case, one way) copy). Figure 22.2 shows a document from Colligo Contributor 3.0.

FIGURE 22.1
Specifying a website in Colligo Reader.

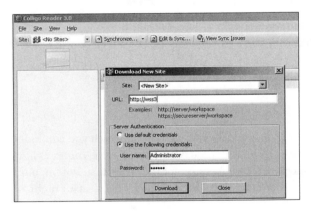

FIGURE 22.2
A document library in Colligo Contributor 3.0.

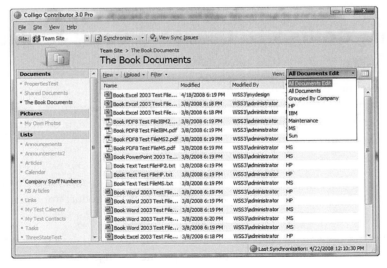

As you can see, both do a good job of simulating the WSS 3.0 look.

Using Save List as Template

Save List as Template and the equivalent Save Site as Template are standard in WSS 3.0. Typically, both create a copy of an existing list/site in another location. However, you can also use them to save your own copy of a list (for instance) in which you have just done a lot of work.

The procedure for using Save List as Template is straightforward. We'll use Save List as Template here. To copy your lists using the Save List as Template option, follow these steps:

1. Open the list. In this case, we'll use The Book Documents document library to show that a "list" could either be a list or a library.

2. Open the site http://wss3 and select The Book Documents from Quick Launch. Select Settings (see Figure 22.3).

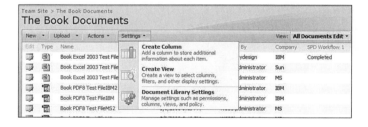

FIGURE 22.3
Accessing document library settings.

3. Select Document Library Settings. The user interface is aware that this is a document library, so the link we use here is Save Document Library as Template (arrowed in Figure 22.4).

4. Select Save Document Library as Template. You get an empty Figure 22.5. Complete it as indicated.

Note

The Include Content option (arrowed in Figure 22.5) is included for most of the lists and library types. If it is not selected, you still get the full structure of the list, but no items or documents. Then it's useful for creating a new list in another site that is based on this revised list. We, however, need the Include Content option; we are saving the list precisely because we amended the content and need a copy of that changed content.

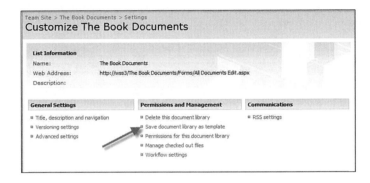

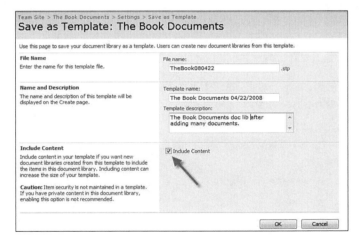

5. Click OK. You now see Figure 22.6.

At the moment, all we have done is save a copy of the List template (with content) in the SharePoint database. If the SharePoint installation crashes, we still lose the information we have just added.

The next step is therefore to make sure we have a copy of the List template on our client PC. To do this, follow these steps:

1. Click List Template Gallery. You now see Figure 22.7.

FIGURE 22.7
The List Template Gallery.

2. We want to save a copy of the third item. Move the cursor over the name (TheBook080422) and right-click (see Figure 22.8).

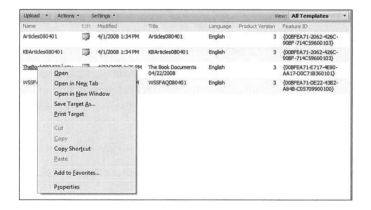

FIGURE 22.8
Right-clicking the template name before saving the template.

3. Select the Save Target As option. You can save this template to your client system (see Figure 22.9).

FIGURE 22.9
Saving an STP file.

You can change the filename. When you name a file, you want to look at the name in a file list and immediately know what it is and when it was saved. That's why I

Note

put both pieces of information in the filename; the date it was stored in your file system might not necessarily be the date the template was created.

In this scenario, if you have a site crash after you save your template (and saved a copy of it on your client), contact the server administrator after he has restored the backup. Tell him you have an intermediate list template. He (or you, if you have rights) can delete the list from his (restored system) version and add it back using your later template.

Note

A template isn't a way to modify a site or list, but it's something with which you can replace an existing list (or site) by first deleting the old site/list and adding it back.

A template is itself a snapshot of the state of the list/site at the time the template was created. A template can only be modified by using it to create a site/list, then amending the site/list, and finally saving a new copy of the template.

Using the Recycle Bins

Recycle Bins were introduced in the SharePoint v3 products. Having them available removes one reason for keeping copies: the incorrect deletion. A link to one of the two Recycle Bins is at the bottom of the Quick Launch section (provided that you have Delete rights).

The basic principle for Recycle Bins is that there are two levels of such bins:

▶ **A Recyle Bin for the user.** Set to a certain number of days (30 days, by default).

▶ **A Recyle Bin for the administrator.** Set to a percentage of the available disk space (default 50%). An administrator could decide not to have Recycle Bins at all or only one of them. Given the extra amount of work the administrator needs to do if Recycle Bins are set to off, it's hard to imagine a good reason to do this.

Figure 22.10 shows the final section of the Web Applications General Settings screen (found by going to Central Administration > Applications Management > Web Applications General Settings).

This is a setting for a particular web application. So, make sure that at the top of this page, you change the settings for web application to reflect the one for which you want to amend the settings (see Figure 20.11).

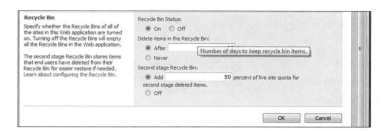

FIGURE 22.10
Specifying the Recycle Bin parameters.

> An off-the-subject but nonetheless important point: Figure 22.11 is where you set the maximum upload size for a document (or in the case of a "multiple upload" the size of a batch of documents) that is uploaded to a library.

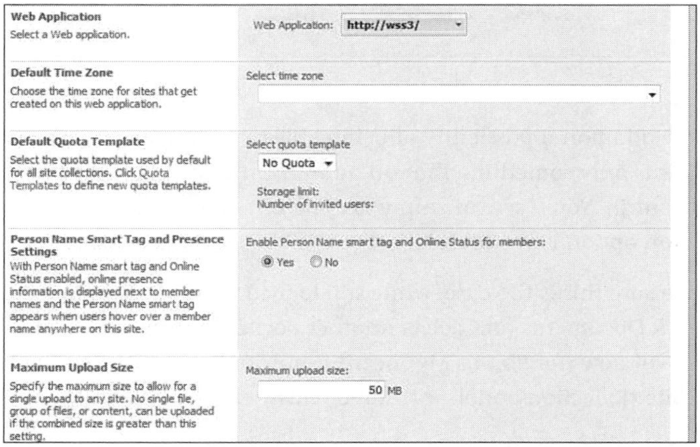

Tip

FIGURE 22.11
Changing the web application and looking at the maximum upload size.

Now let's see how the Recycle Bin works from a user's point of view:

1. (Back in the Team Site) Go to The Book Documents and delete the third item by first clicking the Edit button at the beginning of the row. This action gives you Figure 22.12. Then click Delete Item (arrowed).

2. Now there's a warning: Are you sure that you want to send this to the recycle bin? This warning contains only one button, and the list of documents is shown again, this time without the document (plus columns information— here Company=MS) we just deleted.

3. Go to Recycle Bin at the bottom of the Quick Launch section and select it. Figure 22.13 shows the Recycle Bin for the entire web application, which contains only the document we just deleted.

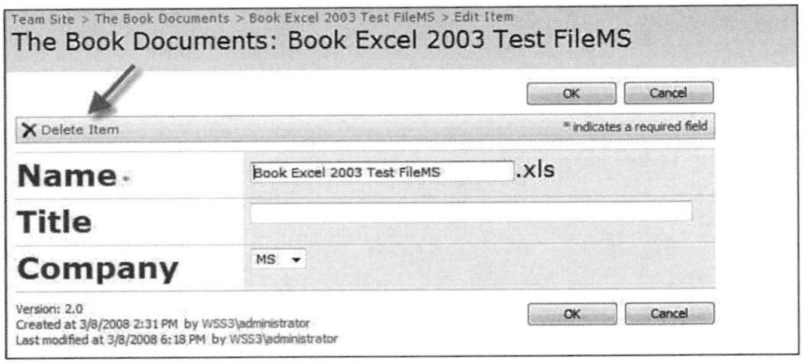

FIGURE 22.12
Deleting a document and its metadata.

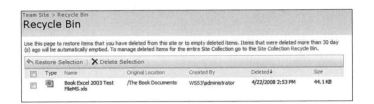

FIGURE 22.13
The Recycle Bin after one document has been deleted.

4. Note the additional possibility of being able to go to the Site Collection Recycle Bin. This is only something that an administrator can do. To prove this, sign in as MyContrib. You'll see an empty Recycle Bin, and the Manage the Entire Site Collection option has vanished.

5. To make sure this is the case, while still logged in as MyContrib go again to The Book Documents and delete another document (say, a PDF one). The Recycle Bin will now (for you as MyContrib) show only the PDF file; the Manage the Entire Site Collection option will still be missing.

6. Log in again as administrator, and your own Recycle Bin still shows only the deleted Excel file. If you click Site Collection Recycle Bin, however, you'll see both (see Figure 22.14).

Restoring (either from Figure 22.14 or from Figure 22.13) is obvious, so it's not covered here.

Let me just emphasize that Figure 22.14 is the (second-level) site administrator's Recycle Bin (http://wss3/_layouts/AdminRecycleBin.aspx) and not the (first-level) Recycle Bin of the administrator (http://wss3/_layouts/recyclebin.aspx). The other way to get to the site administrator's Recycle Bin is (when signed in as administrator) to go to Site Actions > Site Settings and select Recycle Bin from the Site Collection Administration column (see Figure 22.15).

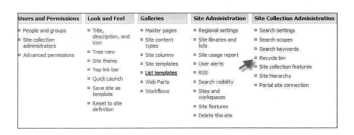

Making Copies Using stsadm

stsadm is the Swiss army knife of SharePoint administrator tools. You can find details on it by going to www.microsoft.com and searching for "Index for stsadm."

Here we only need to look at the backup and restore parameters.

Backup Using stsadm

The manual command-line method for making a backup copy is as follows:

1. Go to the server running WSS 3.0 and open the command prompt (Start > All Programs > Accessories > Command Prompt).

2. Work your way through the directory structure until you reach C:\Program Files\Common Files\\Microsoft Shared\web server extensions\12\BIN (see Figure 22.16).

   Figure 22.16 shows a partial list of the BIN directory. Go to this directory so that you, too, can check that stsadm.exe is included in that directory.

3. Enter the following command:

```
Stsadm -o backup  -filename <filename> -url  "http://wss3"
```

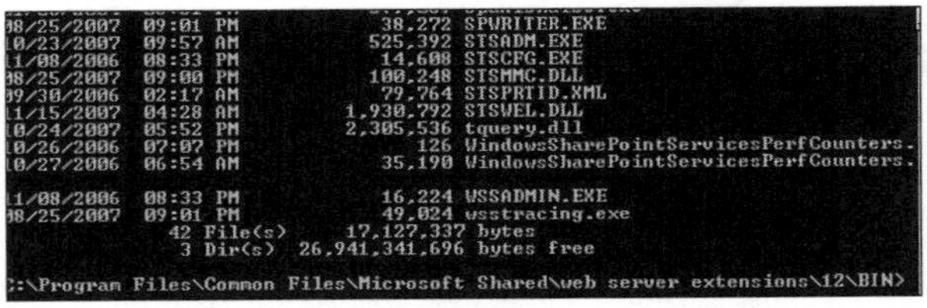

FIGURE 22.16
The correct location at the command-line prompt.

<filename> is the path and filename you want to save the backup as. Note that the filename is surrounded by quotation marks, just like the URL in the preceding example. Figure 22.17 shows this command along with the other backup alternative formats.

Tip

Use something like C:\backupsite1.sp for the filename rather than a name that uses the standard .bak extension so that you can keep all your WSS 3.0 backups separate.

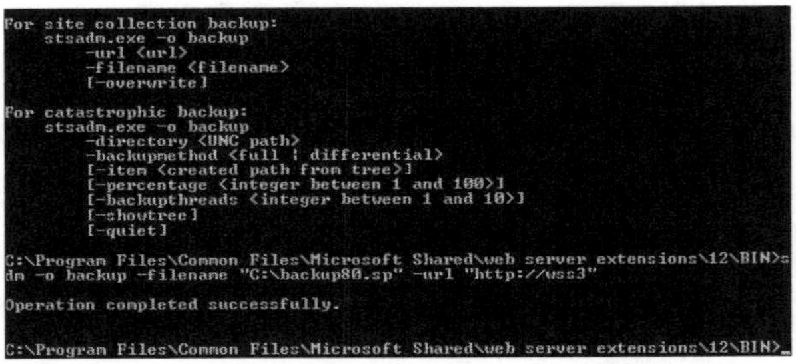

FIGURE 22.17
The stsadm backup command in operation.

Note

Save Site as Template is used for copies of a single site or subsite. stsadm backup is used for a copy of a site collection.

Because stsadm is a command-line tool, you can create a batch file to either make this all work via a single typed command or more commonly to schedule the running of the command.

Here's a suitable batch file:

1. Open Notepad (which is at Start > All Programs > Accessories), and copy the following lines into it:

```
C:
CD\
```

```
CD Program Files\Common Files\\Microsoft Shared\web server
extensions\12\BIN
Stsadm -o backup   -filename %1 -url  %2
```

2. Save this as **SPbackup.bat** in C:\WINDOWS. (C:\WINDOWS is, by default, included in the PATH statement.)

3. To run it, write the following at a command-line prompt:

```
SPbackup   "C:\SPbackup2.sp" "http://wss3:7595"
```

Note

Because these are both parameters, they can be varied every time the batch file is run. If you are scheduling it, have a different filename (and thus a different scheduled job) for every day of the week.

Figure 22.18 shows that batch file running in the command prompt.

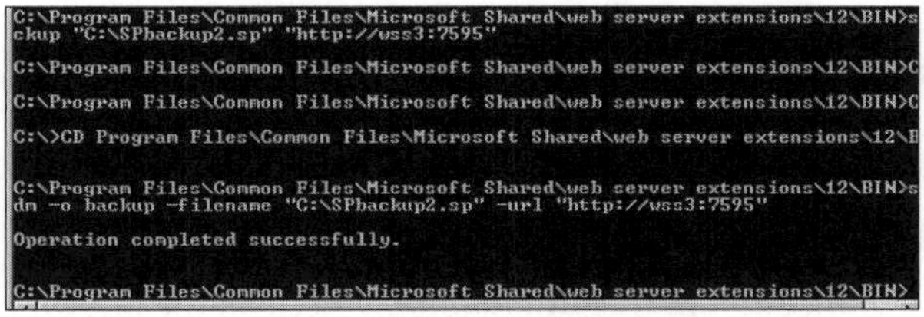

FIGURE 22.18
A batch file version of an stsadm backup.

Restore Using `stsadm`

The `restore` statement is similar to stsadm. Typically, `restore` is only used when needed and would not normally be used as a scheduled task.

The key, however, is that you cannot restore into an existing site collection because the restore itself creates a site collection. This means that you have the following steps:

1. Create a web application (but don't create a site collection).

2. Go down the directory structure until you reach C:\Program Files\Common Files\Microsoft Shared\web server extensions\12\BIN.

3. Enter the following command (which uses the port number of that new web application):

```
Stsadm -o restore -filename <filename> -url "http://wss3:portnumber"
```

This web application will be the original one when used as a genuine restore to re-cover a site collection that has been corrupted in the meantime. It can also be a new web application if the `restore` statement is being used to migrate a site collection from one server (or web application) to another.

Making Copies Using SharePoint Designer 2007

Another backup and restore command set that you can use is the one included in SharePoint Designer (SPD) 2007. The scope of this particular method is different from the scope of the `stsadm` backup/restore method, so there might be reasons why you choose this method even though it is a manual one.

The main attraction of this method is that you can specify exactly what you want to back up. You can, for instance, select to back up just a single site or a site together with its subsites.

Metadata is retained. So, for instance, a typical problem in SharePoint data migra-tion (that the time when a document is uploaded—and the person who uploaded it—is replaced by the time of the restore and the person who did the restore) is avoided and Created/Modified and CreatedBy/ModifiedBy field values are preserved.

Finally, it seems (although I'm hesitant to put my neck on the line for this one) that this method doesn't mean—like most other methods—that the backup and the restore must be done on identical version numbers of the WSS 3.0 (or MOSS 2007) software. With other methods, this can be a nuisance, because it means trying to find just the fix that was made on one server (which upped its version number) but not on the other server.

After all that preliminary information, here are the statements you need:

1. Open the site in SPD 2007.

2. Select Site on the menu line and the subitem Administration.

3. Choose Backup Website (see Figure 22.19).

4. We are now positioned at the subsite called BookSite1. The next screen gives us the option of saving just BookSite1 or BookSite1 plus its subsites (see Figure 22.20). (It's not clever enough to know that it has none!)

   You might think that the Advanced button (in Figure 22.20) will solve that problem by letting you select any site (with or without its subsites). In fact, however, all the Advanced button lets you do is say where to store the temporary backup files before the backup is downloaded to your client (see Figure 22.21).

FIGURE 22.19
Where in SPD
2007 to specify
a backup.

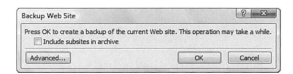

FIGURE 22.20
SPD 2007 back-
up: site or site
and subsites.

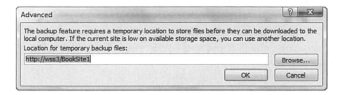

FIGURE 22.21
SPD 2007 back-
up: advanced
setting.

So, if you want to back up BookSite2, for example, cancel this entire procedure and first make sure that SharePoint Designer is open at BookSite2, and only then do Site > Administration > Backup.

5. Here we're just going to use the default location (and thus ignore the Advanced option) and be happy with backing up BookSite1. So, at Figure 22.20, we just click OK.

Figure 22.22 shows the request for where to store the files, and later we can check that location to see what has been stored. We'll find (in this case) a single file called BookSite1Backup.cmp (the name I gave) that has a size of 2599KB.

FIGURE 22.22
SPD 2007 back-up: saving the package.

Restore is the reverse:

1. Create a site using the Blank Site template (File > New > website > SharePoint Template > Blank Site), and most important, change the address to http://wss3/BookSite3 (in this case).

Note

Some books and blogs say that you should do "File > New > website > General > Empty website."

That might have worked in SPD 2007 when it was released, but in SPD 2007 with SP1 it does not work, and step 4 below gives the message that you can only restore to an empty site. Using SharePoint Template and Blank Site does work.

2. Click OK. That site will open in SharePoint Designer 2007.

3. Select Site > Administration > Restore Website.

4. Find the backup file, select Open, and click OK.

Summary

This hour looked at various ways to make copies of a part of a WSS 3.0 installation. We also covered moving data that is stored in a WSS 2.0 site, holding offline copies of data, the Recycle Bin, using Save List as Template, and using both stsadm and Share-Point Designer 2007 methods of backup and restore.

Q&A

Q. *You talked about scheduling a backup using a batch file. How do you do it?*

A. To schedule a backup using a batch file, follow these steps:

1. In Windows 2003, go to Start > Control Panel > Scheduled Tasks > Add Scheduled Task (see Figure 22.23).

2. A wizard guides you through the process. In our case, we need to browse for our batch file because the wizard initially shows only applications that have been installed on the server. Once we browse to C:\WINDOWS and select SPbackup.bat, we get Figure 22.24. We can say when we want the batch file to run.

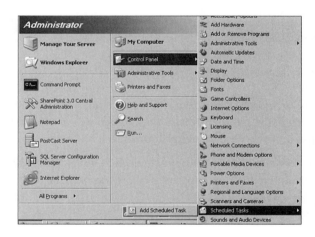

FIGURE 22.23
Selecting scheduled tasks.

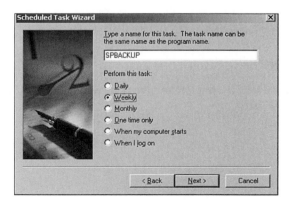

FIGURE 22.24
Specifying the name and how often the task is carried out.

3. You're then asked for the weekly time and day of the week (and given the chance to say every two, three, or four weeks rather than every week). I'm setting it to Sunday.

4. You're then asked for the username under which the task is to be run. Use the default (in our case) WSS3\Administrator.

5. The final screen confirms what we have entered. Click Finish. The scheduled task is ready to run on Sunday.

What will now happen is that on Sunday the task will run as scheduled, and SP-BACKUP will run and (oops!) will wait for data because it is waiting for values for %1 and %2 to be input. (In our earlier test, we entered these by hand.)

There's a simple way to correct this. Create (using the Notepad technique described earlier) for each day of the week different batch files that don't need parameters (in C:\WINDOWS).

For instance, SPbackupmon.BAT would consist of a single line:

```
SPbackup "C:\SPBACKUPMON.SP" "http://wss3"
```

Now when SPbackupmon.BAT has been scheduled to run weekly on Mondays, it will run every Monday at the specified time. SPbackupmon will start and will, in turn, start SPbackup complete with the correct parameters for Monday.

Repeat this for every day of the week (for equivalently named files), and we'll have seven (automatically created) backup copies before they start being overwritten.

Workshop

Quiz

1. Is a Recycle Bin always available to me?

2. Can I use Save Site as Template to save a site and its subsites?

3. Can I use stsadm backup to save a single site?

Quiz Answers

1. A Recycle Bin is always available to you if you have the right to delete items or documents and if the administrator has retained the default value of having a Recycle Bin.

2. No. You can only use Save Site as Template to save a single site. This single site may be a subsite.

3. With `stsadm` backup, you can save only a site collection. Of course, that site collection could consist only of a single site, and in that case, but only that case, you could save a single site with `stsadm` backup.

HOUR 23

Enhancing Your WSS 3.0 Sites: Microsoft Official Possibilities

What You'll Learn in This Hour

▶ Adding foreign-language sites
▶ Adding both types of Microsoft application templates

Adding Foreign Languages

These days, companies work internationally. For this reason, Microsoft provides the possibility of having information and menu items in several languages.

If you've ever seen a Microsoft presentation that includes languages, you've probably seen a web page that is full of useful information and where there are two or more little flag icons in the upper right of the page. The Microsoft presenters will show that when you click the (say) German flag, a German translation of the same page appears.

That kind of functionality uses "variations," which come only with MOSS. It will work only if the site template chosen is a Publishing template.

That "translated" page is not translated by magic, just by clicking an icon. Instead, the variation includes the (translated by someone) German-language version of the content. MOSS supplies only the menus and other things around the content (the basic user interface) that are automatically created in German.

WSS 3.0 offers completely different sites, where everything is in a different language. With WSS 3.0, you get the kind of (say) German language site that you would get if you installed the German version of WSS 3.0. The difference is that this German site occurs within an otherwise normal English-language installation.

Note

> Administration messages always come in the language of the administration site, and that site (and the default site) is always created in the language of the language version of WSS 3.0 that was installed.

Installing and Using Language Packs

Microsoft provides free downloads for language packs. Just as with WSS 3.0, there are both original Language Packs and Language Pack Service Pack 1s. Unlike WSS 3.0, there is no Language Pack including Service Pack 1.

If you have WSS 3.0 (no service pack), you install only the Language Pack. If you have WSS 3.0 including SP1, you first install the Language Pack and then the Language Pack SP1.

Both of the following addresses are for all language versions of the Language Pack. (There is a different download for each different language.) These addresses are both for the 32-bit versions of the downloads. Two equivalent 64-bit downloads are also available.

- ▶ WSS 3.0 Language Pack.

    www.microsoft.com/downloads/details.aspx?FamilyID=36ee1bf0-652c-4e38-b247-f29b3eefa048&DisplayLang=en

- ▶ WSS 3.0 Language Pack SP1.

    www.microsoft.com/downloads/details.aspx?FamilyId=05046B1D-DD7B-456A-8838-8D978C5F3579%20&displaylang=en

Because of the displaylang=en at the end of the preceding address, when the page is accessed, it will show English in the Change Language row. If you want to download the German language version, you need to do the following (note step 2, which is easily missed):

1. Change the language in the Change Language row to German.

2. Click the Change button (also in the Change Language row).

3. Click Download.

The intermediate selection of Change tells the following download which language you want, and it will then download the right one (and you will get German language functionality). Without the selection of Change, the English version would be downloaded.

Figure 23.1 shows the situation after selecting German and then specifying Change.

FIGURE 23.1
Correctly downloading the German language pack.

In other words, if you don't see the language of the Language Pack you are downloading when you click Download, you won't get that language's Language Pack.

At the end of the Language Pack install, you have the opportunity to run the SharePoint Configuration Wizard. If you immediately install the Language Pack SP1 next, there's no need to do that; just go directly to the SP1 install.

Tip

Once the installation of the Language Pack SP1 is done, you must run the SharePoint Configuration Wizard.

When the wizard finishes, don't be irritated if you are transferred to a Welcome page for Search Server 2008. Search Server 2008 is a bit too aggressive in taking over links to standard WSS 3.0 locations. In this case, the test in the next few paragraphs will show you whether the Language Pack has been installed correctly.

You have now installed the Language Pack (and probably also the Language Pack SP1) and the wizard has run. What effect does that have on your WSS 3.0 installation? At first sight, it has absolutely no effect. Everything looks just the same as it was. You see the change only when you create a site. So, let's create a site and see what's changed: Go to http://wss3 in the browser and do Site Actions > Create > Sites and Workspaces.

What you will now see in the Create page is a Language drop-down offering English and German (Figure 23.2, left side). Under it is a full set of the English language templates (the standard ones and the ones we created earlier in the book).

If you select German, you see a selection of sites in German (see Figure 23.2, right side).

These are *only* the standard sites. (But, they are in their German language forms: the two columns are the equivalent of Collaboration and Meetings, and they contain exactly the same site templates that are available in English in the English language list.)

They are thus missing German versions of the ones we have created (Enterprise/Search Center and Custom/Red Site Template). However, there is also a German language pack available for Search Server 2008 that would no doubt also install Search Center in German, making that available in this list, too (Search Server 2008 Language Pack: www.microsoft.com/downloads/details.aspx?familyid=2b7eb5f7-6358-4086-a80f-62f3fb289b24&displaylang=en).

Select the first Site (Teamwebsite) in the leftmost column of the German language template section. Name the site **German Team Site**, and just for fun give it the URL http://wss3/Deutsch. Then click Create.

FIGURE 23.2
Comparing the available English and German templates.

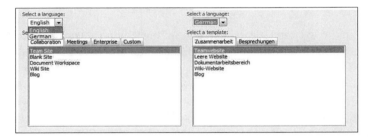

Figure 23.3 shows the site we have now created.

Strangely similar despite the different language for everything, isn't it?

FIGURE 23.3
A German team site.

What else is it important to know about language packs?

You can install as many different languages as you like—that Select a Language drop-down in Figure 23.2 will just get larger. Having installed the different languages, you can have sites in all of them if you feel like it. All, however, are completely independent of one another.

Be aware of the need, in one specific case, to install the English language version of the Language Pack if you installed WSS 3.0 using one of the other language versions of the download. This specific case relates to the 40 application templates that Microsoft supplies by download to anyone who wants them. (The application templates are discussed and worked on in the next section.)

These application templates are all written in English. They will work only in a non-English WSS 3.0 installation if the *English* language pack has been installed.

Using Application Templates

Microsoft provides a set of 40 downloadable application templates they call the "Fantastic 40." They became available several months after the release of the Share-Point v3 products and provide sample sites for 40 different working areas.

To a certain extent, the name Fantastic 40 is justified. They are genuinely different, and in many cases they do have interesting functionality. However, some contain errors. Microsoft states that you can use these templates not only as a sample of what can be done (a valid statement) but also as something you can use as they are or build on for your own applications.

Consider these application templates as inspiration for your site (but then create a site yourself from scratch).

Tip

The Fantastic 40 application templates are all for WSS 3.0. Several months after they were released, a much smaller set of application templates was released for MOSS 2007. (The WSS 3.0 templates can also be used in a MOSS installation.)

Note

There are 2 sets of 20 application templates. No real overlaps exist between the two sets:

▶ **Site Admin Application Templates**. Created as site template files (STP) that you can upload to a Site Template Gallery using the same kind of method we used in an earlier hour to upload a List template.

▶ **Server Application Templates**. Created as SharePoint Solution packages (wsp) that require more work to upload than STP files.

Installing a Site Admin Application Template

From the first set of templates, let's download the Product and Marketing Requirements Planning application template. You can download this template from www.microsoft.com/downloads/details.aspx?familyid=14c8ae74-4953-4e5b-9243-3687515a4437&displaylang=en.

Tip

> If you want to find a list of application templates quickly, go to one of the WSS FAQ sites (such as http://www.wssv3faq.com) and search on "application templates." The links to the individual Fantastic 40 templates all start with *Windows SharePoint Services 3.0*. Add, for instance, "marketing" to the search for the one we need here. Make sure that the one you find says 3.0, because you'll also get hits for the version 2 ones and some have the same name.

Download and run the template using your client. At this point, you are only creating an STP file, not actually doing anything in connection with the WSS 3.0 server.

The final step in the installation asks you where the files should be located. I put them on C: because only two files are generated: ProductPlanning.stp and readme.txt. ProductPlanning.stp is a completely standard site template, so it needs to first be uploaded to a site gallery. Then you can create a new site using this template.

The following steps show how to upload the template to a site gallery:

1. As the administrator, open http://wss3 and choose Site Actions > Site Settings > Site Templates (in the Galleries column). Doing so produces Figure 23.4, where you click Upload.

2. Specify ProjectPlanning.stp (see Figure 23.5). The template is included in the Site Template Gallery.

FIGURE 23.4
The Site Template Gallery (before).

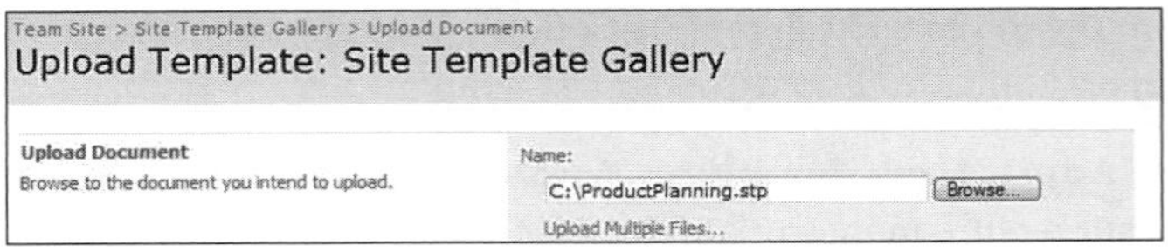

FIGURE 23.5
Uploading a site template.

Note

Watch out. The browser will again show the Upload Template page as in Figure 23.5, only with the entry box empty. Click Site Template Gallery in the menu line (above the Title) to see that the ProductPlanning template has been added to the gallery (Figure 23.4 with an extra row).

The next steps show how to use the template to create a site:

1. Go to Home and choose Site Actions > Create > Sites and Templates. At first, you notice no difference in this page, but then click Custom in the Template Selection section. You'll see a new entry, Product and Marketing Requirements Planning (see Figure 23.6).

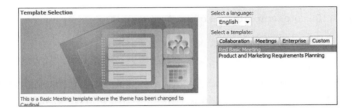

FIGURE 23.6
The revised template selection, including a site admin template.

2. Name the new site **Requirements Planning** and specify the address http://wss3/Planning. Select the Product and Requirements Planning template. A new site will be created that looks (part image only) like Figure 23.7.

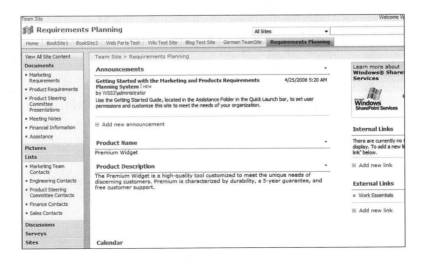

FIGURE 23.7
The Requirements Planning site.

You might generate an error message when you try to add the site. If so, try again but with a marginally different setting. In my case, my failed attempt accessed the website using the TCP (http://192.168.1.198) address, and my successful addition of the site used http://wss3. A temporary communications hiccup between the client and the server might also cause this problem.

All the other stp templates install the same way.

Installing a Server Application Template

The server templates require care. No matter which server template you install, you first must install the template that is called the core template. Then you can install one (or more) of the actual templates.

So, let's install the core template and one actual template:

1. Go to the server. (This installation must be done on the server.)

2. Download the core template
   (www.microsoft.com/downloads/details.aspx?FamilyId=C1039E13-94DA-4D7D-8CAE-3B96FA5A4045&displaylang=en). That gets you a file called
   ApplicationTemplateCore.wsp and another readme.txt. If you specify C: here again, the site admin templates' readme.txt will be overwritten by the server templates' readme.txt.

3. Download the Room and Equipment Reservations template
   (www.microsoft.com/downloads/details.aspx?familyid=3cf62351-d91d-44ee-9169-68303c205292&displaylang=en). (I've chosen this template for a reason.)
   That will get you a file called RoomEquipmentReservations.wsp and (again)
   the server templates' readme.txt file.

For the installation phase of the templates, the core template and the Room Equipment template need to either be located in the bin directory or the Path parameter in the operating system and needs to include C:\Program Files\Common Files\Microsoft Shared\web server extensions\12\BIN (and in that case the following commands can be run from the directory [any directory] containing the two WSP files).

I copy the two files to C:\Program Files\Common Files\Microsoft Shared\web server extensions\12\BIN from the C: drive. (The other option, Path, is probably the better long-term solution.)

Now that the two WSP files are in C:\Program Files\Common Files\Microsoft Shared\web server extensions\12\BIN, do the following:

1. Open the command prompt and work your way down to C:\Program Files\Common Files\Microsoft Shared\web server extensions\12\BIN.

2. Do (this assumes a single-server installation, hence the -local parameter in commands 2 and 5):

    1. `stsadm -o addsolution -filename ApplicationTemplateCore.wsp` `<Enter>`

    2. `stsadm -o deploysolution -name ApplicationTemplateCore.` `wsp -local -allowgacdeployment <Enter>`

    3. `stsadm -o copyappbincontent <Enter>`

    4. `stsadm -o addsolution -filename RoomEquipmentReservations.wsp` `<Enter>`

    5. `stsadm -o deploysolution -name RoomEquipmentReservations` `wsp -local -allowgacdeployment <Enter>`

    Wait for the "Operation completed successfully" message after each of these lines.

Figure 23.8 shows commands 1–5 in the command prompt session.

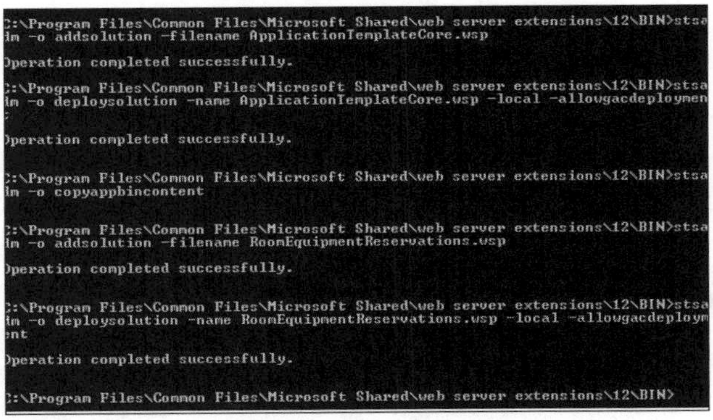

FIGURE 23.8
The full command-line session for core plus template installation.

Tip

If you are installing more than one server template, put all the preceding commands in a batch file so that you can just copy/paste/amend the additional two lines you need for each additional template.

Now, confirm that the operations completed successfully by following these steps:

1. Go back to your client and access the Central Administration.

2. Select Operations > Solution Management (see Figure 23.9).

FIGURE 23.9
Accessing Solution Management.

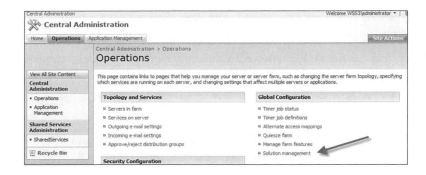

In Figure 23.10, you should see the two new templates with the previously installed Extended Blog Edition.

FIGURE 23.10
Solution Management showing the new WSP templates.

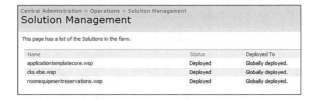

Having made sure they are both (all) marked as Globally Deployed, follow these steps:

1. Go back to the server.

2. Open the command prompt.

3. Enter **iisreset** (see Figure 23.11).

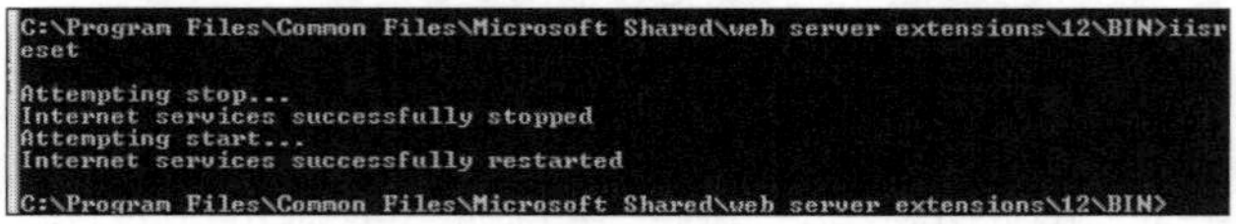

FIGURE 23.11
Doing iisreset.

We can now create a site based on that new template by doing the following:

1. Go to http://wss3 in your client PC and choose Site Actions > Create > Sites and Workspaces. In the Template Selection, you see the new Room and Equipment Reservations template (see Figure 23.12).

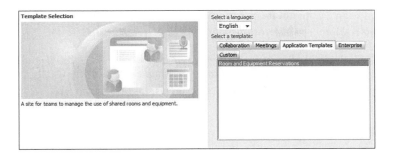

FIGURE 23.12
The revised template selection, including a server application template.

2. Name the site **Room Reservations v1**, and specify the web address http://wss3/Reservations1. Click Create. Figure 23.13 is what you have generated.

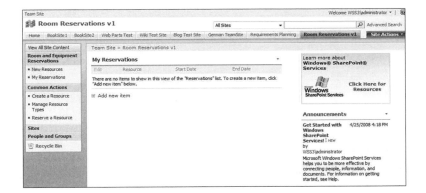

FIGURE 23.13
Room Reservations v1 (the standard version).

The template would be useful if it weren't for the fact that there are some problems with the way this template was done. However, it is available and free, and the SharePoint community can fix it.

Correcting Errors in a Server Application Template

One problem with this template was spotted by early (European) users who noticed that it required U.S. date formats. Fellow SharePoint MVP Steven Van de Craen wrote a revised version called Rooms and Equipment Reservations v2 (UNOFFICIAL), which corrects this error. (The blog talking about this with links to the downloads—note the two different versions for different data formats—is at www.moss2007.be/blogs/vandest/archive/2008/04/21/rooms-and-equipment-reservations-v2-unofficial.aspx.)

His version is an STP template and requires that the core template and the standard Rooms and Equipment Reservations template are already installed.

Go to his web page and follow a standard procedure for first uploading a STP template to the Site Template Gallery and then creating a site that will use this new version. I've done this offline, and Figure 23.14 shows the result.

FIGURE 23.14
Room Reservations v2 (the enhanced version).

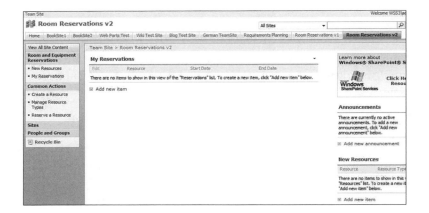

Summary

This hour discussed foreign language packs, which create sites in other languages.

Application templates are supplied with little or no support, and they are best used as samples. The SharePoint community sometimes provides code that extends or corrects an application template.

Q&A

Q. *Which is better, a German language installation with an English language pack or an English installation with a German language pack?*

A. If you install the English version of WSS 3.0, you are installing the version of the code that is used worldwide by the most people by far. In addition, your administrator site will be in English, which means that all error messages will be in English. If you install the German version of WSS 3.0, you install a version that has nowhere near the numbers of the English version. Your administrator site will be in German, so all the error messages will be in German.

If you have an error message you don't understand, search Google for it. If you do, you're likely to find more hits that match your search if the sentence you search for is in English than in German (and your own translation of the German text won't be Microsoft's). There are also more books in English than in German.

My recommendation is to install the English language version of the software and use language packs for the sites.

Workshop

Quiz

1. Are WSS 3.0 foreign language sites translated copies of the English language sites?

2. Is the first step in an application templates installation uploading them to a Site Template Gallery?

Quiz Answers

1. No, the foreign language sites are completely independent and have their own text, which may or may not be a translation of an English language site.

2. Only half of the application templates can be installed starting with that step. The second half (the server application templates) need to be installed using a more complicated approach that requires work on the server.

Enhancing Your WSS 3.0 Sites: Using Third-Party Web Parts

What You'll Learn in This Hour

- ▶ Various third-party web parts
- ▶ Installing and using web parts
- ▶ Pros and cons of free web parts

Using Web Parts to Enhance Your WSS 3.0 Site

WSS 3.0 comes with a large number of built-in web parts. Some of these are used mainly as delivered, whereas others can be modified extensively. MOSS 2007 comes with additional built-in web parts, one of which (the Content Query web part) can be enhanced dramatically with your own code. Web parts can also be created by SharePoint developers, typically using Visual Studio 2005 (and VS 2008).

All these various web parts can enhance websites. But what if you have WSS 3.0 and want to have a function that is perhaps included in MOSS 2007 or requires someone to program it? Are you forced to upgrade or hire a programmer? Given that situation, you can see whether someone or some company has already written such a web part and made it available for use (for a fee or for free).

> **Note**
>
> Other (mainly commercial) applications have to do with SharePoint, promising better administrator tools or improved functionality (such as improved workflows). This hour does not cover those. Instead, we just look at adding web parts.

This chapter is divided into two sections. The first section deals with free web parts, and the second part discusses commercial web parts.

Using Free Web Parts

There are both positives and negatives to using free web parts.

The main positive is that the people who write them and make them available do so to gain the attention and respect of their peers. They have a personal interest in the web part working and working well. A second positive—in some cases—is that sometimes full source code is made available so that others in the SharePoint community can help solve bugs or bring out improved versions.

There are a few negatives, too. For instance, typically (but not always), installation of such web parts requires some hands-on work. Another negative is that the web part's writer might not provide any support. Even if the writer does provide support, that support (and maybe even the website containing the download of the web part) may vanish as the writer moves on to other things.

Be aware of these problem areas and work around them. What you don't typically need to be worried about is the web part destroying your data. What you do need to consider is whether the web part *exactly* meets your requirements, because just as with commercial products, it's unlikely that amendments will be made. After all, it's likely that the web part was written to solve a problem the writer was experiencing; only later did the writer decide to make it available to the SharePoint community.

For long-lasting web parts, use one of the many products on the Codeplex site—especially those in the SharePoint Community Kit.

Free Web Part for RSS Feeds

A RSS Reader web part is available in MOSS 2007 out of the box, but the WSS 3.0 product doesn't have one. For people who want to include some RSS feeds in their WSS 3.0 web pages, that's a major omission.

Note

> Phil Wicklund wrote a RSS Reader web part for WSS 3.0. It is available via Codeplex (www.codeplex.com/RSSReaderWebPart). Click the latest release under Current Release to get the latest downloadable version.

This RSS Reader web part is supplied as a single WSP file (RssReaderWebPart.wsp), so you need to download it to the server's hard disk (to C:\) and deploy it. To do this, follow these steps:

1. Go to the usual bin location (C:\Program Files\Common Files\Microsoft Shared\web server extensions\12\BIN).

2. Execute the following statement:

```
STSADM -o addsolution -filename c:\rssreaderwebpart.wsp
```

> The installation instructions provided by Phil Wicklund say that you need "either WSS_Medium or Full trust in the web.config file of the web application that you're adding it to." Ignore this instruction and see what happens.

3. Run Central Administration and click Operations. Select Solution Management (arrowed in Figure 24.1).

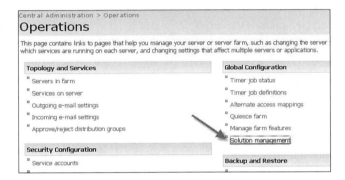

FIGURE 24.1
Starting Solution Management.

You are shown a list of SharePoint solutions that should be available on your site. Now, the RSSReaderWebPart needs to be deployed.

3. Click rssreaderwebpart.wsp. This starts the process of deploying it.

4. Select Deploy Solution (see Figure 24.2) and accept all the defaults in the Deploy Solution page which follows.

```
Central Administration > Operations > Solution Management > Solution Properties
Solution Properties

Deploy Solution  |  Remove Solution  |  Back to Solutions

Name:                                    rssreaderwebpart.wsp
Type:                                    Core Solution
Contains Web Application Resource:       Yes
Contains Global Assembly:                No
Contains Code Access Security Policy:    No
Deployment Server Type:                  Front-end Web server
Deployment Status:                       Not Deployed
Deployed To:                             None
Last Operation Result:                   No operation has been performed on the solution.
```

FIGURE 24.2
Confirming the solution properties.

Now that the web part has been deployed globally, we can leave the server and go back to the client PC.

The next steps show how to use the RSS Reader web part we've just added:

1. Open the site in the browser at http://wss3 (that is, the default site) and select Site Actions > Edit Page. Click the Add a Web Part link in the rightmost column.

2. Figure 24.3 shows part of the list of web parts currently available to us. This includes the RSS Reader web part. Select that and click OK.

FIGURE 24.3
The list of web parts, including RSS Reader.

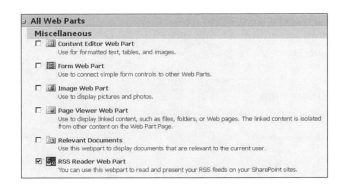

3. Figure 24.4 shows the top of the resulting rightmost column. To "specify the feed," click the upper-right downward arrow (see Figure 24.4).

FIGURE 24.4
How to modify the RSS Reader web part.

Clicking that arrow opens a new pane (see Figure 24.5).

4. Select Modify Shared Web Part and (as shown in Figure 24.6) add an RSS feed. You also need to specify whether just the titles or the whole text should be visible.

FIGURE 24.5
Starting to modify the RSS Reader web part.

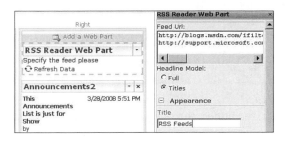

FIGURE 24.6
Specifying the feeds for the RSS Reader web part.

5. Click OK. Control is returned to the default page. At this point, choose Exit Edit Page.

   If you see Figure 24.7, you'll know that you shouldn't have disregarded the earlier warning about web.config. I wanted you to ignore the warning so that you encountered this problem; it demonstrates one of the issues with free web parts. The next steps will solve it.

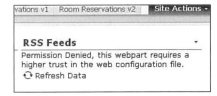

FIGURE 24.7
Permission denied for the RSS Reader web part.

6. Go to the server and look for the web.config for this web application. The way I usually do this is to do a search on the server for web.config and try to work out which is the right one to change. (If I can't work it out, I change them all.)

   Figure 24.8 gives part of such a list on the server. The default web application is at port 80, so the config.web at ...\virtualdirectories\80 is the one to amend.

   This looks right (and WSS_Medium is specified there), so what's the problem?

FIGURE 24.8
The first trust-level location in web.config.

```
</SharePoint>
<system.web>
    <securityPolicy>
        <trustLevel name="WSS_Medium" policyFile="C:\Program Files\Common
        <trustLevel name="WSS_Minimal" policyFile="C:\Program Files\Commor
    </securityPolicy>
```

The problem is that the writer's instructions in codeplex for the web part were incorrect. In those instructions, he said that WSS_Medium was enough. In fact, Full is necessary as he told me in an email. Figure 24.9 shows the change that was necessary (in a different part of the web.config file).

FIGURE 24.9
Amending web.config in the correct place.

```
            <add name="SharedServicesQuickLaunchProvider" description="Quicl
            <add name="UsagePagesSiteMapProvider" description="Provider for
        </providers>
    </siteMap>
    <trust level="Full" originUrl="" />
    <webParts>
        <transformers>
            <add name="TransformableFilterValuesToFilterValuesTransformer" ·
```

As a result of that change, the web part now produced the information shown in the default page's rightmost column (see Figure 24.10).

FIGURE 24.10
The working RSS Reader web part.

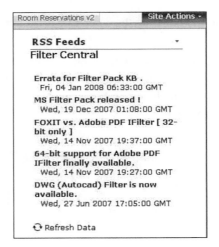

Room Reservations v2   Site Actions ·

RSS Feeds   ▾
Filter Central

Errata for Filter Pack KB .
Fri, 04 Jan 2008 06:33:00 GMT
MS Filter Pack released !
Wed, 19 Dec 2007 01:08:00 GMT
FOXIT vs. Adobe PDF IFilter [32-bit only]
Wed, 14 Nov 2007 19:37:00 GMT
64-bit support for Adobe PDF IFilter finally available.
Wed, 14 Nov 2007 19:27:00 GMT
DWG (Autocad) Filter is now available.
Wed, 27 Jun 2007 17:05:00 GMT

↻ Refresh Data

Note

This example shows the pros and cons of using free third-party web parts:

Pro: If you have problems, you can contact the writer who may help you move forward. The web part is free, so you don't need permission to buy it.

Con: The installations generally require manual work. Web parts are written for a specific environment (here, Full).

To get this web part listed in your set of web parts, go the Web Parts Gallery. Select Site Actions > Site Settings > Web Parts (in the Galleries column). Click New. A list of web parts appears, including the RSS Reader. Select it and click Populate Gallery. The web part is listed as both a solution and as a web part.

Using Commercial Web Parts

The two companies that make the largest number of commercial web parts are KWizCom (www.kwizcom.com) and Bamboo Solutions (http://store.bamboosolutions.com/). This section briefly looks at a web part from Bamboo Solutions. In addition, we look at a very useful low-priced web part from a Swiss company, Advis.

All three companies have trial versions of their web parts. Typical prices these days are around $500 per server, but they vary a lot. All three companies mentioned here are open about their prices and make it relatively easy to download and order them.

Web Part from Bamboo Solutions

Instead of having web parts from both KWizCom and Bamboo Solutions in the book, this hour includes details of a Bamboo Solutions web part. Similar details for a KWizCom web part are available on the website of the book.

Getting a trial version from Bamboo Solutions involved registering, adding the free trial version to the shopping basket, and "buying it" via several screens. Getting a paper about it (good and detailed, but with no installation instructions) required the same steps.

This section looks at the Chart Plus web part. The trial product download is a zip file containing a Setup.bat and four directories, so you first have to extract it to a directory on the server somewhere (see Figure 24.11).

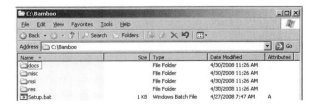

FIGURE 24.11
The contents of the Bamboo zip file.

Follow these steps to install the web part:

1. Run setup and select the web part. This gives you Figure 24.12.

FIGURE 24.12
Starting the Bamboo Chart Plus Web Part Wizard.

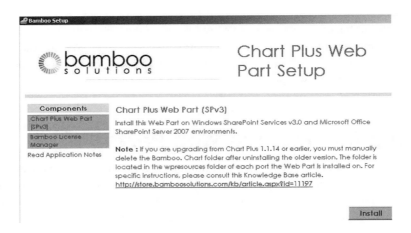

2. Click Install. This results in Figure 24.13.

FIGURE 24.13
Bamboo lets you specify where the web part is to be used.

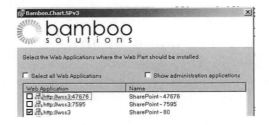

An "Installation complete" message appears. This message indicates errors and directs you to a log file to see them. (They are a warning only.)

3. Move to the client and access http://wss3. Select Site Actions > Edit Page > Add a Web Part. Figure 24.14 shows the relevant part of the current list.

FIGURE 24.14
Adding the Bamboo ChartPlus web part.

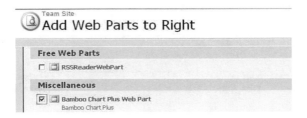

4. Click Add. The web part is visible but it needs configuring. Select the small downward arrow at the top right to get the additional box where it can be configured.

Figure 24.15 is one section of the configuration box, with several things filled in. You get a drop-down with a complete selection of the lists in that web collection. When you select one, the other related entry fields then contain suitable field names and so on.

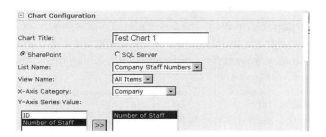

FIGURE 24.15
Configuring the
Bamboo Chart
Plus web part.

With less than 5 minutes of work adding and configuring the web part, you get the result of the Bamboo Chart Plus web part (see Figure 24.16).

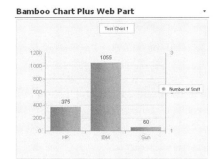

FIGURE 24.16
A working Bam-
boo Chart Plus
web part.

Web Part from Advis

At Advis, I chose the Change My Password (v3) web part (http://sharepoint.advis.ch/WebParts/ChangeMyPasswordV3/tabid/114/Default.aspx). This web part allows local users (and AD users) to change their passwords, which means that if you have local users you don't necessarily need to give them (security challenged) permanent passwords. (Advis also has a Change My Expired Password web part that might save administrators even more time!)

You must register at Advis, but once you do, you can access a page that includes the download link and a link to the (good) manual.

Installation requires a small amount of manual effort and does not install with a single click, like the Bamboo web part. However, it is considerably cheaper than the web part from Bamboo Solutions (at $129 per server), so having to write a single `stsadm` statement on the server is forgivable.

The zip file contains two files: a CAB file and a PDF file with the manual.

Follow these steps to install the Advis web part:

1. After extracting the zip file to the server's hard disk, open the command prompt and go to the usual bin location (C:\Program Files\Common Files\ Microsoft Shared\web server extensions\12\BIN). Run the following statement (assuming you extracted the files to C:\Advis):

   ```
   STSADM.exe -o addwppack -filename C:\Advis\ChangeMyPassword_v3.0.0.0.CAB -
   globalinstall -force
   ```

2. Go back to the client and access http://wss3. Select Site Actions > Edit Page > Add a Web Part. Figure 24.17 shows part of the list.

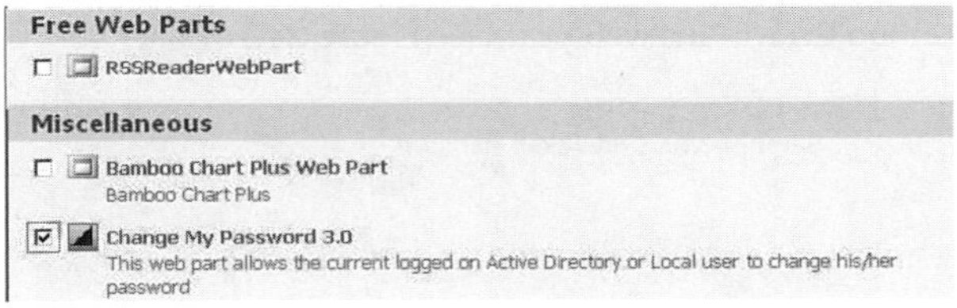

FIGURE 24.17
A list of web parts, including the Advis one.

This brings up the screen in Figure 24.18, which shows the effect of not yet paying for the nontrial version.

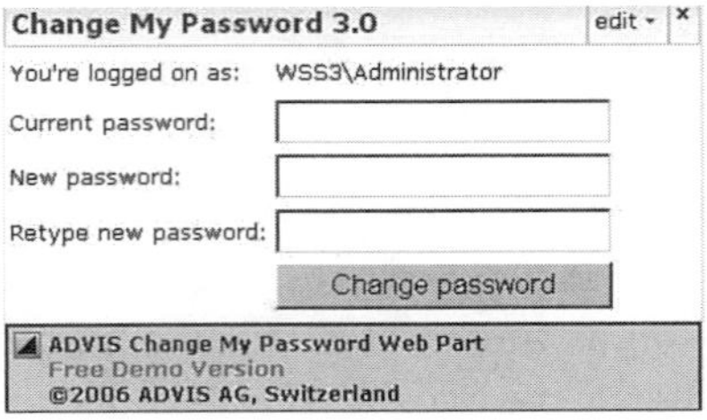

FIGURE 24.18
The web part as it appears in the trial version.

Again, further settings are obtained by clicking the top-right downward arrow. To test it properly, however, we need to change the user to, for instance, MyContrib. So, stop editing the page (Exit Edit Page) and change the user to MyContrib. Now enter the current password (MyContrib) and a new password (twice) and select Change Password. Check the new password works by going back to Administrator and then back again to MyContrib.

After you change the user to MyContrib but *before* you try to change the password, go to the server and access the user MyContrib there. Make sure that the field User Cannot Change Password is turned off.	***Tip***

When you change the password using this web part, you will probably receive a login box for MyContrib. The first time this happens, enter the *old* password. The second time this happens, enter the new password.	***Note***

Summary

This hour discussed how to add functionality to your websites by installing free and commercial web parts.

Q&A

Q. *How do I find all the free and all the commercial web parts?*

A. No sites specialize entirely in keeping track of web parts. On my WSS FAQ sites (the WSS v3FAQ list), I have two views: one for commercial products (V) and one for free products (X). Both list more than 100 WSS-related products, some of which are web parts.

Workshop

Quiz

1. What are the negative aspects of using free web parts?

2. Why is it worth paying for a commercial web part?

Quiz Answers

1. There are various possible answers: not so well tested, manual installation required, security concerns, and not full featured.

2. Commercial web parts are well tested, have automatic installation, are security-conscious, and they're full featured.

Index

overlapping, 249

synchronizing, 250

Captaris Workflow 6.5, 297

CAPTCHA support for blogs, 188-189

CD/DVD (VM installation), Web:415

Central Administration site, 47-48

Change My Expired Password web part, 383

Change My Password web part, 383-384

changing

passwords, 383-384

port number, 57

Chart Plus web part, 381-383

CMS 2002 (Content Management Server), 9-10

CodePlex, 10, 185

Codeplex SharePoint Community Kit, 376

Collect Feedback workflow, 296

Collect Signatures workflow, 296

Colligo

Contributor, 344

Reader, 343-344

colors of Data View web parts, 337-340

columns

creating, 105-108

defined, 106

deleting, 116-117

document libraries versus Office products, 230-232

Edit column, 109-111

commercial web parts, 381-385

community, 376

Company Header section (reports), 289

conditional formatting of Data View web parts, 338-340

conditions in workflows, 318, 324

configuring

Alternate Access Methods (AAM), 50-52, 54-56

blogs, 185

Search, 48, 50

Windows Server 2003, Web:400-402

connecting to the Internet, 72

connections

to servers, 247

to web parts, 341

contacts

bulk-transfers, 255-256

defined, 124

linking

to Outlook 2003, 255-256

to Outlook 2007, 251

content

brainstorming site content, 157-158

documents list, 158-161

unformatted content, 163

Content Editor web part, 130-131

Content Management Server (CMS 2002), 9-10

Content Query web part, 375

Contribute permission level, 36

copies

Colligo

Contributor, 344

Reader, 343-344

Recycle Bins, 348-350

restore, 353-354

Save List as Template, 345-348

scheduling backups with batch files, 357-358

SharePoint Designer 2007, 354-356

stsadm, 351-353

crawling (searches)

defined, 209

Lotus Notes, 218

MOSS 2007, 215

Search Server 2008, 216

Search Server 2008 Express, 216-219

WSS 3.0, 215

Created field, 166-167

creating

Access 2007

lists, 272

tables, 269-271

blog posts, 184-185

blogs, 69-70, 184-185

Sams **Teach Yourself**

When you only have time
for the answers™

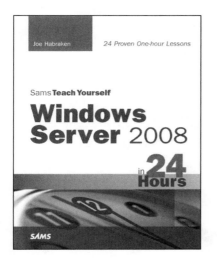

Whatever your need and whatever your time frame, there's a Sams **TeachYourself** book for you. With a Sams **TeachYourself** book as your guide, you can quickly get up to speed on just about any new product or technology—in the absolute shortest period of time possible. Guaranteed.

Learning how to do new things with your computer shouldn't be tedious or time-consuming. Sams **TeachYourself** makes learning anything quick, easy, and even a little bit fun.

Windows Server 2008 in 24 Hours

Joe Habraken
ISBN-13: 978-0-672-33012-4

ASP.NET 3.5 in 24 Hours

Scott Mitchell
ISBN-13: 978-0-672-32997-5

Visual Basic 2008 in 24 Hours

James Foxall
ISBN-13: 978-0-672-32984-5

SQL in 24 Hours, Fourth Edition

Ryan Stephens
Ron Plew
Arie Jones
ISBN-13: 978-0-672-33018-6

Microsoft SQL Server T-SQL in 10 Minutes

Ben Forta
ISBN-13: 978-0-672-32867-1

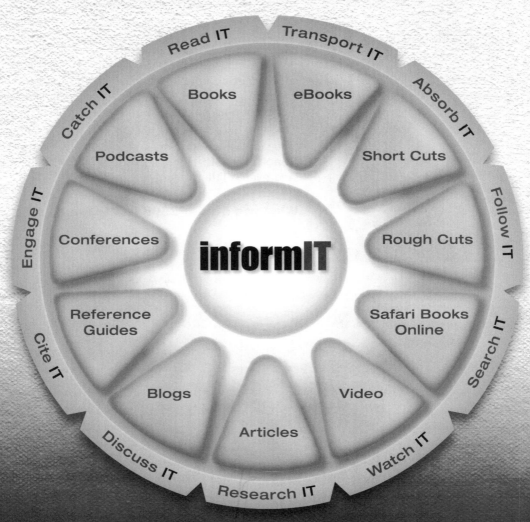

Learn IT at InformIT

Go Beyond the Book

11 WAYS TO LEARN IT at **www.informIT.com/learn**

The digital network for the publishing imprints of Pearson Education